IMAGES
of America

LAFAYETTE'S LEXINGTON

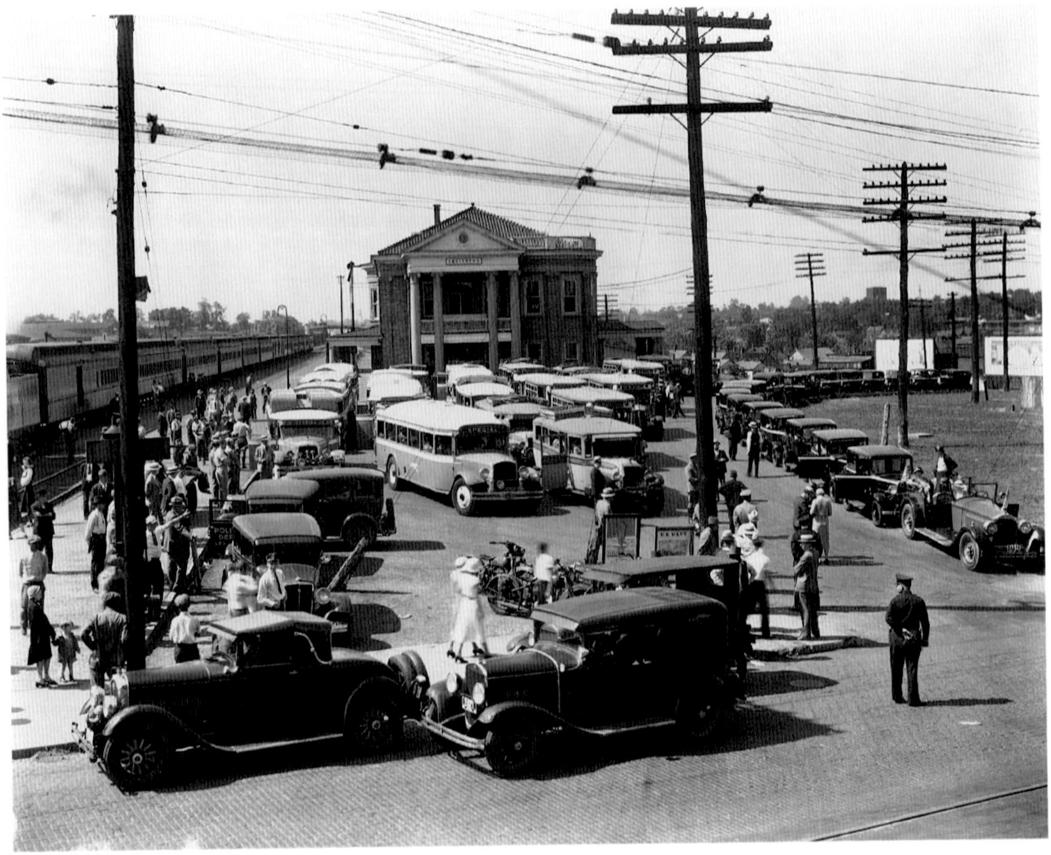

IMAGES
of America

LAFAYETTE'S LEXINGTON

Thomas M. House and Lisa R. Carter

ARCADIA
PUBLISHING

ISBN 978-0-7385-1552-6

Published by Arcadia Publishing
Charleston, South Carolina

Printed in the United States of America

Library of Congress Catalog Card Number: 2003107142

For all general information contact Arcadia Publishing at:
Telephone 843-853-2070
Fax 843-853-0044
E-mail sales@arcadiapublishing.com
For customer service and orders:
Toll-Free 1-888-313-2665

Visit us on the Internet at www.arcadiapublishing.com

Frontispiece: Southern Railway Depot on South Broadway, May 1932. (1322)

Contents

Acknowledgments

First and foremost, we are grateful beyond measure to Bob and Ida Long and the staff of the Lafayette Studio for creating such a remarkable visual record of Lexington's past. This book is but a sampling of their work, drawn from the Lafayette Studio Collection at the University of Kentucky Library. Our thanks also goes to Gerald J. Munoff, former curator of the photographic archives at the University of Kentucky, for recognizing the value of this collection and overseeing its acquisition by the University of Kentucky Libraries.

The authors also wish to thank Bettie L. Kerr, Burton Milward, Gregory A. Waller, George C. Wright, and John D. Wright Jr., for their writings and insights on the history of Lexington. We are also grateful to B.J. Gooch, Jim Birchfield, Terry Birdwhistell, Bill Cooper, Bill Marshall, Claire McCann, Frank Stanger, and Jeff Suchanek for their help with research and other aspects of the preparation of this book. Additionally, we would like to express our appreciation to Connie Schooler, who provided valuable insight into the lives of Bob and Ida Long. The contributions of these people made this book more accurate and informative, and certainly made our work much easier. We are responsible for any errors or omissions.

Thanks to all those students and volunteers who have helped sort, organize, and identify the negatives and prints in the Lafayette Studio Collection. There have been too many to name them all here, but Karla Dooley, Hugh Henderson, Gwynne Schwartz, Amy Walveart, and David Wells deserve special thanks for their outstanding contributions.

We are grateful to the members of the staff of the Lexington Public Library who maintain the wonderful research collections in the Kentucky Room of the Central Library. Our research was made much easier because these were available, well organized, and well maintained. We especially want to thank Patrick Lynch, Robin Rader, Jan Marshall, Wayne Johnson, Clay Redding, Melissa Gibson, Chris Walls, Heather Wingfield, and Leah Thompson. Very special thanks goes to Todd Lemley whose assistance went well beyond the call of duty.

Thanks also to Brad Carrington and his staff for simplifying the liberal use of the University of Kentucky Libraries' newspaper microfilm during this project.

Special thanks to Sallie Powell, at the University of Kentucky Medical Center Photography Department who, using Bob Long's original negatives, produced the prints used in this book. Her technical skills, attention to detail, and artistic eye, greatly enhanced the quality of the images reproduced here.

Tom would especially like to thank his colleagues at the University of New Hampshire, Mylinda Woodward, Becky Ernest, Roland Goodbody, Bill Ross, Justina Lane, Dan Cheever, and Kathy Arbogast, who covered for him while he was away working on this book. Thanks too, to his parents, Jack and Mary Frances House, and to his mother-in-law, Nell Webb, who provided board, lodging, and transportation during his research trips to Lexington.

Lisa would like to express her appreciation to all of her colleagues at the University of Kentucky Special Collections and Archives, whose assistance with the activities of the Audio-Visual Archives facilitated the development of this project.

Finally very special thanks and love go to Jo Nell and Ben. Without their encouragement, support, understanding, and patience, this book could not have been completed.

INTRODUCTION

Robert James "Bob" Long, the eldest son of Richard Thomas and Sarah Emma Long, probably developed his lifelong love of new technology and gadgets while riding streetcars around Lexington with his father, a motorman with the Belt Electric Line Company. Richard Long moved his family from Mercer County to Lexington and took the motorman's job in 1890, the same year the company initiated Lexington's first electric streetcar service. It is possible that Bob Long was visiting his father at the Loudon Avenue streetcar barn on the day, in 1897, that noted Lexington photographer Captain Isaac Jenks came to take a group portrait of the motormen (Kerr, p. 67). This could have been the event that sparked the boy's interest in photography and led him to take his first photograph the following year, at the age of ten. Bob Long's youthful fascination with photography would never leave him, and eventually led to a 40-year career in photography and the establishment of the Lafayette Studio, some 25 years after he took his first photograph.

By 1911, Bob Long was working as an electrician and the following year the Lexington City Directory lists his occupation as "machine operator" at the Orpheum Theater. Soon after he began work at the Orpheum, Bob Long met Ida Nelson of Wayne County, West Virginia, who was working as a chorus girl. They were married in 1916. Three years later, while Bob was still working as a projectionist at the Orpheum, he and Elmer Bryant opened a film processing business as a sideline. Bryant quickly sold his part of the business to his partner, and Ida Long began working in the film processing business with her husband.

Around 1921, Edward L. McClure joined the Longs in opening the Acme Photo Company, which operated out of the Long's apartment at 147 West Main Street. The Long's photo processing business had now expanded to become a full photographic studio. In 1920, Bob Long's former business partner, Elmer Bryant, joined with McClure and several other partners to establish the Kentucky News Pictorial Company, a motion picture production company that shot newsreel footage in and around Lexington in late 1920 and early 1921. Bob Long worked as a cameraman on at least one Kentucky News Pictorial Company production. In 1922, he also served as cameraman on Associated First National's production, The Crossroads of Lexington (Waller, pp. 267-268). Both the Acme Photo Company and the Kentucky News Pictorial Company closed after being in business for only a few years. By 1923, Bob and Ida Long had moved out of their room at 147 West Main and were boarding at 243 North Limestone. They were operating a photographic studio in rooms 14 and 15 in the New Johns Building, at 108 Walnut Street, near the corner of Main and Walnut. In addition to his work as a freelance motion picture cameraman, Bob Long, along with Elmer Bryant, was working as a projectionist at the Kentucky Theater, which had opened in October of 1922.

It was in the rooms in the New Johns Building on Walnut Street that the Longs first began doing business under the Lafayette Studio name. By 1925, they had moved their business to 311 West Main, and were living in rooms above the new studio, which was located on the north side of Main Street between Mill and Broadway. An advertisement in the 1925 Lexington City Directory listed their services as commercial photographers and Kodak finishers. They also offered "moving pictures made to order."

In its new location, the Lafayette Studio's business began to grow, and by the early 1930s, Bob Long had given up his job as a projectionist at the Kentucky Theater. Ida Long was doing the portrait work in the studio, and Bob was handling the commercial photography assignments. In spite of the deepening effects of the Depression, their business continued to expand. In July of 1931, they were able to buy out a rival studio, the Starman Studio, located at 301 West Main. At about the same time, they also bought a house on Idle Wilde Court. Instead of moving into their new home right away, the Longs rented it out and continued to live in rooms over the studio until the late 1930s.

When the Longs took over the Starman Studio, they added two new employees, bringing the total to nine, and moved the Lafayette Studio into the much more spacious Starman Studio quarters. Around this time, W.C.G. Long came to work for his brother as a darkroom technician. W.C.G. would continue to work at the studio until the mid-1970s. In the late 1930s, Ida Long's niece, Rose Marcum, would also begin working at the studio, doing negative retouching, hand tinting, and painting miniatures on glass. Her work won several awards for the studio.

It was also in the 1930s that Richard Clark began working for the Longs. Both Ida and Bob Long preferred to use large format cameras for almost all of their photography. These large cameras produced images on negatives that measured 5x7 inches or 8x10 inches. While the large negatives made it possible to produce remarkably crisp and detailed prints, it was always a challenge to move and set up the bulky cameras. Richard Clark often traveled with Bob Long on assignments to help with these cameras. Clark also made frames and did other jobs around the studio and would work there until the mid-1960s.

In 1941, the Long's again moved the Lafayette Studio to new quarters at 141-143 North Limestone. This would be the final home of the studio under their ownership. The Lafayette Studio was firmly established as one of Lexington's leading commercial photography studios, and Bob and Ida Long continued to run the business for another 18 years. Then, in 1959, after 40 years in the photography business, they retired and sold the Lafayette Studio to Coy Goforth and Chester Wainscott. Goforth left the business around 1962. Wainscott continued to operate the studio on North Limestone until 1984 when he moved to 111 South Limestone. He closed the studio the following year.

When they first moved into their home in the late 1930s, Bob Long immediately began to indulge his inventive spirit. An April 5, 1959 Lexington Herald-Leader article, written at the time of the Longs' retirement, mentions several of Bob Long's hobbies and the effect they had on their home on Idle Wilde Court. He installed an elaborate sound system that would allow music to be piped into any room in the house and out to the patio. He also built a recording studio in the basement where he recorded demo tapes for local performers. In his backyard, Long built an elaborate fountain that was illluminated by colored lights and could produce a variety of spray patterns. The Longs often entertained friends and family in their basement recreation area, which Bob had equipped with a jukebox, a television, a piano, and a bar.

Bob Long died on October 10, 1971 at the age of 83, and Ida Long died on December 22, 1975. She was 78. Lexington is indebted to Bob and Ida Long who devoted much of their lives to creating a photographic record of the city as it developed through the decades of the 1920s, 1930s, 1940s, and 1950s. Lexington's historical record is remarkably richer because of their devotion to their business, their art, and their community.

In 1981, the University of Kentucky Libraries purchased a significant portion of the Lafayette Studio's commercial photograph collection from Chester Wainscott. The photographs reproduced in this volume are drawn exclusively from that collection of over 10,000 negatives and prints. Over the years, library staff, students, and volunteers have worked to sort, organize, identify, and preserve the material in the collection. Housed in the Libraries' Special Collections and Archives Department, the collection is open to researchers by appointment only. The numbers in parentheses at the end of the captions are studio order numbers used to organize and locate the negatives in the collection.

one

Lexington's Lafayette Studio

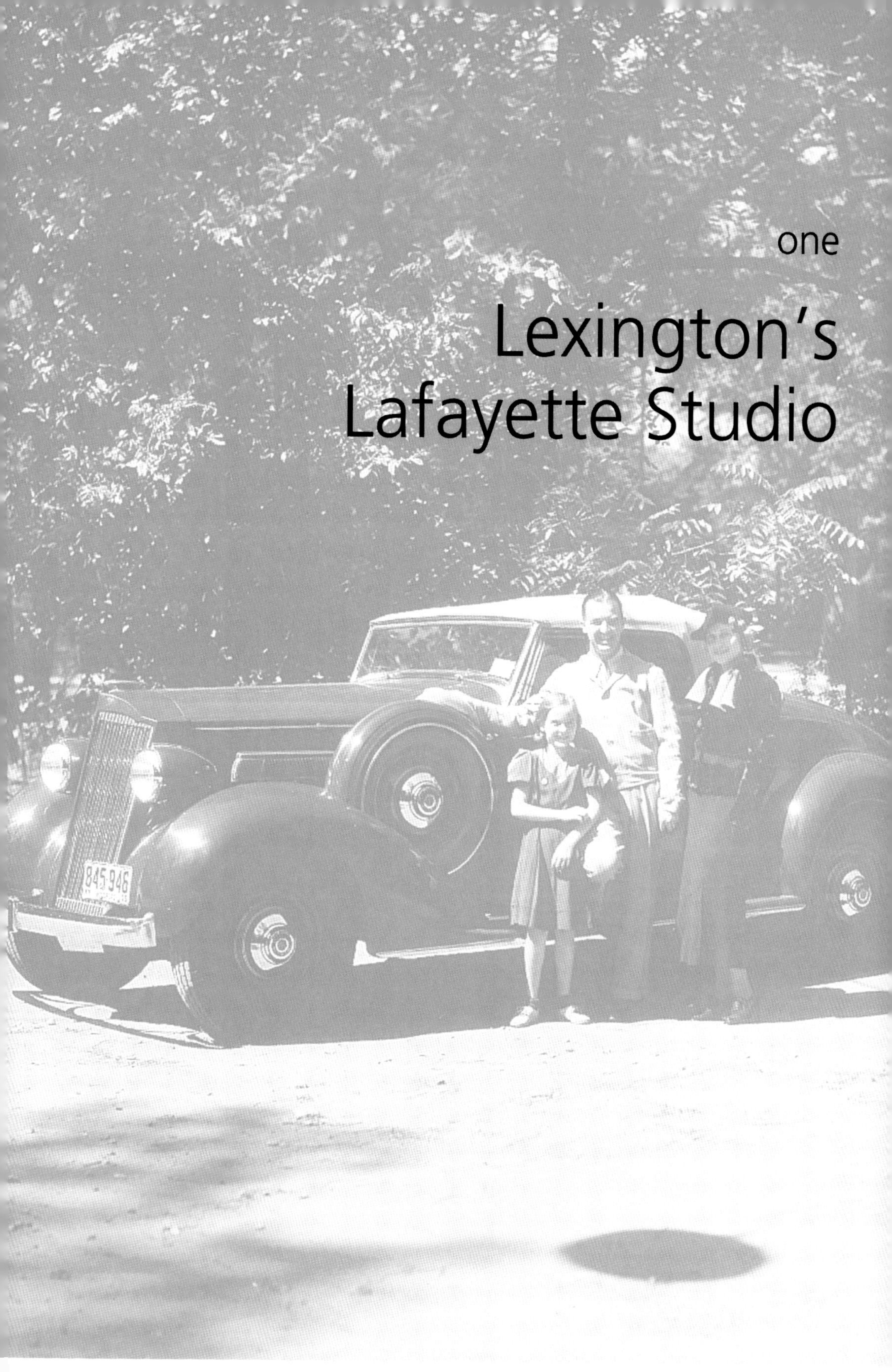

Starting with a photo processing business which they ran out of the rooms on East Main Street where they lived, Bob and Ida Long developed a business that would not only survive, but prosper during the Great Depression, and the War years. Due to their hard work, and their skill and talent as photographers, the end of the 1940s saw the Lafayette Studio well established as the leading commercial photography studio in Lexington.

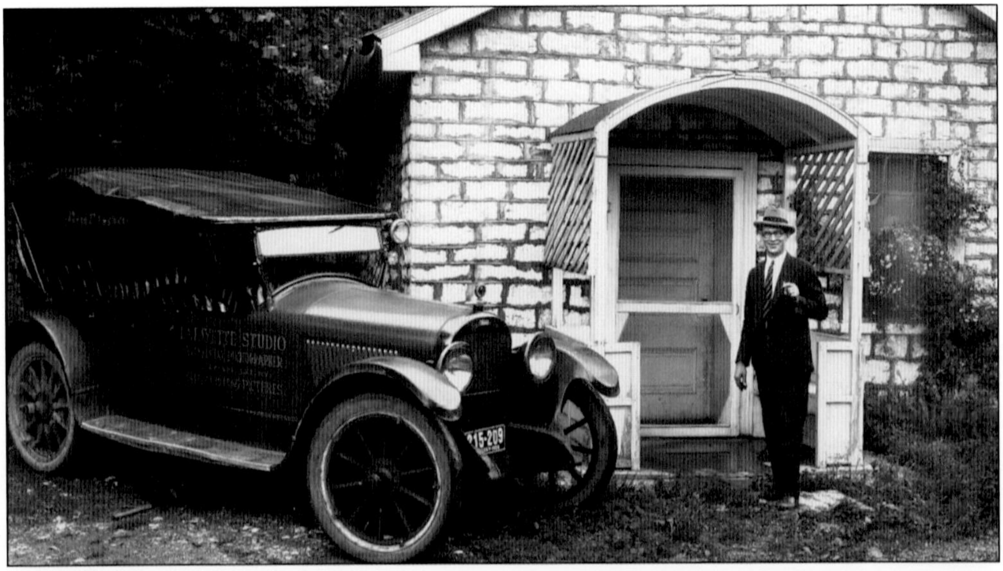

Robert J. Long, August 1947. In an April 5, 1959, *Lexington Herald*-Leader article, written at the time of Ida and Robert J. "Bob" Long's retirement from the Lafayette Studio, Bob Long explained that he always smoked cigars because they were better than matches for lighting flash powder, the predecessor of flashbulbs and electronic flash. The Lafayette Studio car in this photograph is believed to be a Lexington Minute Man Six. In 1909, a company formed by Dr. F.F. Bryan, Fred Coates, V.K. Dodge, and Kinzea Stone produced the first Lexington at a plant on West Main Street just west of Calvary Cemetery. In 1911, the Lexington plant moved to Connersville, Indiana. (5859)

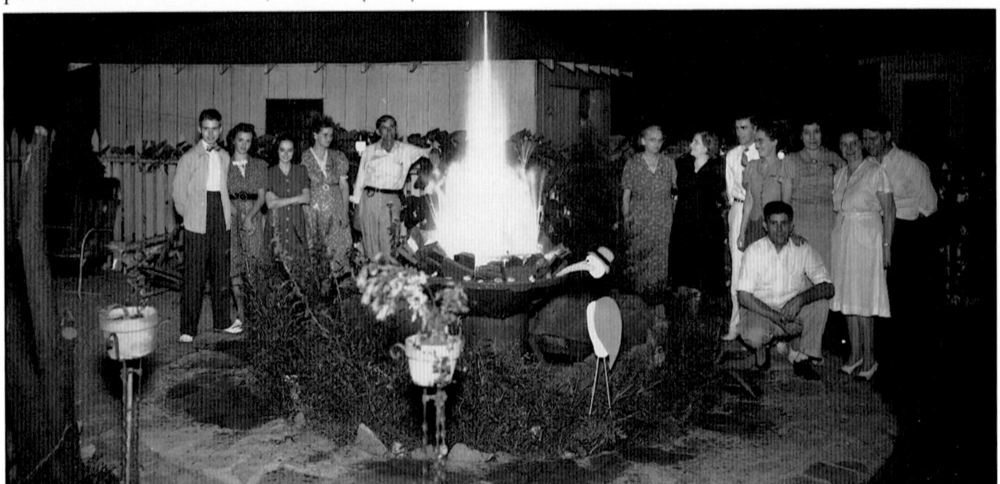

Friends and family around the fountain at the Longs' home on Idle Wilde Court, *c.* 1940. Ida Long, in the dark dress, is the second person from the left in the group to the right of the fountain. Bob Long, who as a young man had worked as an electrician, built this fountain which was illuminated by colored lights and could produce a variety of spray patterns. It was controlled by a theater marquee control panel. (4535)

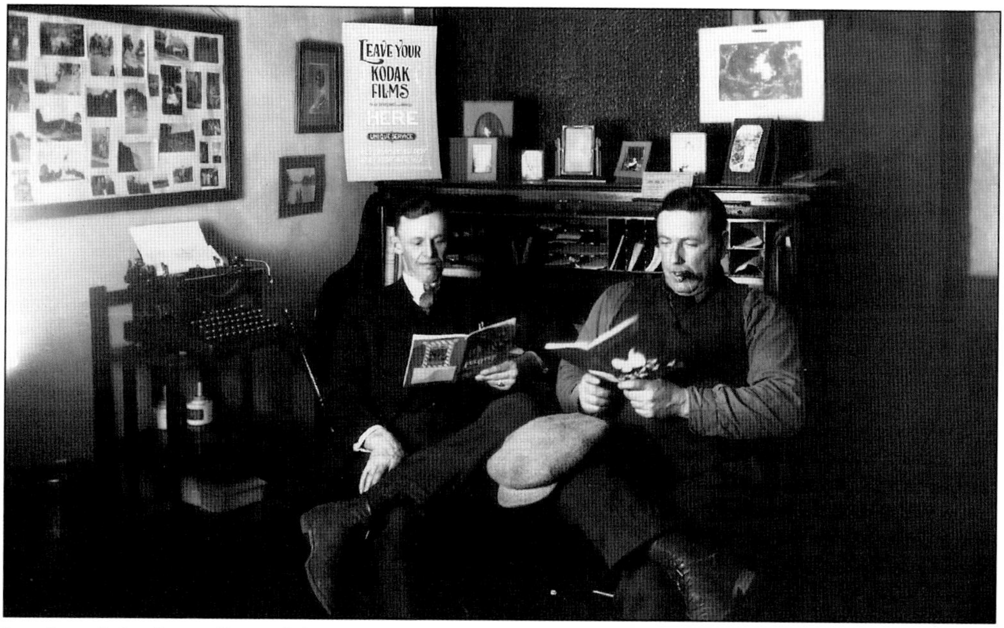

Interior of the first offices of the Lafayette Studio, New Johns Building, 108 Walnut Street, c. 1924. Leonard Ishmael (at left) and an unidentified customer were photographed in the first home of the Lafayette Studio. The sign above Ishmael advertises the studio's "unique service, nice enlargements from small Kodak negatives." The studio remained at the Main and Walnut Street (now Martin Luther King Boulevard) location for about a year before moving, c. 1925, into new quarters at 311 West Main. (1885)

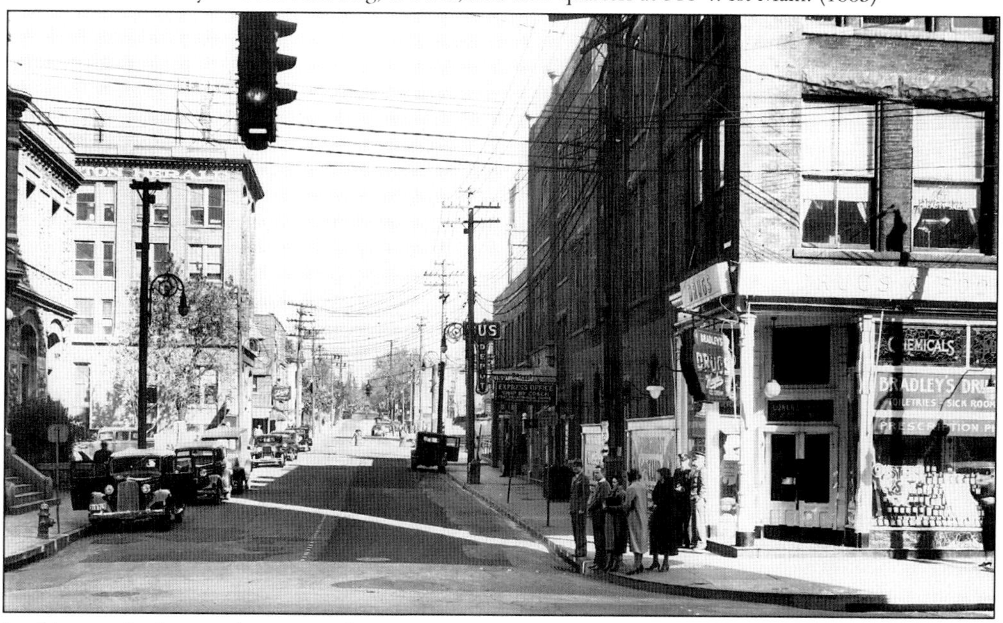

Looking north along Walnut Street from the Main and Walnut Intersection, November 7, 1934. In 1923, rooms 14 and 15 of the New Johns Building served as the first home of the Lafayette Studio. This photograph, taken several years after the studio had moved to new quarters at 311 West Main, shows the New Johns Building at 108 Walnut (now Martin Luther King Boulevard), one door south of the Bus Depot at 110 Walnut. (3296)

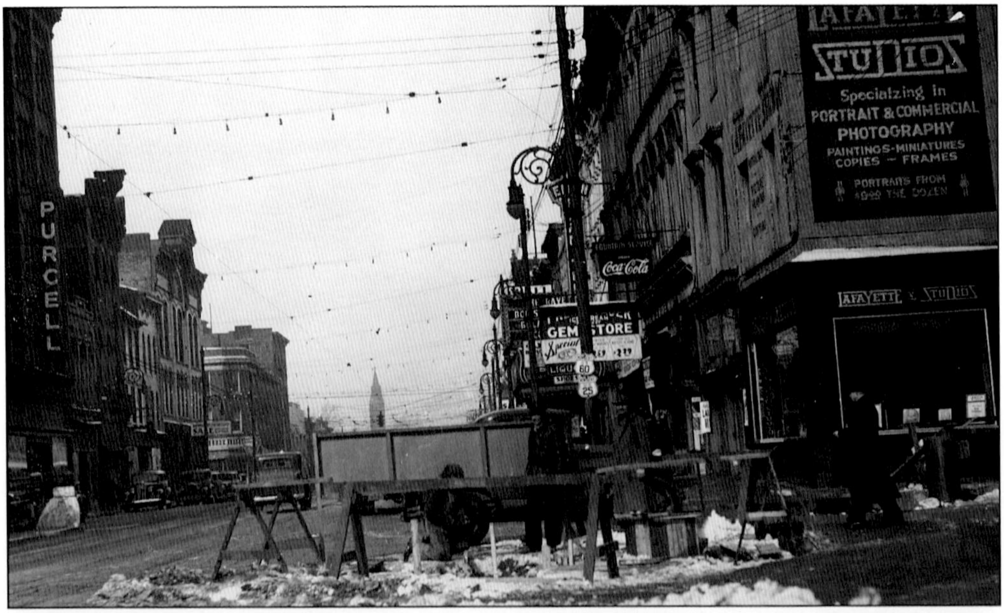

Third home of Lafayette Studio, northeast corner of Main and Mill Streets, 1936. The studio remained in offices at 311 West Main until 1931 when Bob and Ida Long purchased the Starman Studio and consolidated the two businesses under the Lafayette Studio name at the location of the Starman Studio, 301 West Main. At least for Bob and Ida Long, running a photography studio seemed to have been a Depression-proof business. (3088)

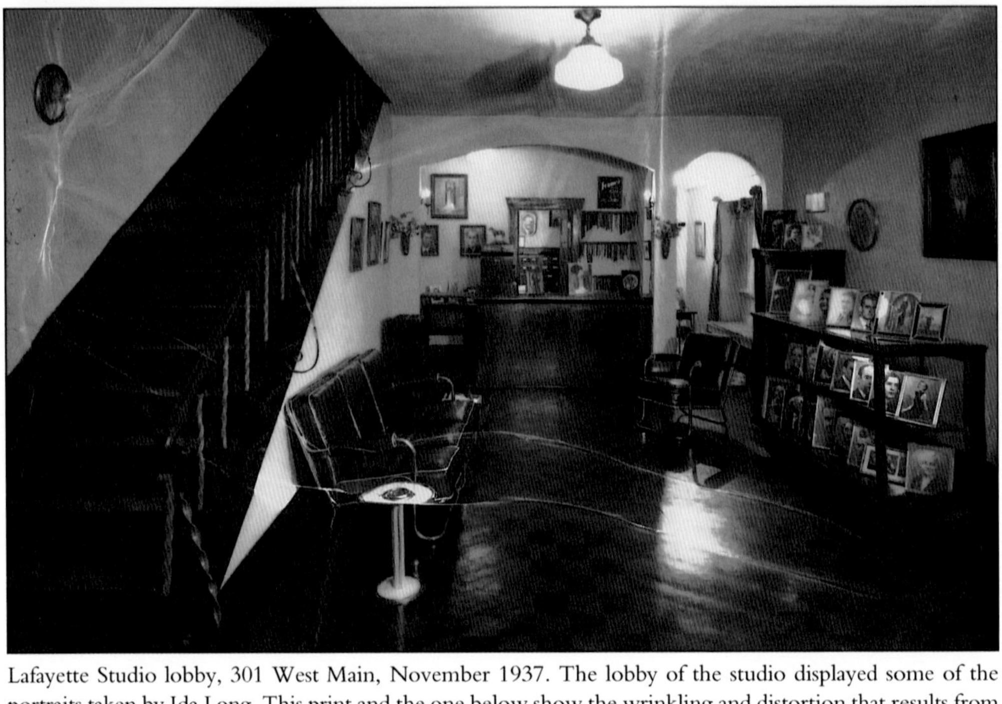

Lafayette Studio lobby, 301 West Main, November 1937. The lobby of the studio displayed some of the portraits taken by Ida Long. This print and the one below show the wrinkling and distortion that results from the deterioration of the safety film produced during this period. Unfortunately, a significant portion of the negatives in the Lafayette Studio collection are now threatened by this deterioration. (3835)

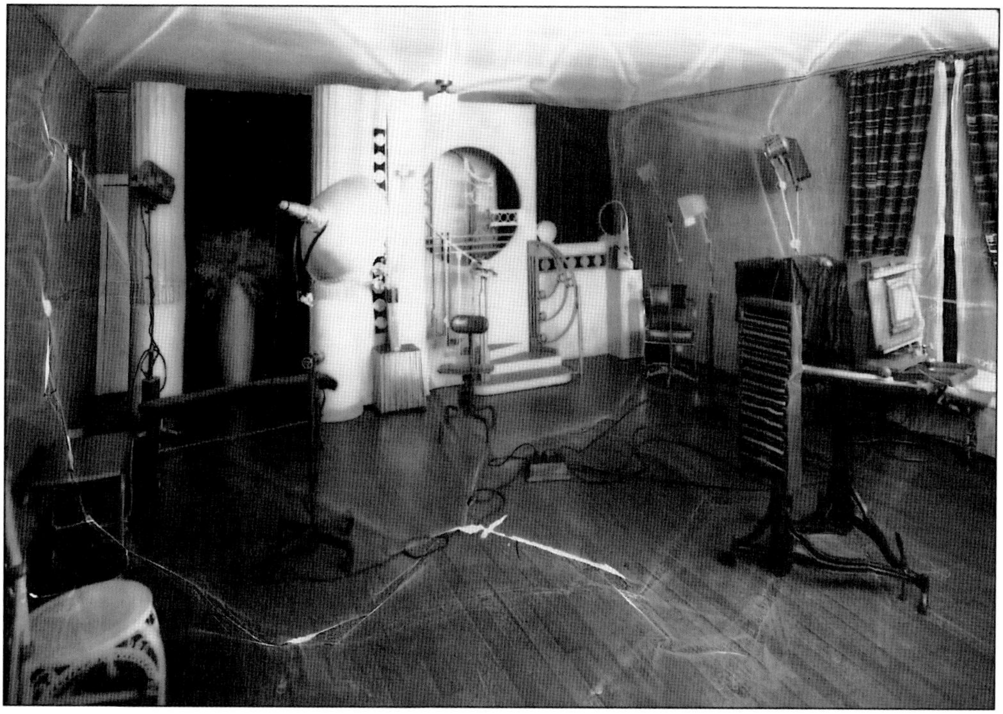

Above: Ida Long's portrait studio, 301 West Main, November 1937. Ida Long did the in-studio portrait photography. The April 5, 1959 Lexington Herald-Leader article mentions that on one occasion she photographed 150 people in one day. Note the large camera at right that was used to capture images on large negatives that measure 5x7 inches or 8x10 inches. The Longs used large format negatives and cameras when taking almost all of their photographs. (3835)

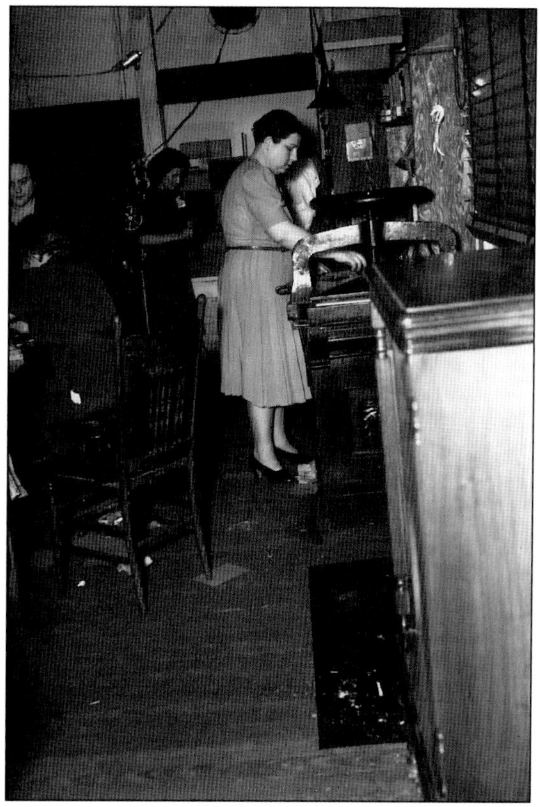

Right: Interior of Lafayette Studio, 301 West Main, December 1940. The purchase of the Starman Studio and the move into larger quarters on the northwest corner of Main and Mill Streets allowed the Longs to hire more employees. A 1931 advertisement announcing the relocation of the studio also mentioned that with the recent addition of two new employees, the studio now had a total of nine. (4624)

COMMERCIAL PHOTO PRICES

A- One view in city limits $4.00, additional view at same time $3.50,
quantities views at $2.00 each negative, two prints with each order.
Flash light of room, no living subjects, first flash $5.00, additional
flash-$4.50 each. Electric lighted, same price.
Banquets--8 x IO, $5.00; 7xII, $7.50; 7 x I7, $IO.00.
Corpse photographs, 8 x IO, $5.00 & $7.50 - two prints included; additional prints glossy finish, 75¢; additional prints, rough finish
$I.00. Folders 25¢ extra.
5 x 7 negatives - first view $3.00, additional view at same time,
$2.50; quantities views at $I.50 each negative, two prints with each
order.
Out of town, regular price with an additional charge of 25¢ per mile
one way, and $I.00 charge per hour for standing time after the first
hour on location. No charge made for the first hour. Where transportation is furnished an additional charge of $I.00 per hour standing
time is made after the first hour. Time is to start at the time of
leaving the Studio.

B- Camera man by day (8 hrs.) $I5.00. When it is necessary for camera
man to stay over-night at location, hotel lodging is to be paid by the
party having the work done.
Negatives are the property of the Studio unless agreement is made
for their sale at the time work is being done. When sold the price
is 8 x IO $3.00 each. 5 x 7 $2.00 each.

PRICES OF PRINTS IN QUANTITY LOTS

C- 7 x I7 glossy prints, not mounted, are
$I.00 each in quantities less then 25. Linen backs 50¢ extra. Mounts 50 extra
75¢ " " " of 50 prints " " 25¢ " " " "
50¢ " " " " I00 " " " 25¢ " " " "

D- 8 x IO glossy prints, not mounted, are
75¢ each in quantities less than I2. Linen backs 25¢ extra Mounts 25¢ extra
50¢ " " " of 25 prints. " " I5¢ " " 20¢ "
35¢ " " " " 50 " " " I0¢ " " 20¢ "
25¢ " " " " I00 " " " 07¢ " " I5¢ "

E- 5 x 7 glossy prints, not mounted, are
50¢ each in quantities of less then 6, Linen backs I5¢ extra Mounts 20¢ extra
35¢ " " " " I2 prints. " " I5¢ " " I5¢ "
25¢ " " " " 25 " " " I0¢ " " I5¢ "
20¢ " " " " 50 " " " 09¢ " " I2½¢ "
I5¢ " " " " I00 " " " 06¢ " " I0¢ "

F- Commercial tinting,
Plain, $3.00 each, extra.
Fancy, $5.00 " "

G- Prices subject to change without notice

H- Copy work, 8 x IO negative $2.00, 5 x 7 negative $I.50, one print with
each order.

I- Develope 5 x 7 negatives I0¢ each, $I.00 per dozen

J- Monthly construction contracts in city limits, exterior, sixe 8xIO
I negative & 2 prints, linen backs $4.00, additional views at same
time $3.00, additional prints at 50¢ each: 2 negative 2 prints each
linen backs$6.00, additional views at same time $2.00. additional
prints at 50¢ each. Old additional prints in quantities see sec. D.
For interiors where flash is used add 50¢ extra for each negative where
powder is used, flash bulbs will be charged as amount used. For out
of town work see sec. A. Any printing or titles on negatives to be
paid by person having work done.

Studio commercial photo prices, c. 1935. While Ida Long's portrait work was a major part of the studio's business, commercial photography became increasingly important as Lexington's economy continued to recover from the effects of the Depression. This price sheet lists some of the commercial photography services the studio offered. Photographs from the studio's commercial files provide one of the most significant visual records of Lexington's development during the 1930s, 1940s, and early 1950s. (3469)

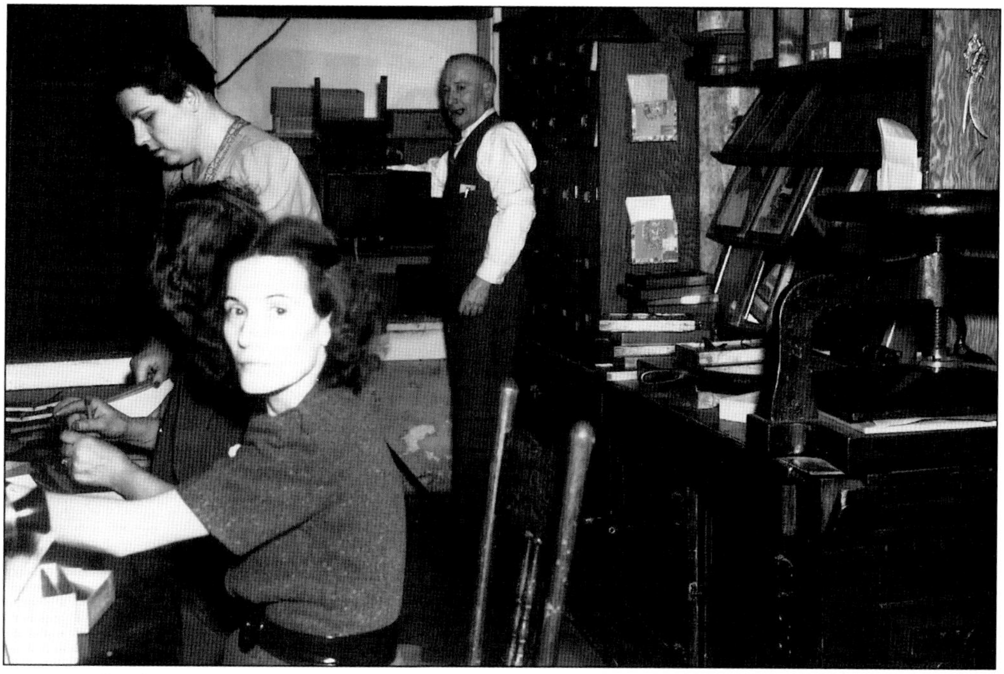

Interior of Lafayette Studio, 301 West Main, December 1940. In addition to portrait and commercial photography, the studio also provided picture-framing services, sold and processed film, shot motion pictures, and produced miniatures and oil paintings. Rose Marcum, in the foreground looking at the camera, was Ida Long's niece. She specialized in negative retouching, hand tinting, and miniature painting. Her work won several awards for the studio. The other workers in this photograph are unidentified. (4624)

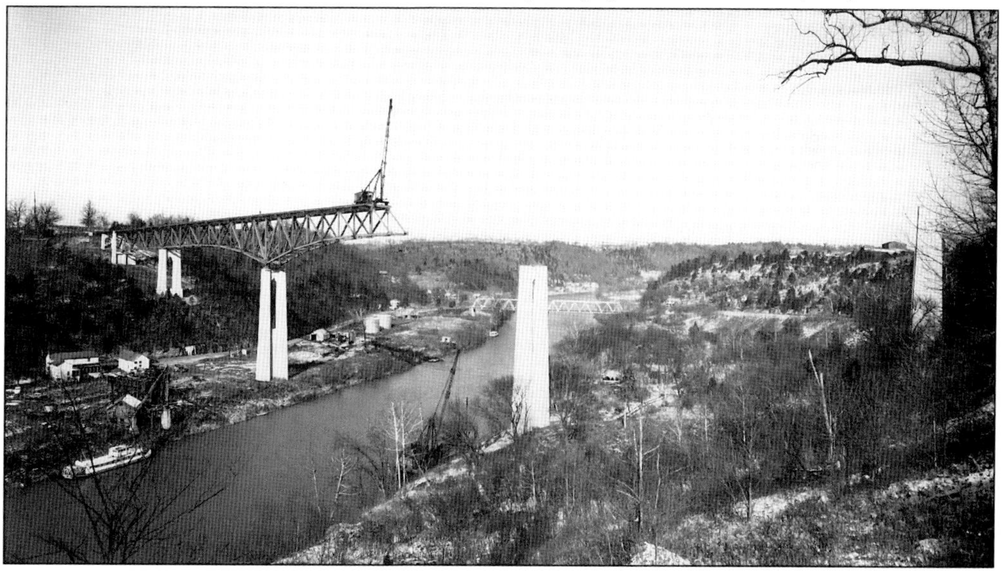

Clay's Ferry bridge under construction, December 1944. Many photographs in the Lafayette Studio collection were produced to document the progress of various construction projects in Lexington and surrounding areas. Construction work on the Clay's Ferry bridge started in 1941. The bridge, which spanned the Kentucky River to connect Fayette and Madison Counties, was not completed until 1946. The grand opening was held on August 17, 1946. (5302)

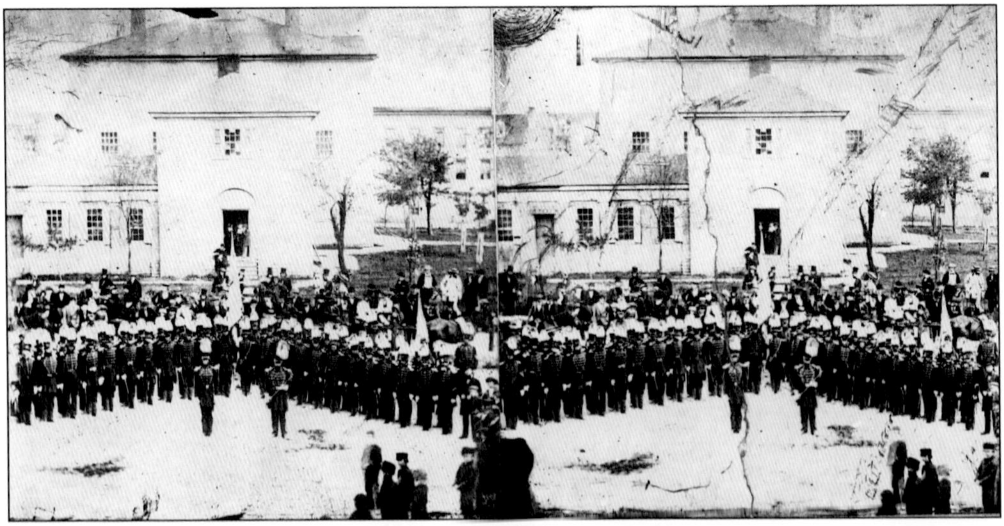

Lexington Chasseurs on Cheapside, July 4, 1860. The studio also did "copy work," making copy negatives and prints from existing photographs. This is an example of a copy photograph of a card-mounted stereoview albumen print showing the Lexington Chasseurs, a noted military group, in formation outside the west wing of Lexington's third courthouse during Fourth of July celebrations. (4026)

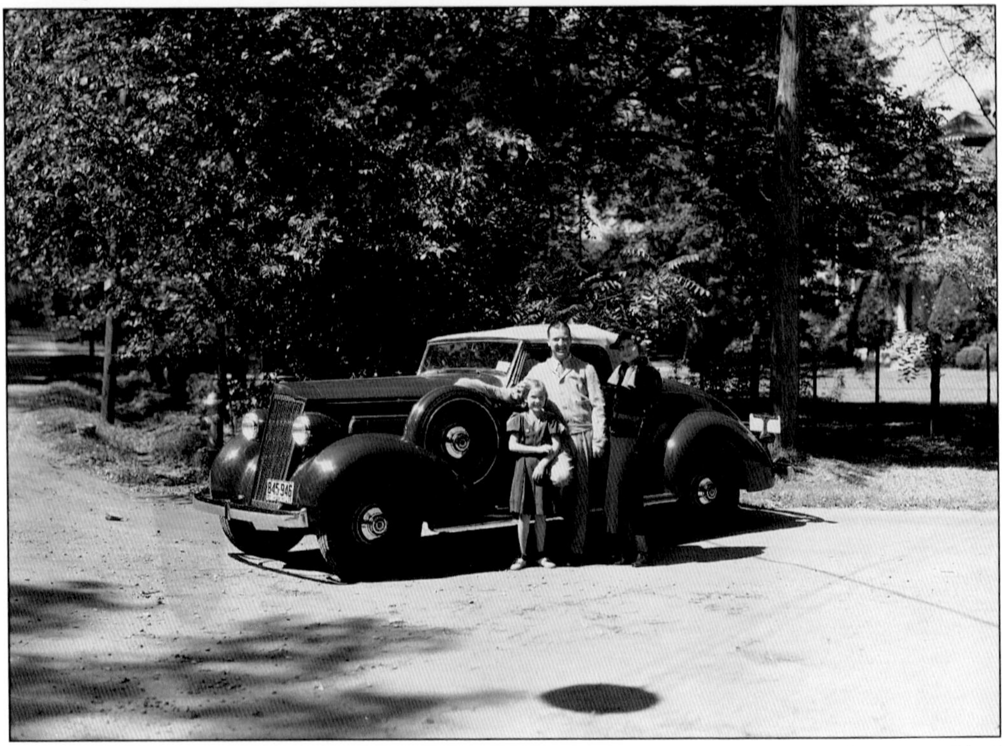

Albert Benjamin "Happy" Chandler, with wife Mildred "Mama" Watkins Chandler and daughter Mildred "Mimi," September 1935. Bob and Ida Long were often hired to photograph prominent Kentuckians. Albert Benjamin "Happy" Chandler, two-term Kentucky governor (1935–1939, 1955–1959), United States senator (1939–1945), and commissioner of baseball (1945–1951), is one of the most photographed celebrities in the Lafayette Studio Collection. (3344)

Right: Miss Kentucky Pageant, Joyland Park, August 18, 1932. Bob Long also covered various ceremonies and community events. This photograph shows Governor Ruby Laffoon crowning Miss Kentucky of 1932, Evelyn Dean, 19-year-old daughter of Mr. and Mrs. Hite T. Dean of Lexington. The finals of this Miss Kentucky beauty pageant were held at Joyland Park, located a few miles north of Lexington on Paris Pike. (1371)

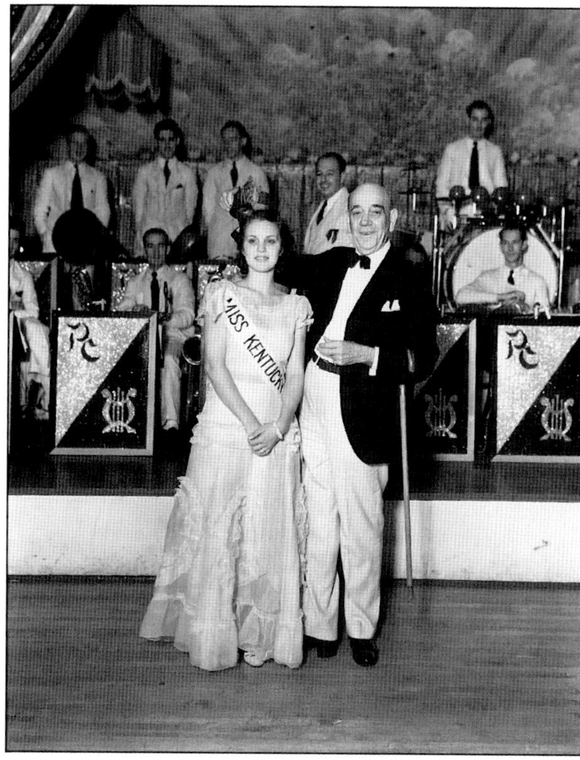

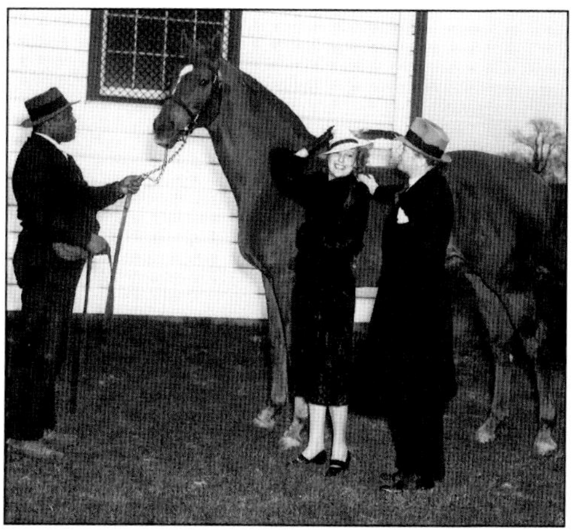

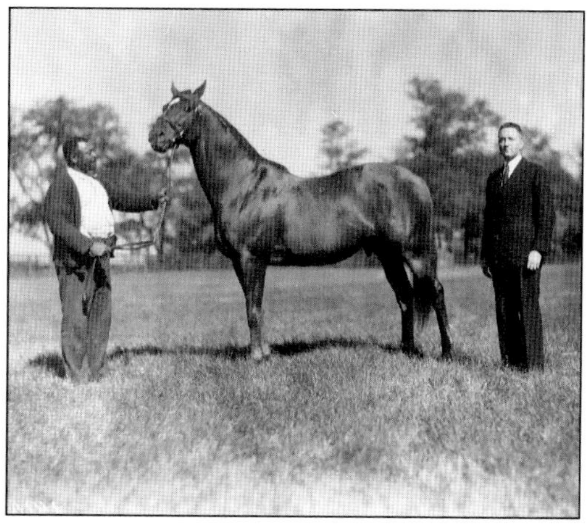

Above left: Actress Jeannette McDonald with Man O' War, April 1939. Other than A.B. "Happy" Chandler and the Kentucky Theater, Man O' War is the most photographed "celebrity" in the Lafayette Studio collection. Many visitors to Lexington arranged to have photographs made with the famous thoroughbred. Here, actress Jeannette McDonald and an unidentified man (right) have their portrait taken with Man O' War and groom Will Harbut (left). (4221)

Above right: Admiral Richard E. Byrd with Man O' War and groom Will Harbut, October 1932. Man O' War was foaled on March 29, 1917, at Nursery Stud near Lexington. Purchased as a yearling by Samuel Riddle, owner of Faraway Farm on Huffman Mill Pike, Man O' War won 20 of 21 races. He avenged his only loss to a horse named, appropriately enough, Upset, by defeating Upset decisively in six subsequent meetings. Man O' War died on November 1, 1947. (1410)

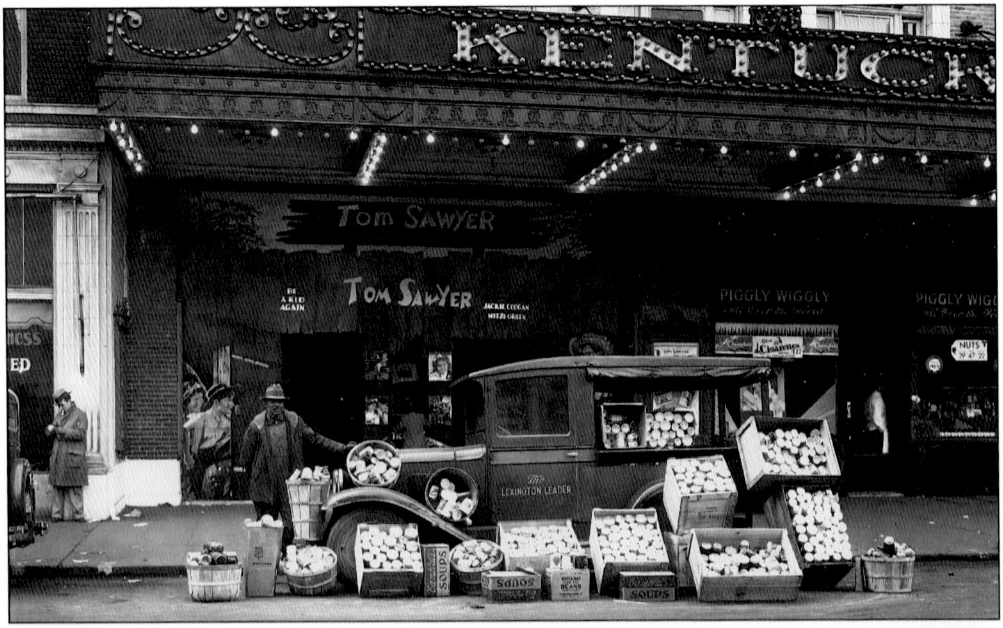

Canned goods collected at the State and Kentucky Theaters, December 21, 1930. Bob Long often took photographs for the Lexington newspapers and for the Lexington Police Department. This photograph showing the canned goods collected at the benefit showings of The Border Legion at the State and Kentucky Theaters was probably taken for The Lexington Leader. The event was sponsored by the Family Welfare Society, and the canned goods collected were to be distributed to needy elderly citizens at Christmas. (827)

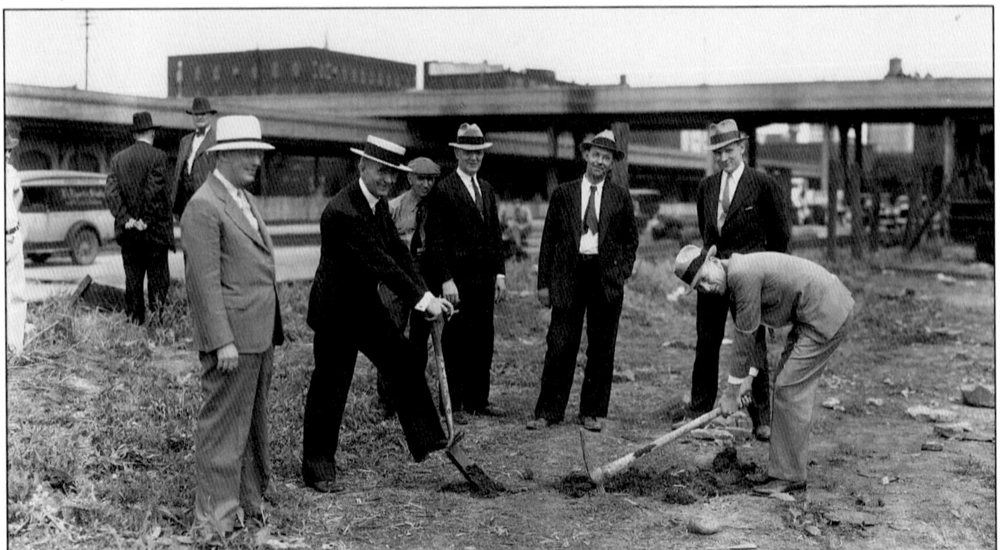

Groundbreaking for Lexington's first P.W.A. project, May 14, 1934. Another newspaper photograph shows city leaders and engineers, from left to right, as follows: Walter G. Rehm (president of the Lexington Board of Commerce), Mayor W.T. Congleton (with shovel), F.W. Phelps (resident city engineer), A.W. Howard (assistant P.W.A. engineer), J. White Guyn (city engineer), Leo Butler (president of Northern States Contracting Company), and City Manager Paul Morton (with pick). Lexington's first P.W.A. project was the construction of storm sewers in the downtown area. (1931)

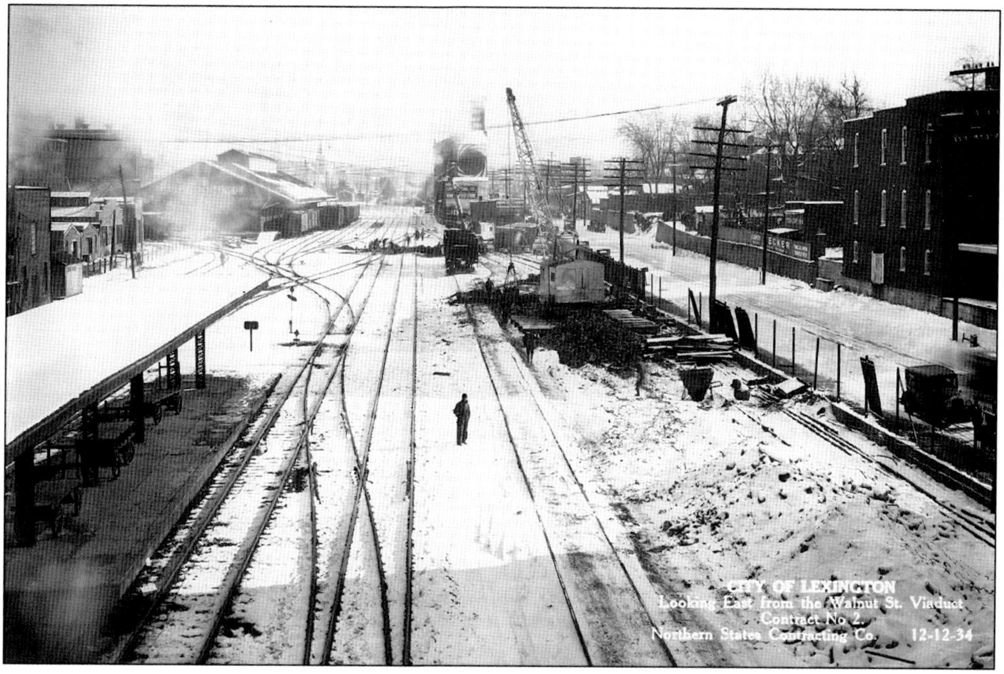

P.W.A. storm sewer project seen looking east from the Harrison Avenue viaduct (now Martin Luther King Boulevard), December 12, 1934. Work is underway on the P.W.A. storm sewer project. The storm sewers were constructed to prevent the recurrence of floods that had plagued the downtown area for years. (3330)

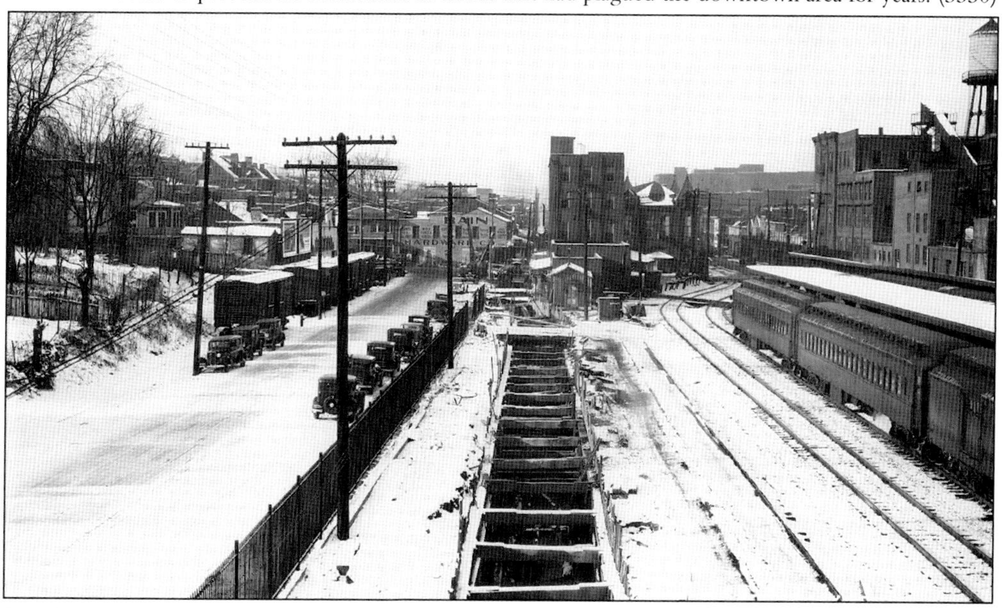

P.W.A. storm sewer project seen looking west from the Harrison Avenue viaduct (now Martin Luther King Boulevard), December 12, 1934. Northern States Contracting Company was awarded the contract to build the storm sewers. The construction project provided jobs for many Lexingtonians during the mid-1930s. At right, a passenger train is waiting at the depot behind Union Station, which opened on the southwest corner of Harrison and East Main on August 4, 1907. Torn down in 1960, it was located where the County Clerk's Building and parking structure are today. (3330)

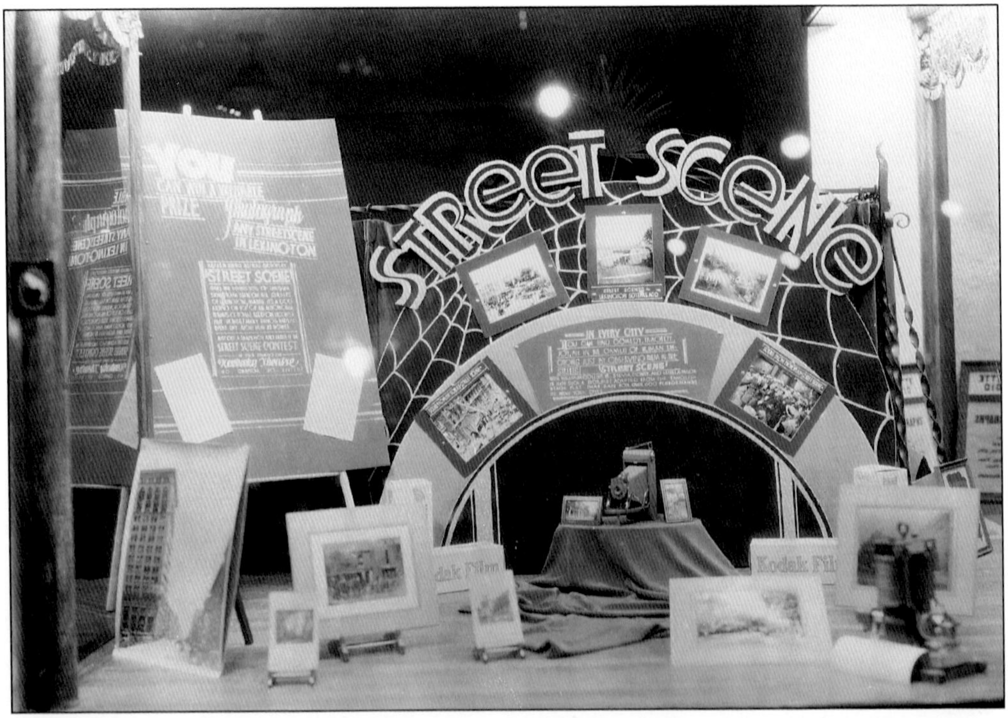

Window display for *Street Scene* photography contest, c. 1930. Many of the studio's photographs were taken for advertising purposes. This window display advertised a photography contest which ran in conjunction with the showing of *Street Scene* at the Kentucky Theater. The Lafayette Studio and the Kentucky Theater sponsored the contest that encouraged Lexingtonians to photograph the "unusual scenes to be seen on the streets of Lexington." (1775)

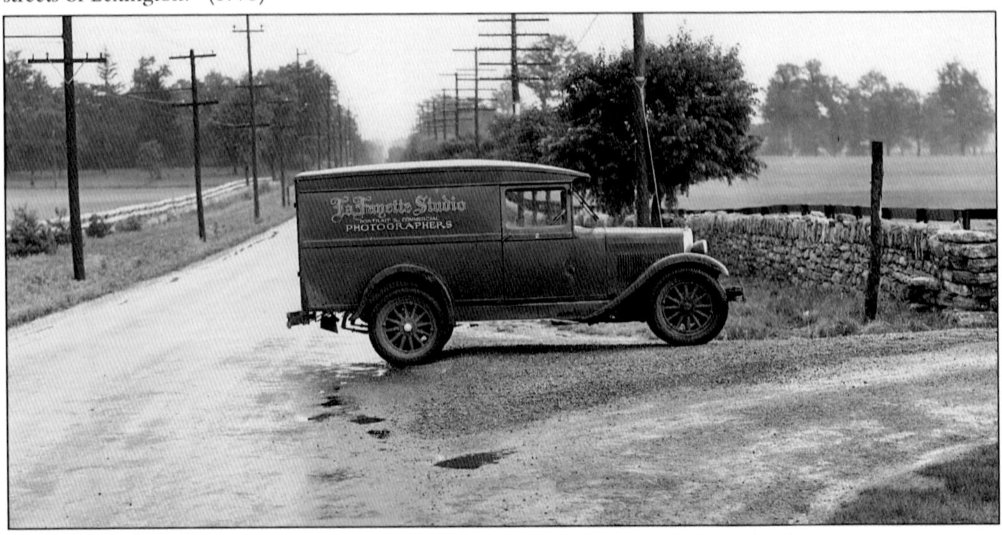

Lafayette Studio truck, c. 1939. Over the years, the studio had several trucks and at least one car that were used to transport the large cameras and other photographic equipment needed to do photography in the field. Richard Clark, who began working for the Longs in the mid-1930s, often accompanied Bob Long on photographic assignments to help him with his camera equipment. Clark continued to work at the studio until the mid-1960s. (2174)

two

Welcome to Lexington

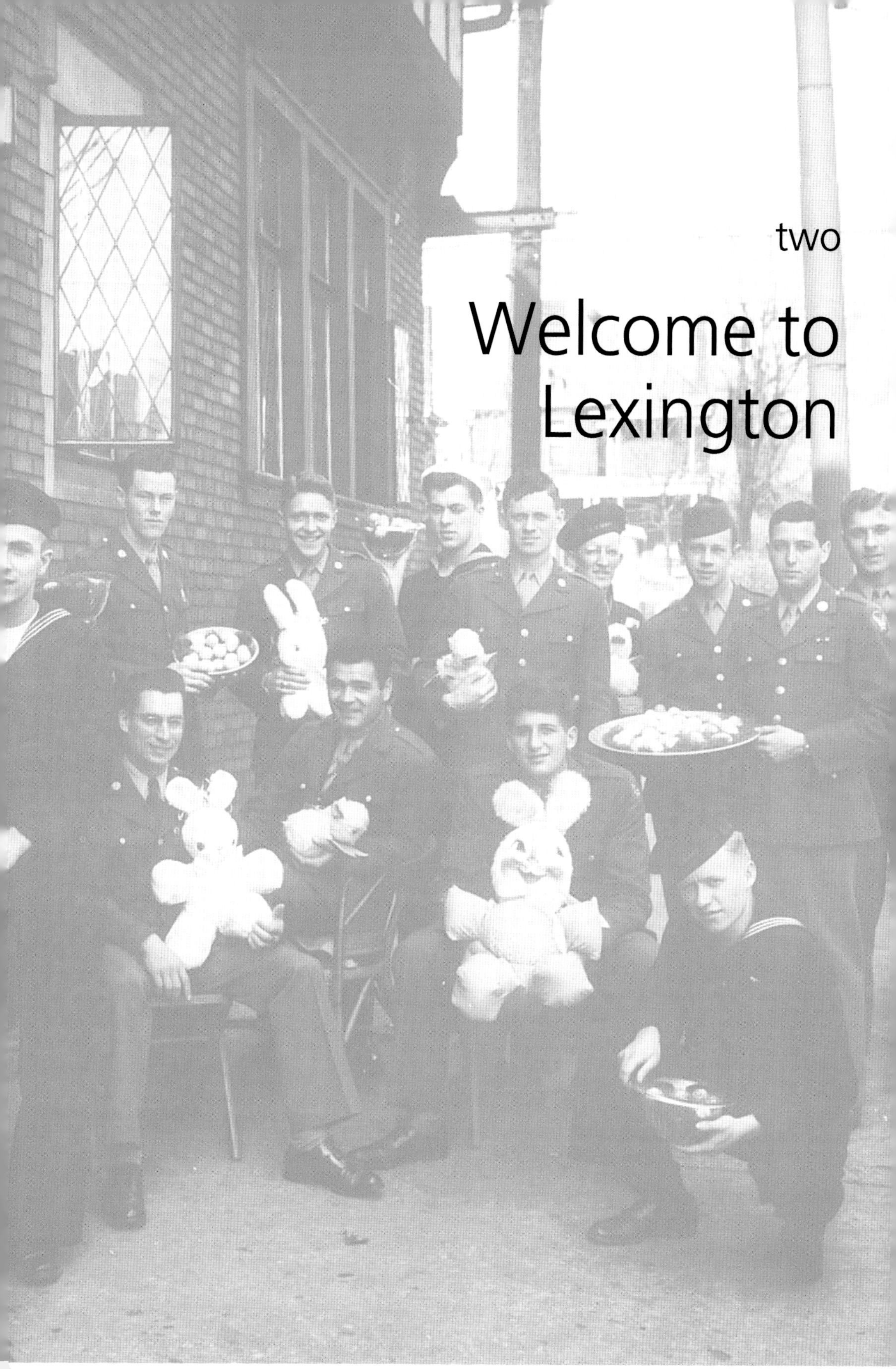

The growth of Lexington in the 1930s and 1940s reflected the civic pride, social concern, and public spirit of the community. Lexingtonians actively participated in community development by participating in civic groups and politics, promoting educational and cultural growth, increasing public safety, and supporting the national war effort. Bob Long captured this dynamic as he photographed the activities taking place around the town.

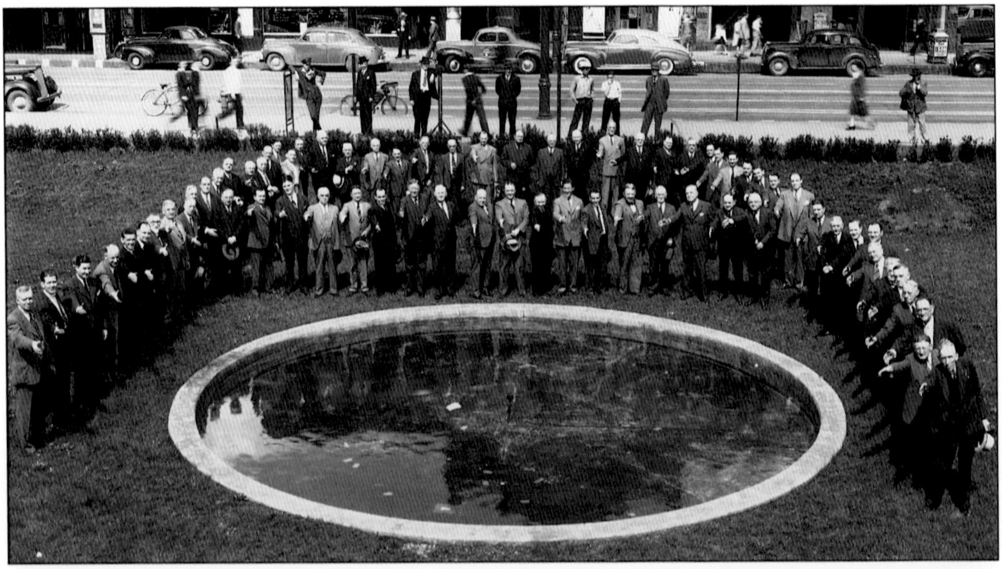

Rotary Club at Union Station, April 1941. On April 27, 1941, the Lexington Rotary Club welcomed delegates from around Kentucky to Lexington for a three-day conference, by extending the right hand of fellowship in front of Union Station. The Rotarians were treated to tours of horse farms, a golf tournament, bowling, and theater parties. Business sessions were held in the Phoenix and Lafayette Hotels and the Ben Ali Theater. (4693)

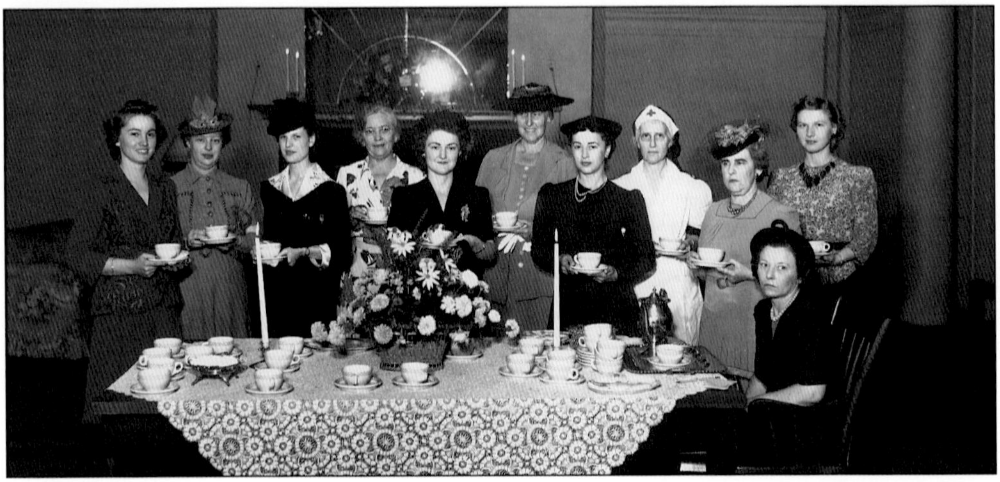

Victory Club tea at the Y.W.C.A., September 24, 1942. The Y.W.C.A., active in Lexington since the early 1900s, provided classrooms, a gymnasium, a boarding house for girls, and a cafeteria for business and professional women, as well as the general public. Here, the Signal Corps Victory Club, which was composed of wives of Signal Corps trainees and the directors of the Lexington Y.W.C.A., held a tea in the honor of new members. The women pictured here, from left to right, are as follows: Mrs. L.B. Tooley, Mrs. C.B. Lacey, Mrs. T.B. David, Mrs. Maud A. Foy, Mrs. G.W. Shaw, Mrs. Frank L. McVey, Mrs. K.A. Halverson, Mrs. W.D. Reddish, Mrs. Collis Ringo, Mary Louise Dobbs, and Mrs. I.L. Dutton (seated). (4945)

Right: Elks at the Henry Clay Monument, May 30, 1934. The Elks closed their annual statewide conference by laying a wreath at the tomb of Henry Clay during their memorial services in the Lexington Cemetery. Elks groups became active in Lexington as early as 1888, when Lodge #85 was organized with the assistance of Louisville Elks. The Henry Clay Monument, originally completed on July 4, 1861, has long been a favorite Lexington landmark. (1637)

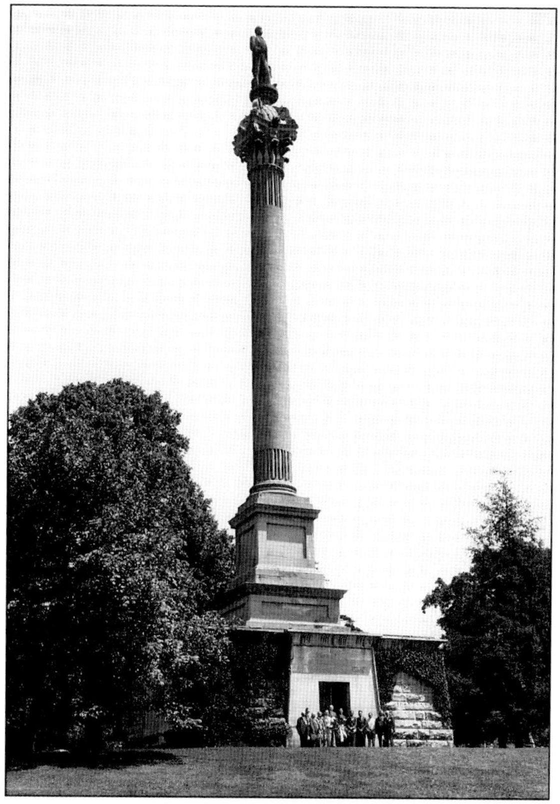

Below: Dedication of the historical marker at Ashland, April 18, 1936. Ashland, the home of Henry Clay, was the first spot of historical significance in Lexington to receive an historical marker. The Historical Marker Society first met on January 4, 1936 to plan the marking of 21 historical sites in Central Kentucky. Pictured from left to right are Society members: R.W. Davis, Tom R. Underwood, Charles Staples, Glenn Weinman, Henry Clay Bullock, Judge Samuel M. Wilson, Lieutenant Governor Keen Johnson, Baylor Landrum, R.M. Wheeler, Samuel Look, Thomas Platt, and Earl Wallace. (3135)

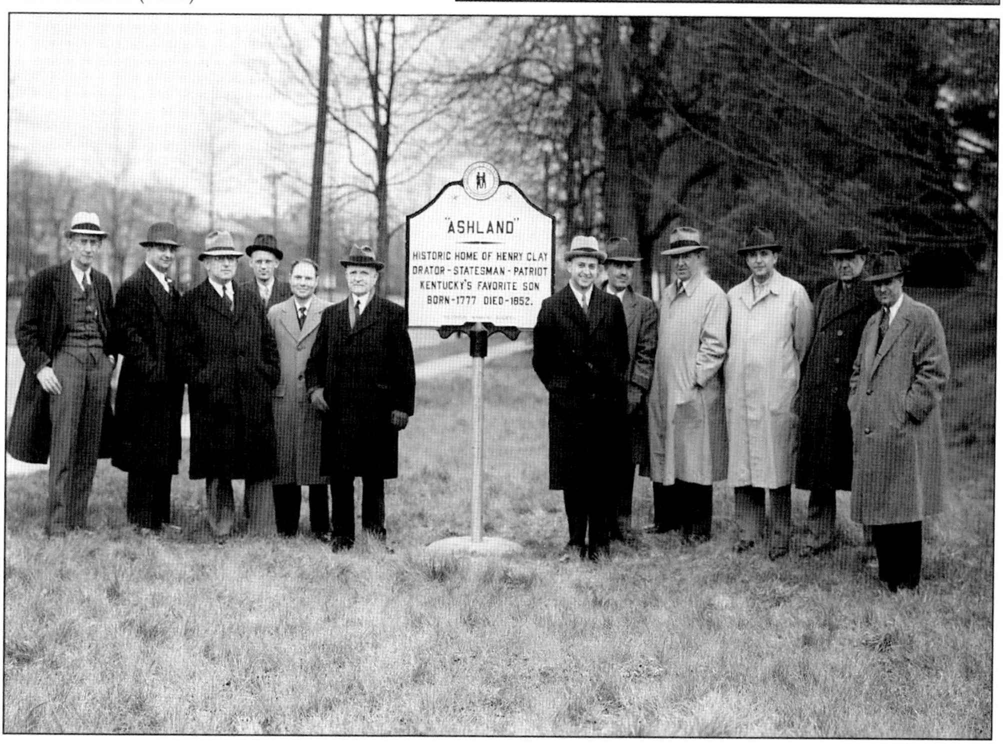

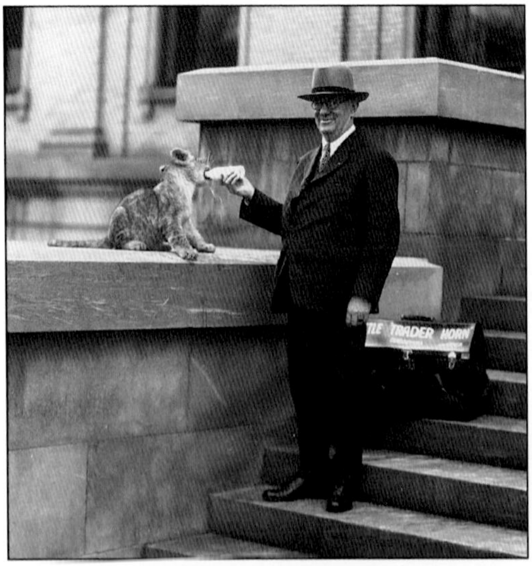

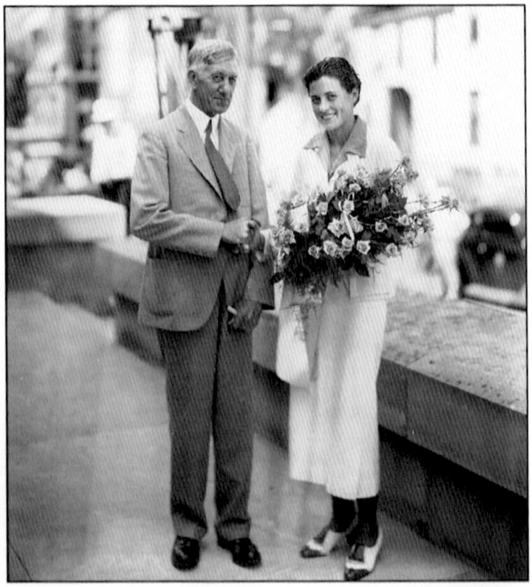

Above left: Mayor O'Brien, April 1931. Another member of the Historical Marker Society not included in the photograph above was James J. O'Brien, the 35th mayor of Lexington, who served from 1928 to 1932. He posed here with a Nubian lion cub on the doorsteps of City Hall to promote the film Trader Horn which was playing at the Ben Ali Theater. The lion was a gift to the film's star, Edwina Booth, from an East African tribe's chief. (880)

Above right: Marion Miley with Mayor Thompson, August 1935. Charles R. Thompson, mayor from 1934 to 1935, posed on the steps of city call with Marion Miley to celebrate her victory in the western women's golf tournament. Miley went on to become the top woman golfer in the United States in 1937. On September 28, 1941, she and her mother were killed by robbers at the Lexington Country Club where the two women resided. (3347)

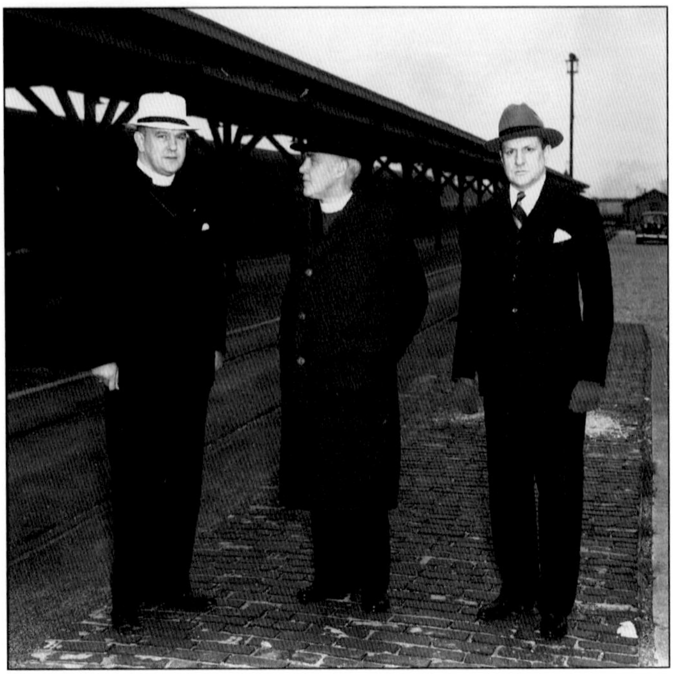

Left: Reverend Derwyn Trevor Owen and Dr. John W. Mulder with Mayor E. Reed Wilson, May 1939. Continuing the mayoral trend of being photographed with local and national celebrities, Mayor Wilson, who held the office from 1936 to 1939, visited with Reverend Owen and Dr. Mulder, the popular pastor of the Church of the Good Shepherd on East Main. (4263)

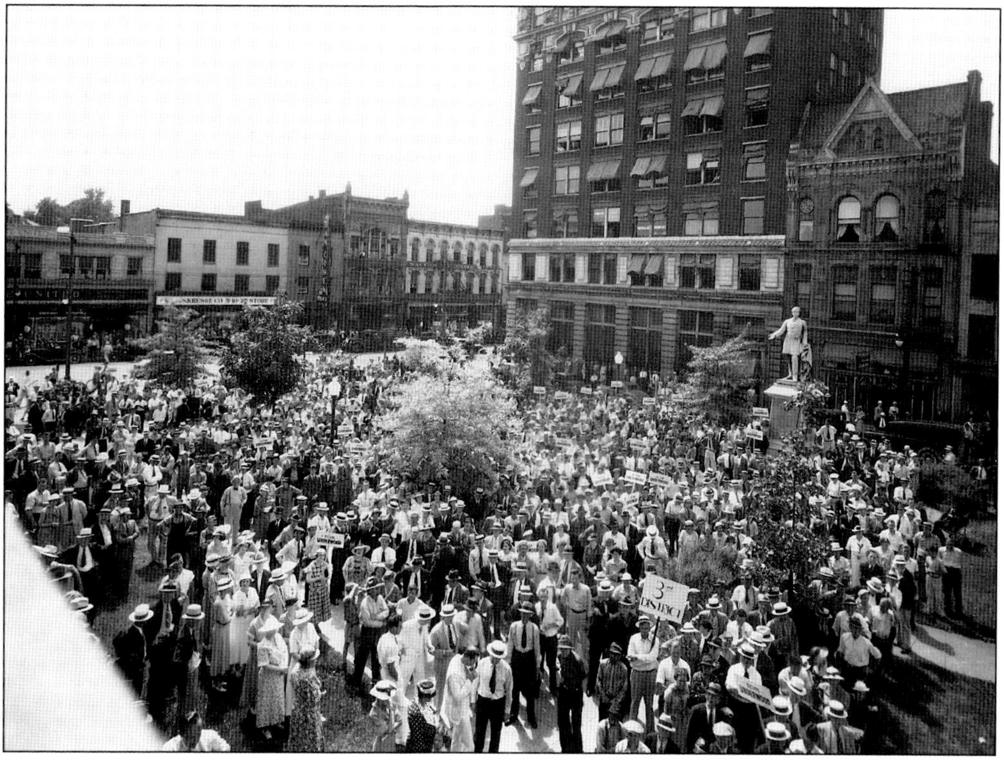

Democratic Convention, June 8, 1936. Kentucky is known for its colorful political history, and Lexington's has proven just as interesting. Here, Fayette County Democrats met in Cheapside for their quadrennial convention, where the group split over the appointment of chairman. While the advocates for Mr. G. Allison Holland gathered on the Main Street end of Cheapside, the supporters of Mr. Frank L. McCarthy called a "rump" convention on the Short Street side. (3184)

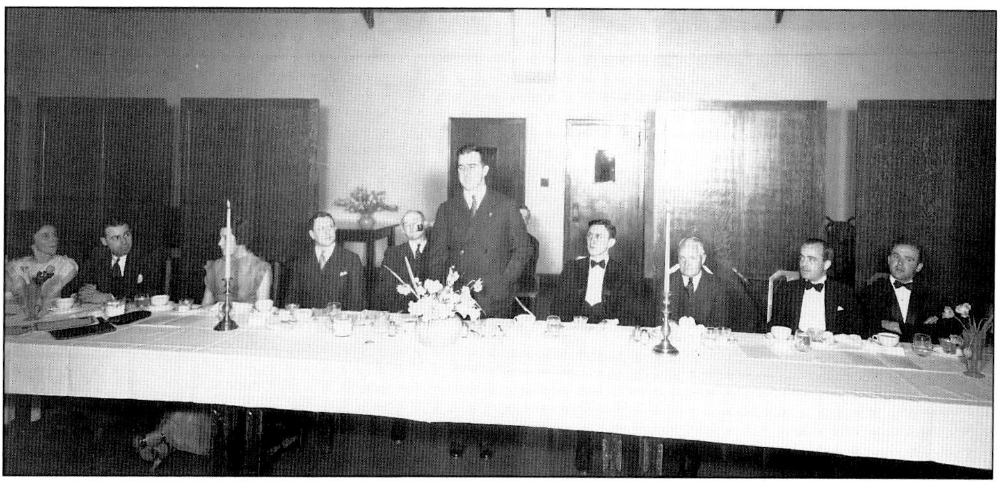

Democratic Club banquet at the University of Kentucky's McVey Hall, May 5, 1936. A.B. "Happy" Chandler, governor of Kentucky from 1935 to 1939 and 1955 to 1959, was known for improvements in education, roads, health, and welfare, and for his sometimes unorthodox methods. On this occasion, he spoke to the Young Democratic Club of the University of Kentucky. Felix H. Winston, director of the Young Democratic Clubs of America, and Lieutenant Governor Keen Johnson were also in attendance. (3150)

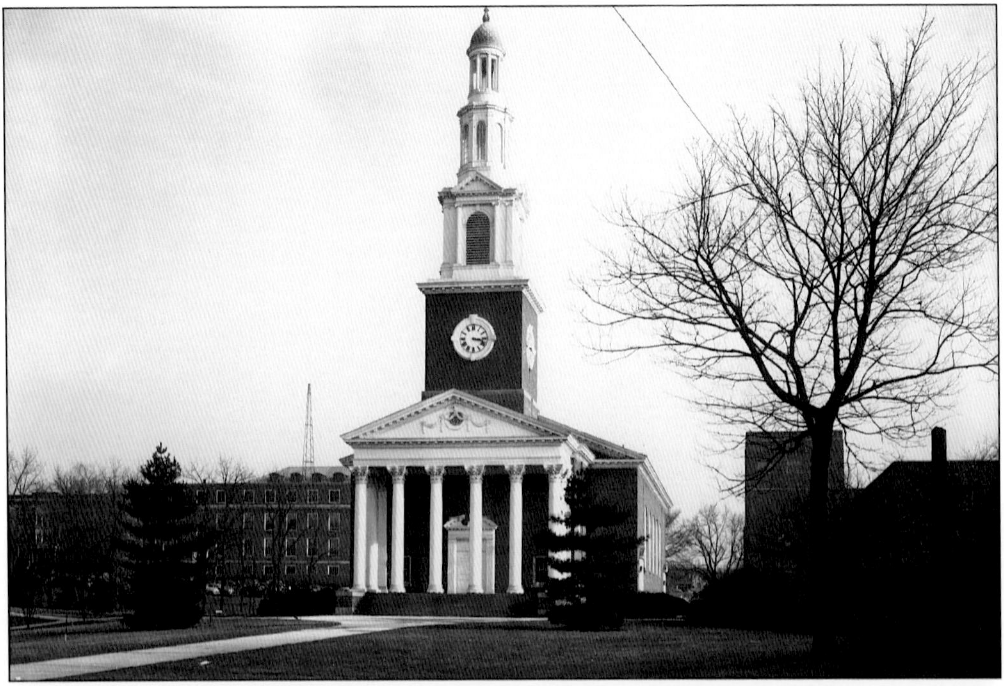

Memorial Hall at the University of Kentucky, February 1947. Lexington has long served as a major center of education in Kentucky, and the city's institutions of learning have had significant impact on the greater community. The University of Kentucky has contributed notably to the physical, cultural, and social shaping of the city. In 1929, the university and the community dedicated Memorial Hall to Kentuckians who died in World War I. (5771)

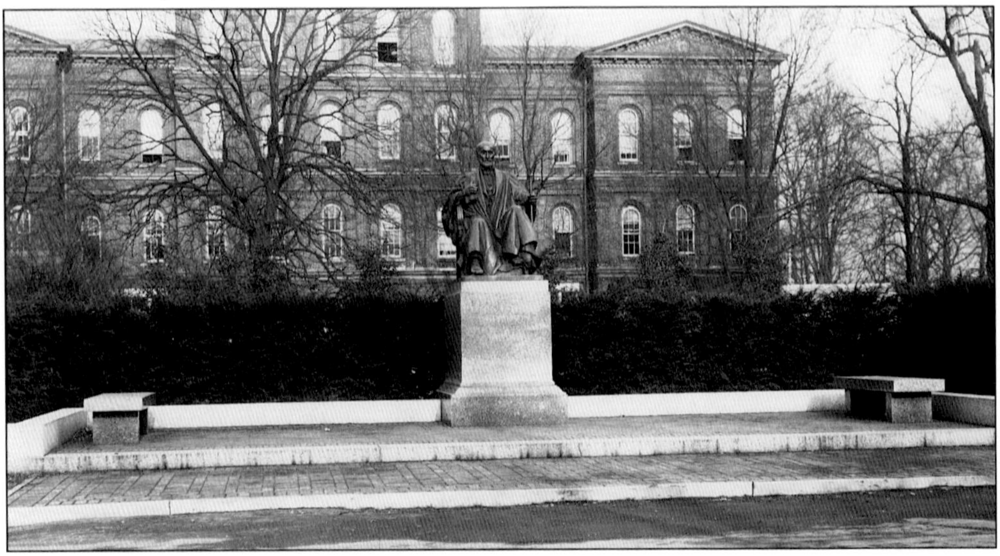

Patterson Monument, January 1938. A memorial to Dr. James Kennedy Patterson, this statue was created by the distinguished American sculptor, Henry Augustus Lukeman, and dedicated on June 1, 1934. President Patterson persistently promoted the idea of a state university in Lexington during the University's nascent years. In saving "the seed for the next generation," he prepared the school to become an active educational and social force in the city. (3891)

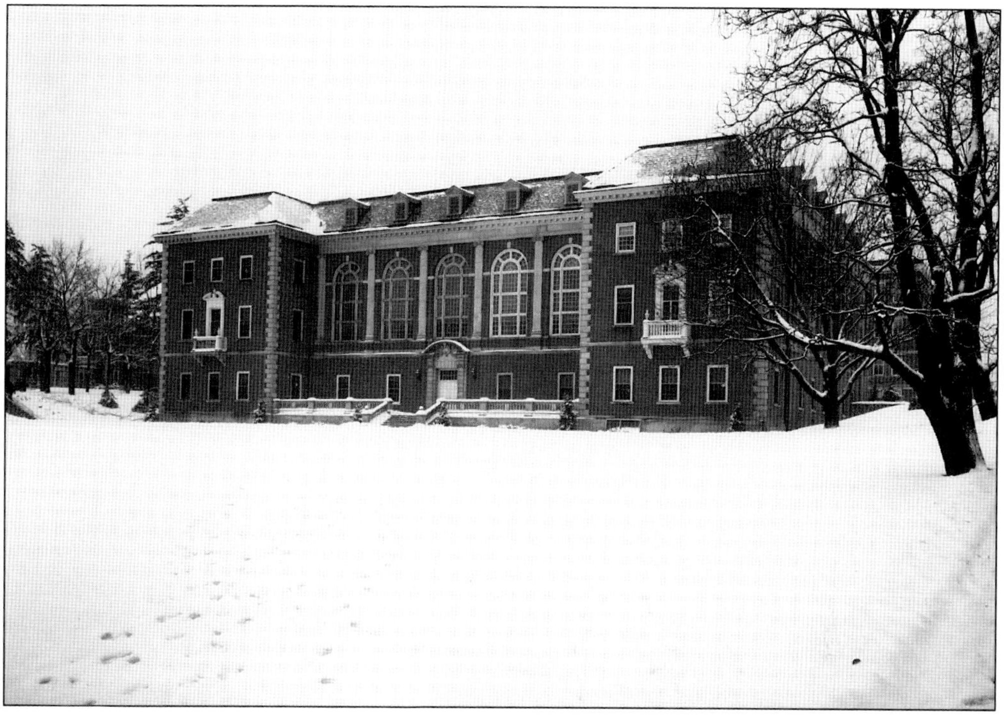

Above: Library at the University of Kentucky, January 1940. As the university has grown, so has its need for improved library facilities. The second of three main libraries, this building was dedicated on October 23, 1931, and later named after the first university librarian, Margaret I. King. The library originally cost $400,000 and was heralded by Dr. John H. Finley, associate editor of the New York Times and dedicatory speaker, as "a magnificent depository for noble works of the thinkers of the past." (4412)

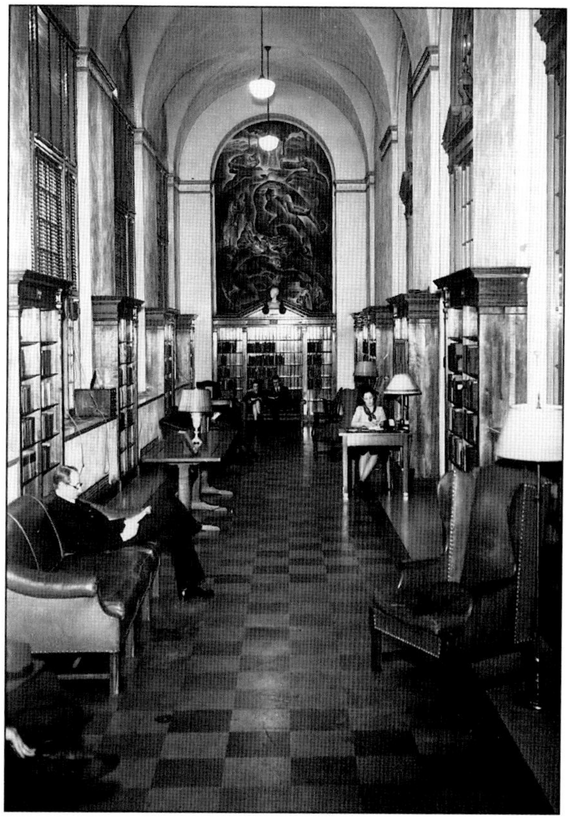

Right: Browsing room at the University of Kentucky Library, February 1939. The main browsing room of M.I. King Library featured two murals painted by Frank W. Long of Berea, Kentucky. The theme is "Rural Life in Kentucky," and this painting depicts the labor of a rural economy. The murals now decorate staff offices adjoining the Great Hall. This photograph and the one above were taken for issues of the Kentuckian, the University of Kentucky's yearbook. (4174)

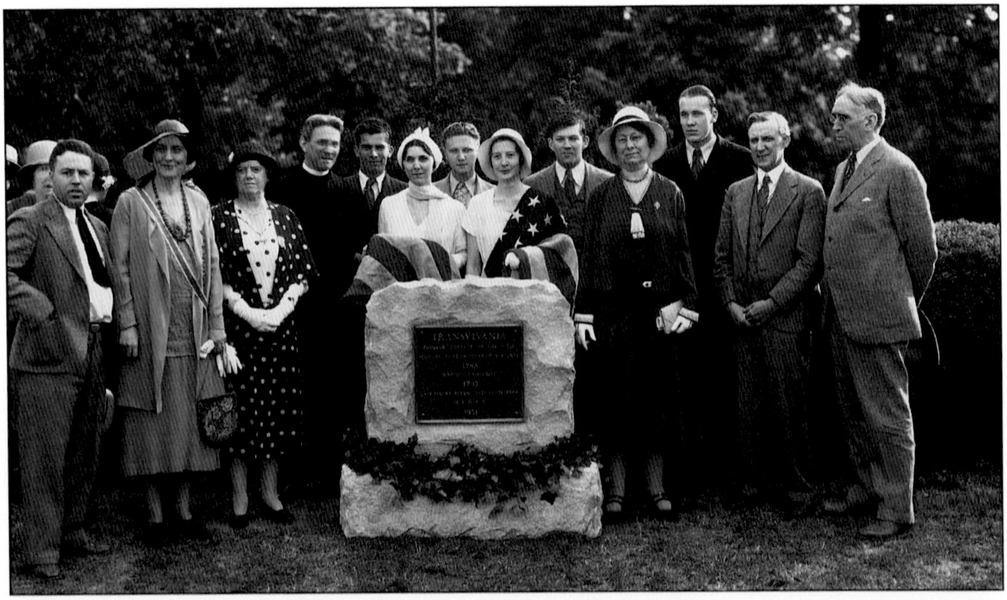

Dedication of monument at Transylvania, June 2, 1931. Transylvania University, Lexington's first institution of higher education, was moved here permanently from Harrodsburg, Kentucky, in 1793. This monument marks the site of the original building and reads, "Transylvania, pioneer college of the West, founded by the Legislature of Virginia in 1780. Moved to this site in 1793—Erected by Bryan Station Chapter of the Daughters of the American Revolution, 1931." Members of the D.A.R. pictured here include: Mrs. Stanley Forman Reed, Mrs. E.B. Sweeney, Ann Art Milward, Celeste Thompson, Mrs. B.F. Buckley Sr., with Dean C.P. Sparling, Arthur Braden (president of Transylvania), and Frank L. McVey (president of the University of Kentucky). (1042)

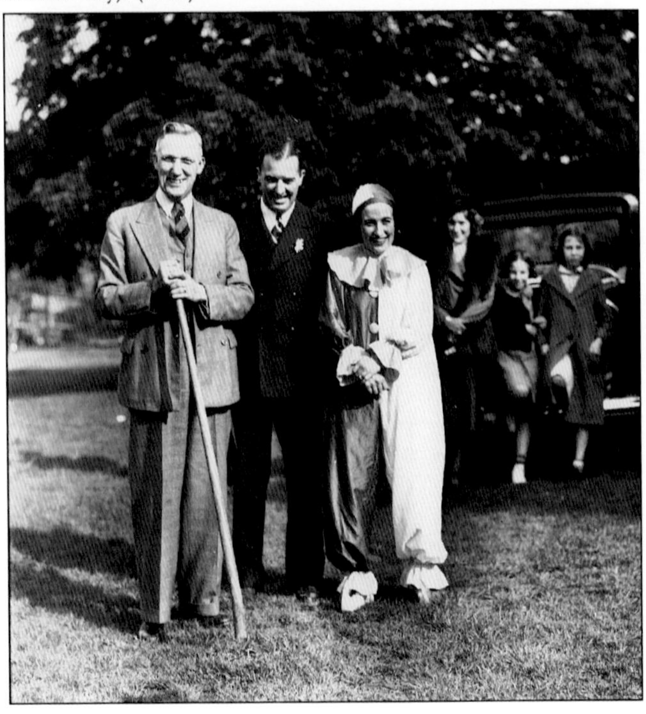

Transylvania Day, May 1, 1937. This celebration marked the 157th anniversary of Transylvania College with a parade, an outdoor luncheon, musical programs, and a court of honor. The events were a part of the community's three-day Pioneer Festival and featured the crowning of Miss Transylvania and Mr. Pioneer by Governor Chandler (a Transylvania alumnus), shown here with Louise Hood (the court jester) and Dr. Arthur Braden (Transylvania president). (3715)

Right: Jefferson Davis bust at Morrison Chapel, Transylvania College, October 21, 1931. In another dedication at Transylvania, the United Daughters of the Confederacy presented this bust of Jefferson Davis, a student of the college in 1824 who later became president of the Confederacy. The bust was set in bronze by Augustus Lukeman, the widely known sculptor who would later create the Patterson statue erected at the University of Kentucky. (1774)

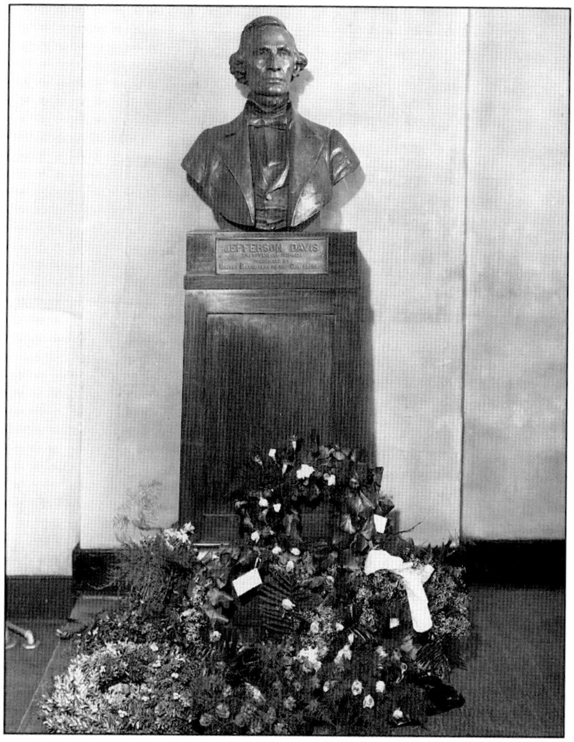

Below: Morrison Chapel at Transylvania College, October 21, 1931. "Old" Morrison, the main building at Transylvania College, was built with money donated by James Morrison at his death in 1823. Dedicated in 1833, the structure remains a symbol of Lexington's cultural and educational heritage. The design of the building, by Gideon Shryock of Lexington, has become incorporated within the city's seal (Wright, John D., p. 33). (1772)

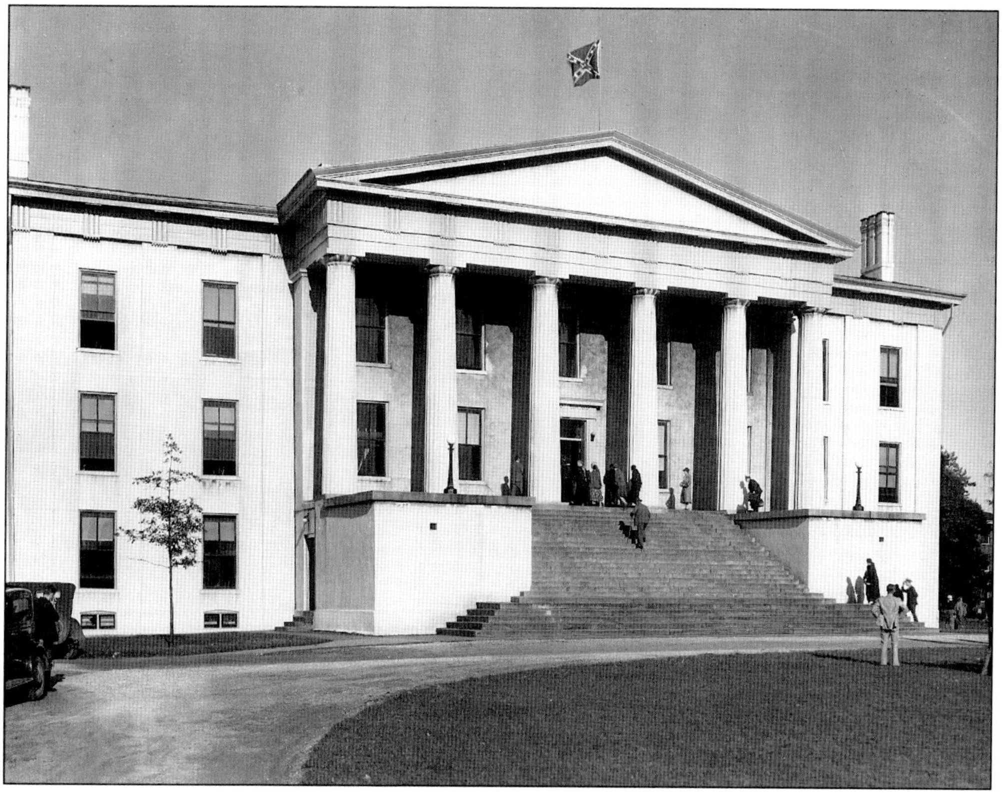

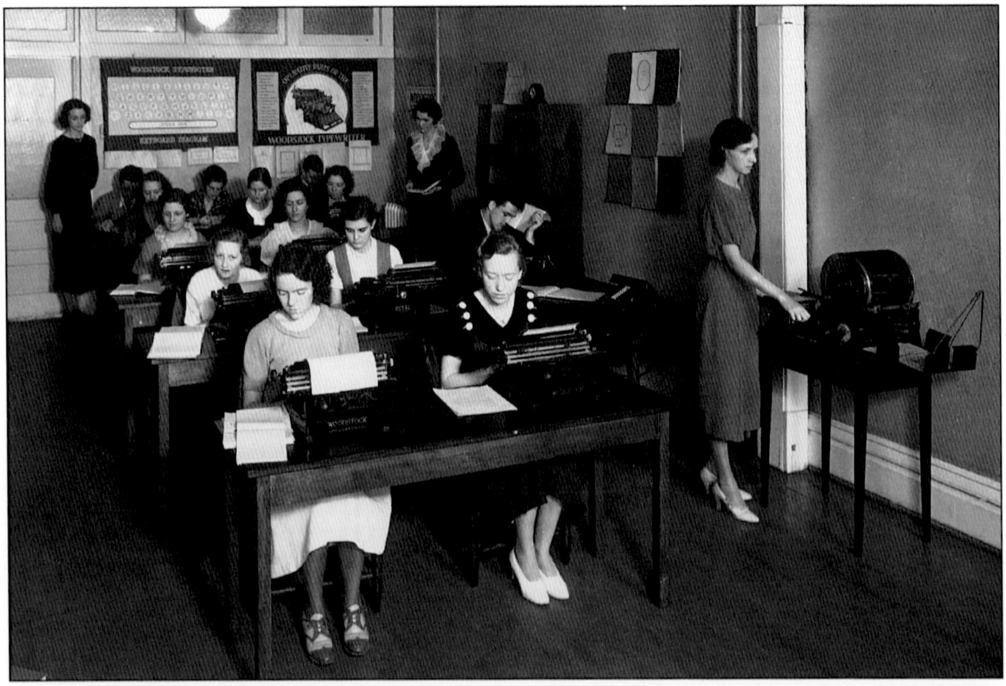

Lexington Business College, May 1933. In 1933, the Lexington Business College was located at 229 West Short Street. The school was run by Sara C. Sayre and was advertised as "Central Kentucky's Newest 'Accredited' Commercial College" and the "only Kentucky school teaching Speedwriting." While this school only existed for approximately five years, it was just one of the many post-secondary alternatives available to the people of Lexington. (1732)

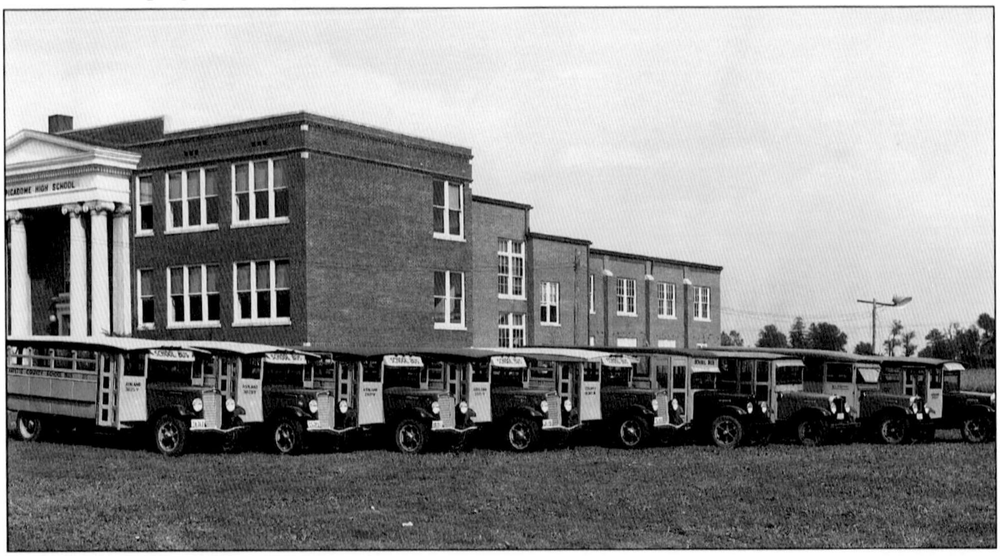

Fayette County school buses, c. September 11, 1934. The public school system was growing and changing in the 1930s and 1940s. This photograph was taken five days before the county schools finally opened for the year, with a projected enrollment of 4,500 after a delay due to an outbreak of infantile paralysis. These empty school buses are parked outside of Picadome High School, which was built in 1928 and torn down in 1976. (1552)

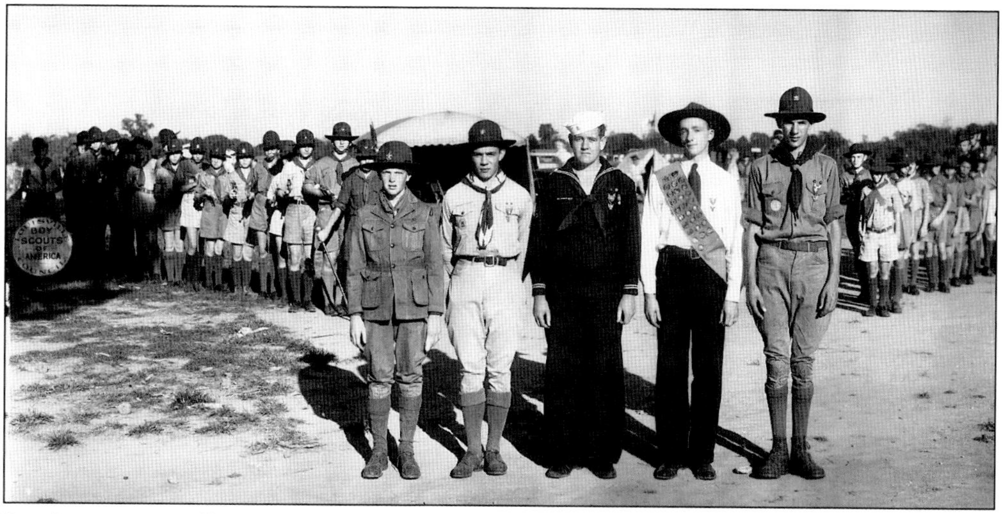

Boy Scouts Camparall Parade, September 30, 1933. In addition to educational opportunities, numerous extracurricular activities were available to Lexington youths. The Boy Scouts became active in Lexington in 1919. In September of 1933, over six hundred scouts gathered in Castlewood City Park for a camparall. This one hundred-piece Louisville Scout drum and bugle corps, lead a parade of scouts from the campground, through downtown to the University of Kentucky campus, where the scouts watched a football game. (1691)

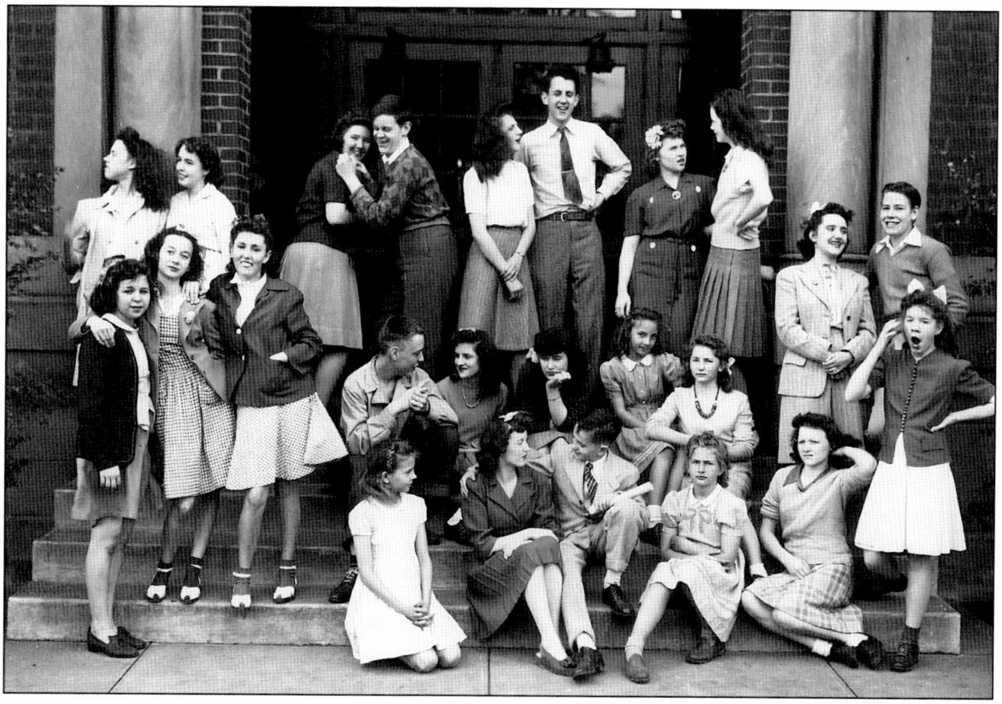

Lexington Children's Theater, May 1944. The cast of Teen Town posed for this publicity photo to advertise their performance on Saturday, May 13, 1944. The play was written by members of the Lexington Children's Theater staff and edited by the actors to suit the individuals. The organization started in the 1939-40 season with the production of five plays and continues to provide entertainment and dramatic experience for Lexington's youth. (5198)

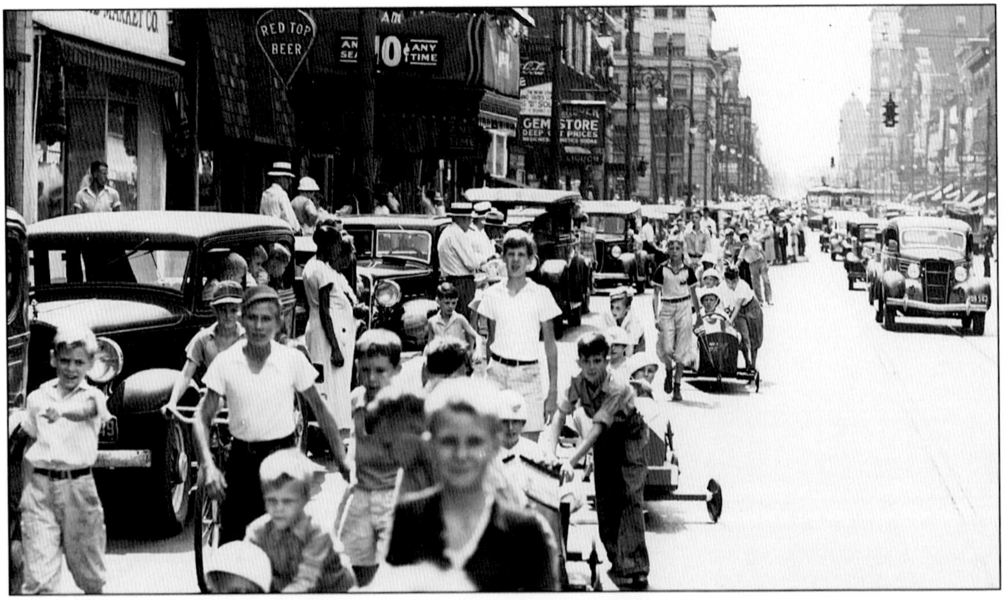

Soap Box Derby, July 29, 1936. The city's first All-American Soap Box Derby, sponsored by The Lexington Herald and L.R. Cooke Chevrolet, took Lexington by storm in July of 1936. During this parade, 90 boys moved their cars west down Main Street to Leestown Pike, where they raced down the viaduct. Seven thousand Lexingtonians watched 14-year-old Leonard Dyer, a resident of the Odd Fellows Orphan Home, speed to victory. (3215)

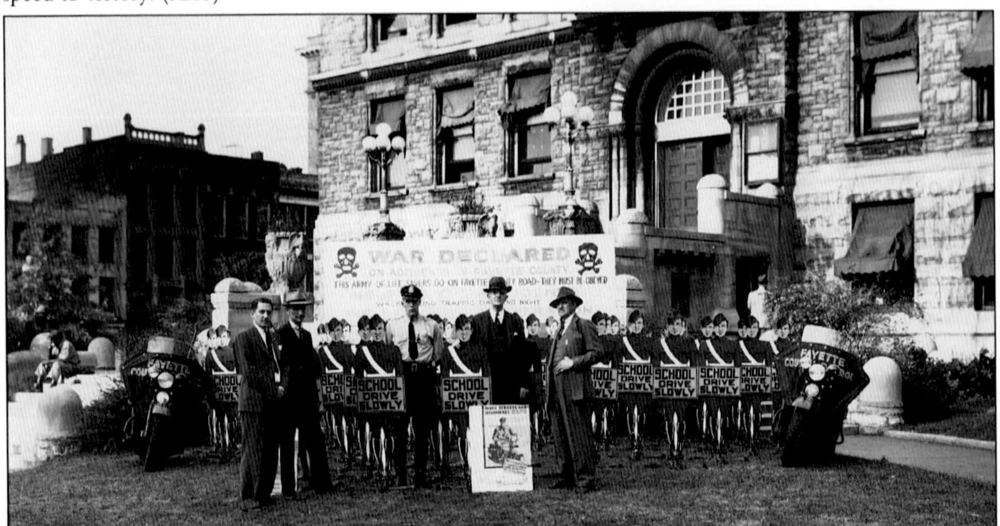

Safety Boy patrol signs on the courthouse lawn, October 1940. Slower driving was promoted in this campaign to increase student safety through the installment of these Safety Boy signs on roads near Fayette County schools. Their purpose was to remind drivers, as Chief of Fayette County Police J.W. McCord advertised in The Lexington Leader, that "recklessness, carelessness, thoughtlessness, fast driving, and plain old everyday discourtesy cause most of the accidents." The officials active in the campaign included the individuals pictured here. From left to right are: Louis Rives (county magistrate), H.D. Coleman (patrol captain), Charles Fentress (patrolman), Judge W.E. Nichols, and W.C. Uhlman (from the Kentucky Peace Officers' Association). (4579)

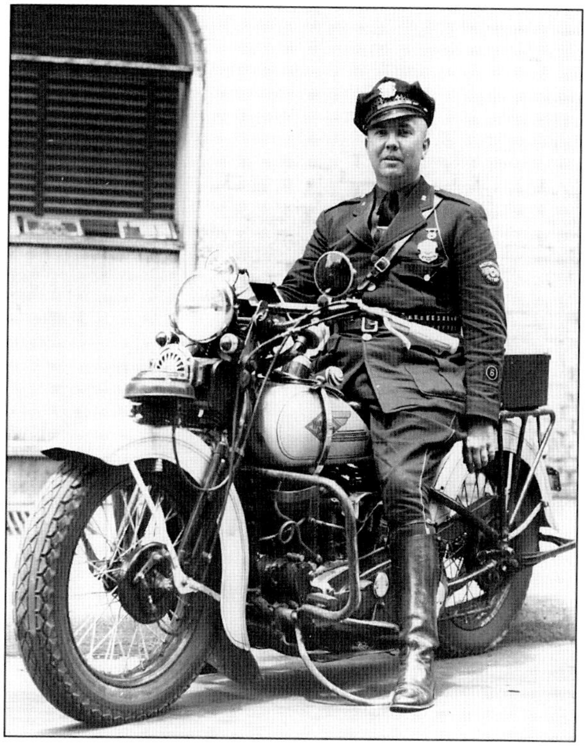

Right: Police officer W.C. Jordon, May 1937. The Lexington Police Department employed the latest in patrol technology to enhance traffic safety. On March 31, 1934, The Lexington Herald reported that new motorcycles purchased by the city would enhance a campaign to stop speeding and reckless driving. Police Sergeant William Jordon, shown here with his vehicle, served the Lexington Police Department for 26 years. (3747)

Below: Pistol squad, August 1931. The Lexington Police Department's efforts to improve public safety included skill enhancement and continuing education for its officers. This pistol team, dressed in new uniforms, participated in small arms matches and national police school at Camp Perry. The team included the following members, shown from left to right: A.A. Thornton, Linzie Leighton, L.E. Henderson, J. Howard Wills, Clyde O. Mattox, G.W. Maupin, and William Maupin (their mascot). (1797)

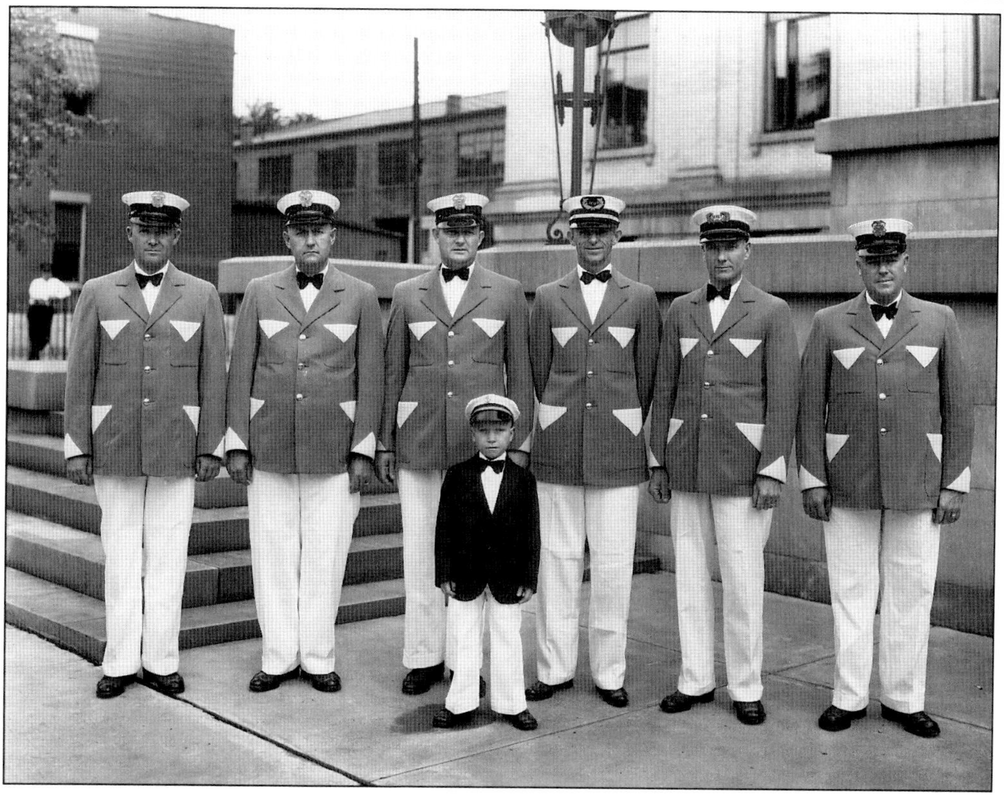

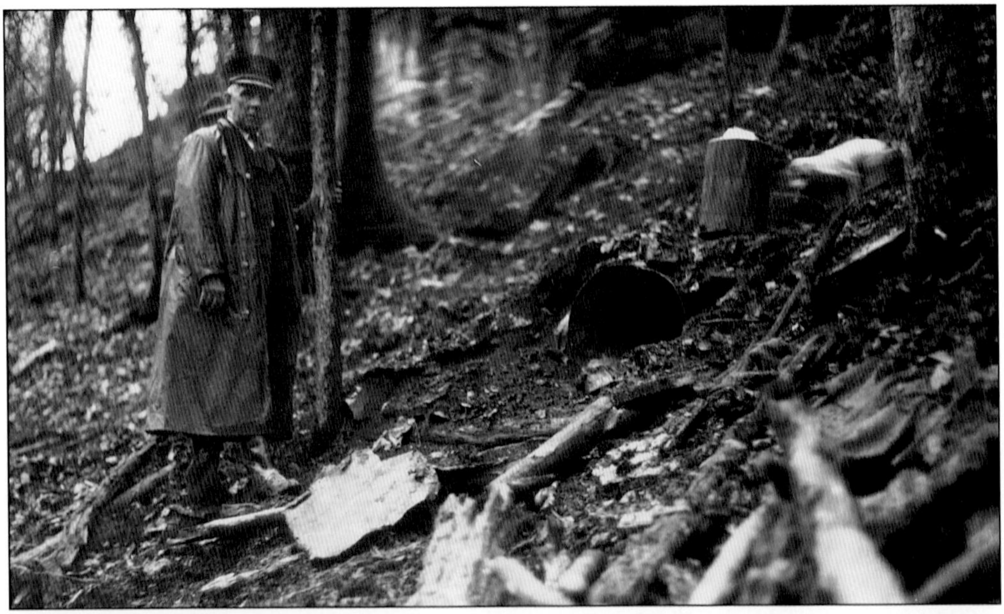

Raid on moonshine still, 1931. Prohibition kept Lexington police officers active in a region that was known for its historic local distilleries and private alcohol production. Raids on moonshine stills such as this one resulted in frequent arrests during the 1920s and into the 1930s. In addition, local distilleries, some of which had remained in operation under federal permit, often became victims of thieves (Wright, John D., p. 169). (1071)

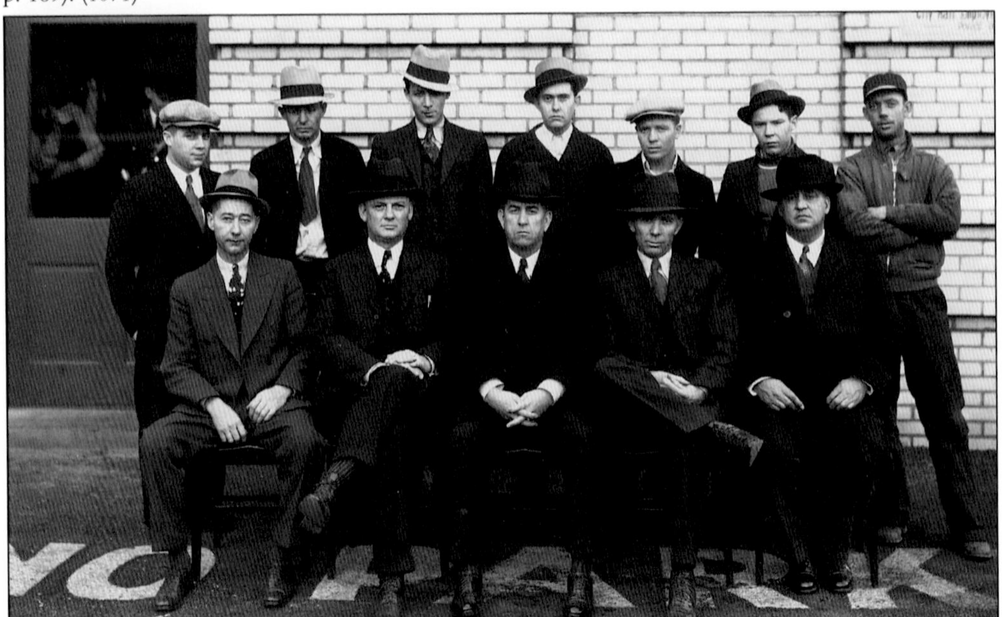

Police officers and bank robbers, January 1933. Lexington's police were also involved in arresting this band of thieves for bank robberies in Stamping Ground, where a cashier was killed; in Simpsonville, where bank employees were locked in a vault; and an attempted robbery in Moorefield. The robbers and police officers posed for this photograph while the Scott County Circuit Judge considered requests for a Special Grand Jury to indict them. (1464)

Right: Fire Department display, August 1932. The fire department contributed to public safety by promoting fire prevention in addition to firefighting. This display, which advertised the movie Flames, includes these "Friendly Suggestions" from Fire Chief C.J. Henry: "1. Don't throw lighted matches around carelessly. 2. Never look for trouble around an automobile by open light. 3. Don't be reckless with gasoline or other inflammables. 4. Pull aside when you're driving and hear the sirens. We have to get where we're going rapidly." (1358)

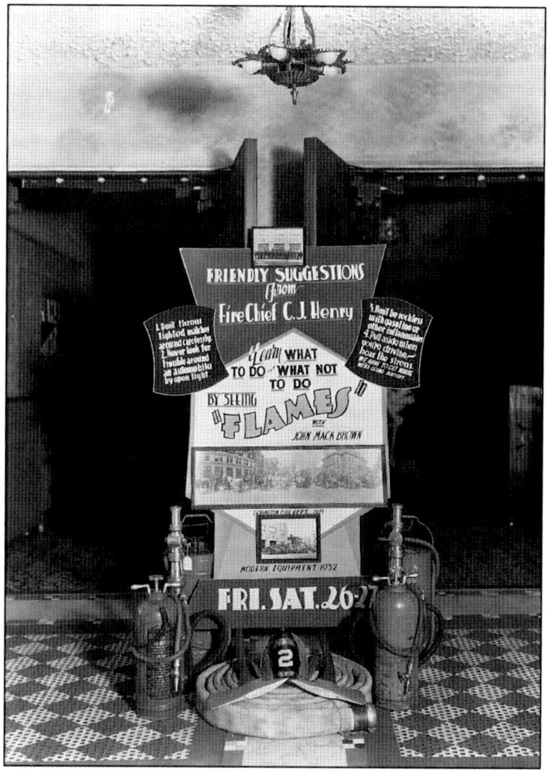

Below: Central Fire Station and fire truck, June 1941. The first formal firefighting company in Lexington was instituted in 1790 and was called the Union Company. By 1941, the city fire department was well established and in the process of being modernized. Station 1 (pictured here) became the headquarters for the Lexington Fire Department in June of 1929. Modern fire trucks helped the men of the department meet the challenges of fighting fires in the expanding city. (4725)

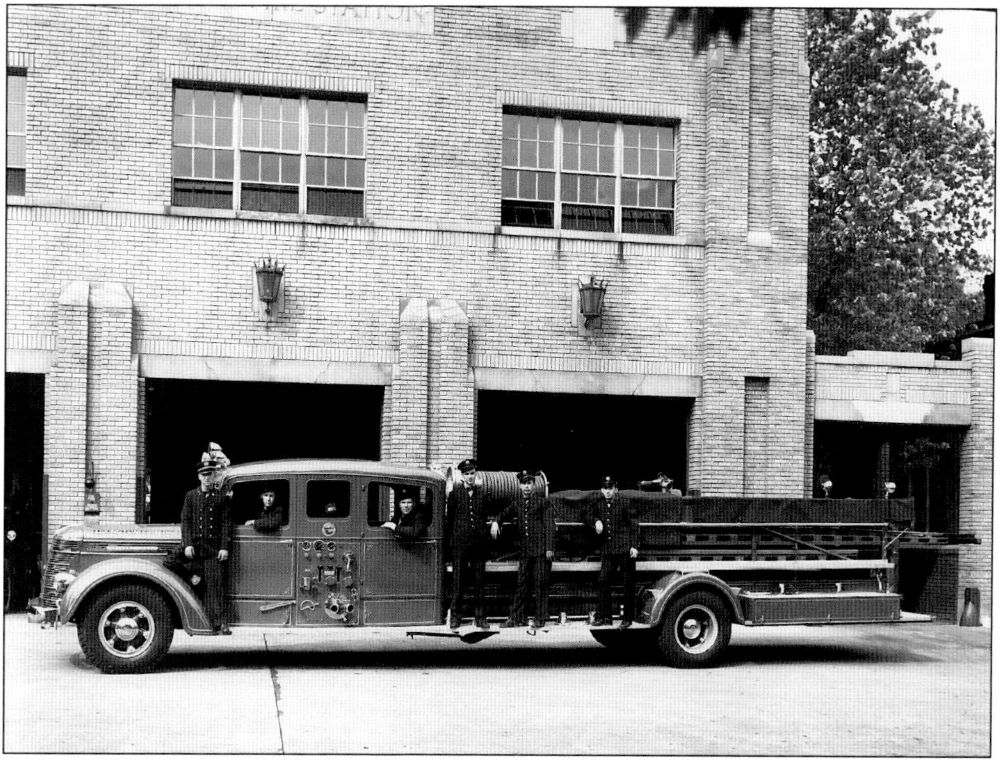

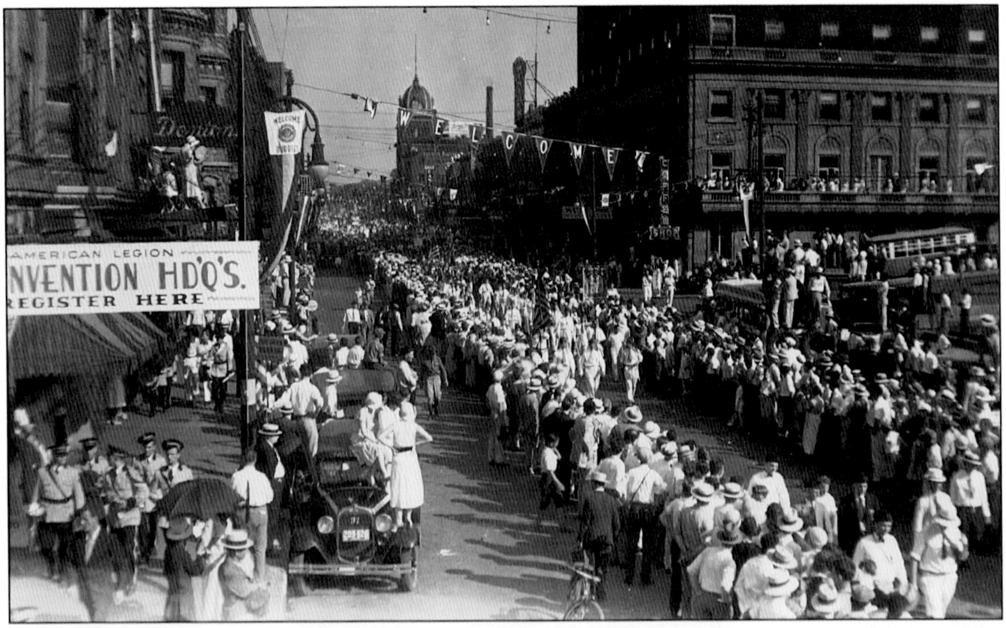

American Legion parade, July 27, 1931. The World Wars impacted Lexington as they did all communities throughout the United States. Veterans from the first World War formed the American Legion, dedicating themselves to community service. Three thousand Kentucky Legionnaires came to Lexington, on July 27, 1931, to meet for their 13th annual conference. City businesses closed and WHAS broadcast the event as the Legionnaires and the Legion Auxiliary paraded down Main Street. (1105)

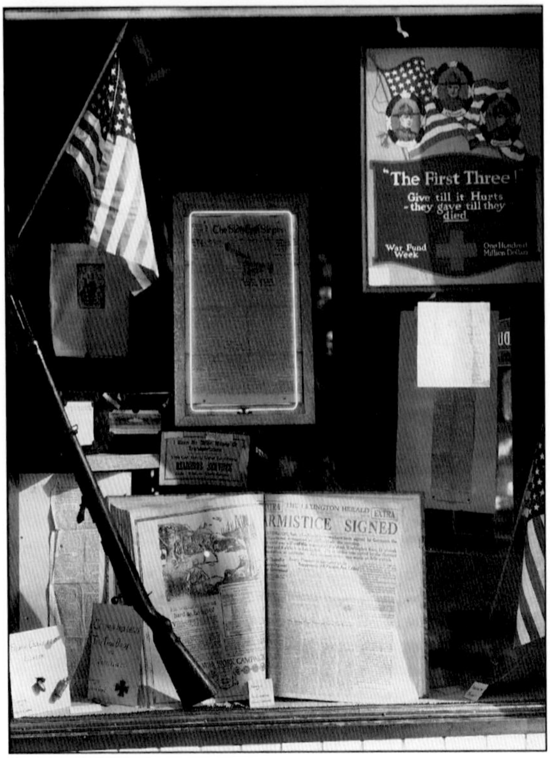

War poster display. The day World War I ended was also celebrated with parades and by local businesses which created displays. This Armistice Day display pulled together posters, newspapers, and war artifacts to remind Lexingtonians of the luxury of peace. The bound newspaper proclaiming "Armistice Signed" was furnished by the Lexington Public Library while a French cigarette lighter and a German Iron Cross were lent by Mr. Carter Coons. (U-967)

Right: Signs at the Royal Cafe, February 1943. By February of 1943, signs of World War II were prevalent throughout Lexington. On the wall of the Royal Cafe, next to the signs discouraging profane language and noting that college students would not be issued membership cards, patrons were encouraged to "Knock Off A Japanazi" by taking their "Change In War Stamps" and to show a "Thumbs Up for Victory." (5018)

Below: Ellis Drug window display, October 1943. Local businesses contributed to the war effort in many ways. Ellis Drug, at 141 North Broadway, did their part with this display which encouraged their customers to "Back the Attack" by purchasing war bonds and to bolster the troops through National Letter Writing Week. By the seventh war bond drive in 1945, Lexington residents had purchased over $16 million in bonds (Wright, John D., p. 190). (5106)

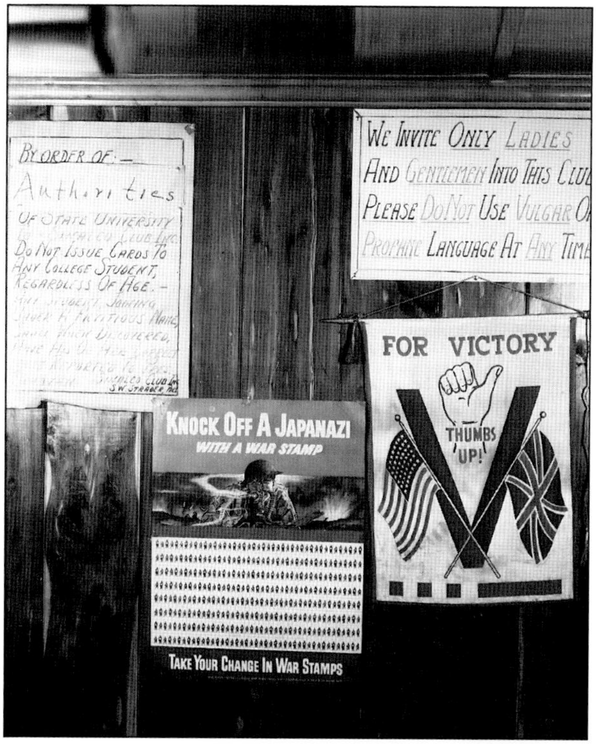

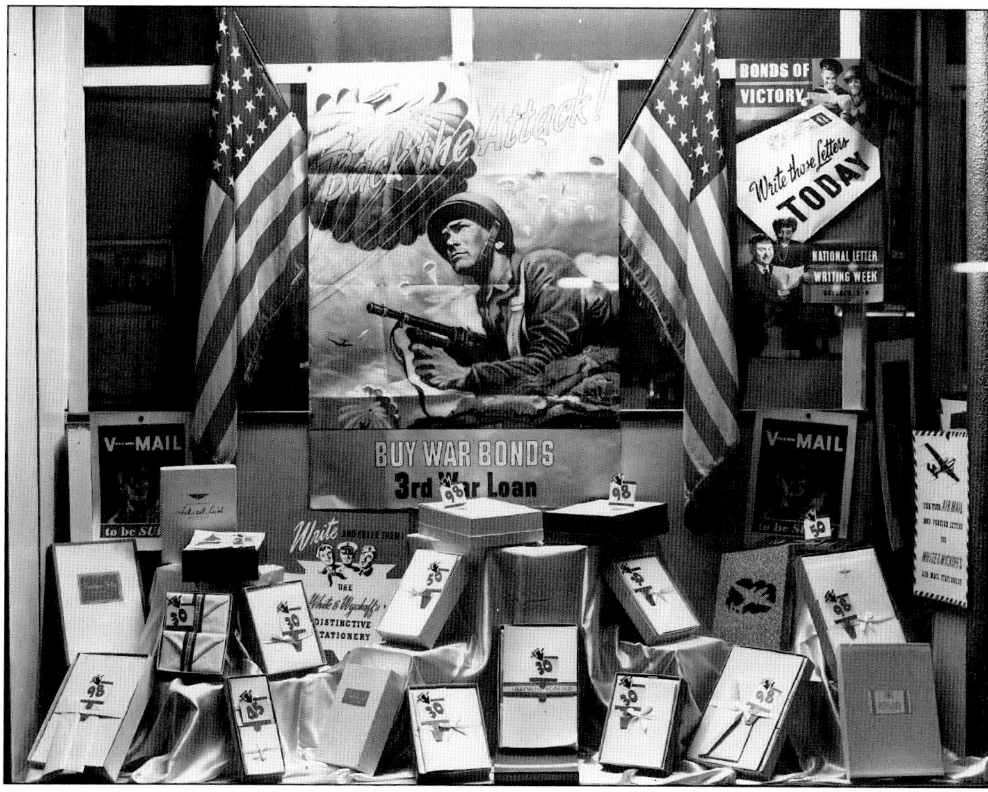

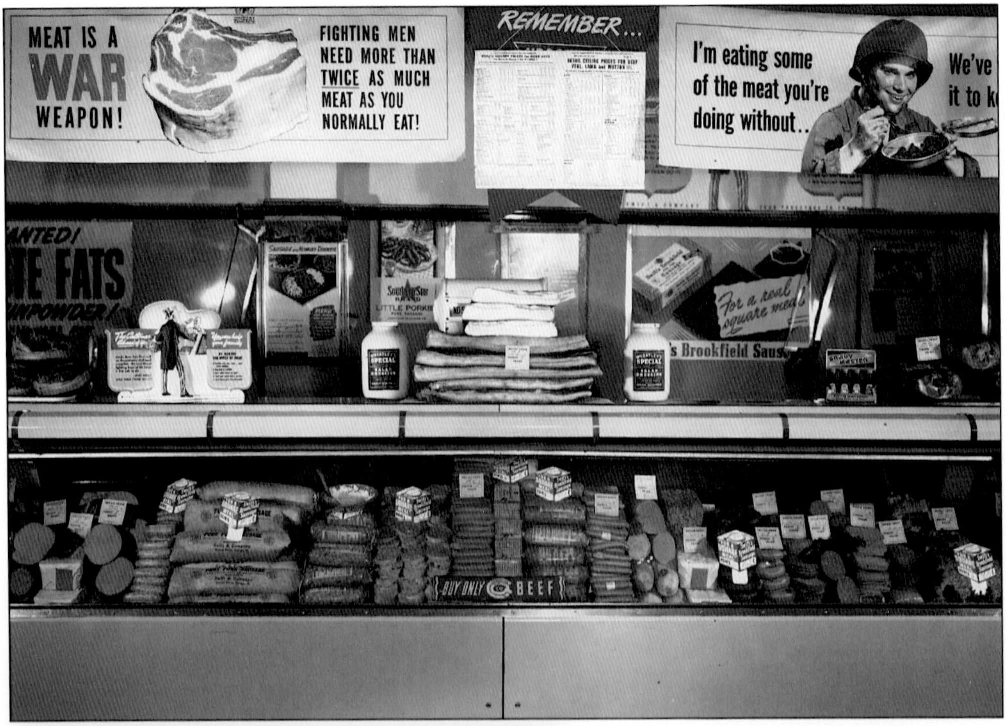

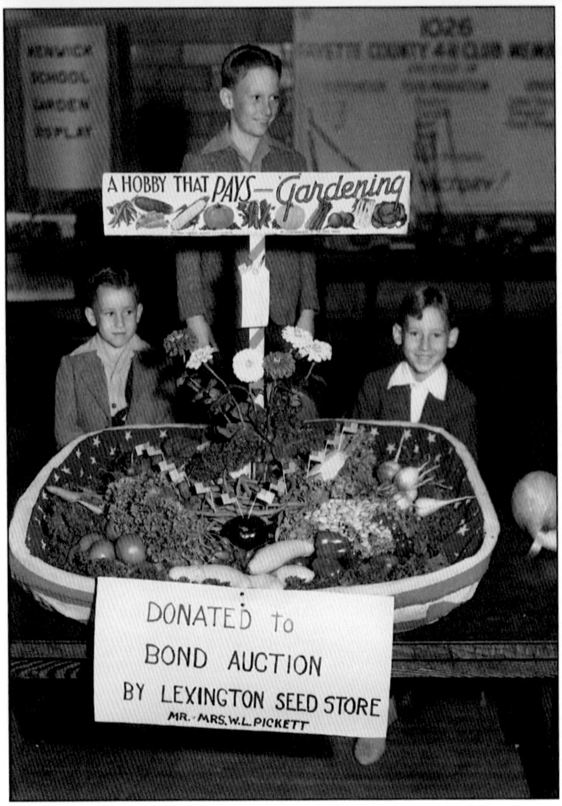

Above: Kroger Store meat counter, November 1943. Lexington joined the rest of the country in rationing goods such as meat, sugar, tires, and gasoline. While encouraging the purchase of meat "for a real square meal," Kroger's backed rationing efforts by featuring patriotic ideas such as "Meat is a War Weapon" and "The Customer Ahead of You" is Uncle Sam. Many Lexington businesses supported the war effort by promoting conservative consumerism. (5122)

Left: Pickett family contribution to war bond auction, September 23, 1943. Individuals and nonprofit organizations chose to contribute to the war effort in several ways. Organized in 1930, the Kenwick Junior Garden Club held a harvest festival on September 23, 1943, which included a war bond auction. Over $5,000 worth of bonds were sold through the auctioning of exhibits. The Pickett family's entry is proudly displayed here, representing the Lexington Seed Store. (5101)

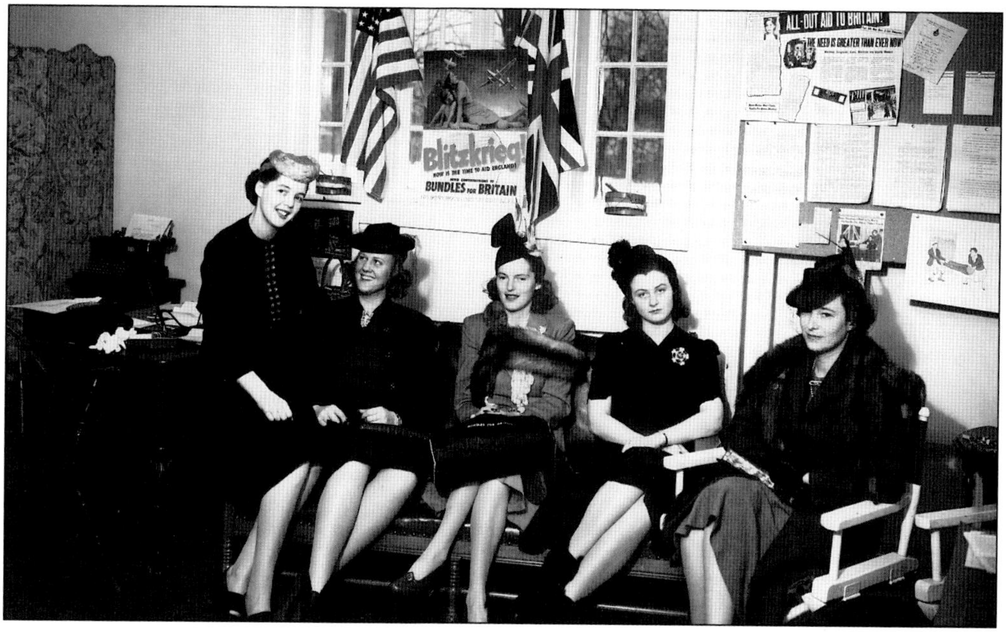

Bundles for Britain, February 27, 1941. Lexington women collected clothing and other articles as part of the "Bundles for Britain" campaign. The Lexington unit arranged a benefit-style show at the Phoenix Hotel which starred models Mrs. John Lacey, Mary Elizabeth Clay, Evelyn Beard, Ann Clay, and Mrs. Clay Simpson. The proceeds went to medical relief for England. Over five hundred women turned out and contributed about $270 for the crusade. (4675)

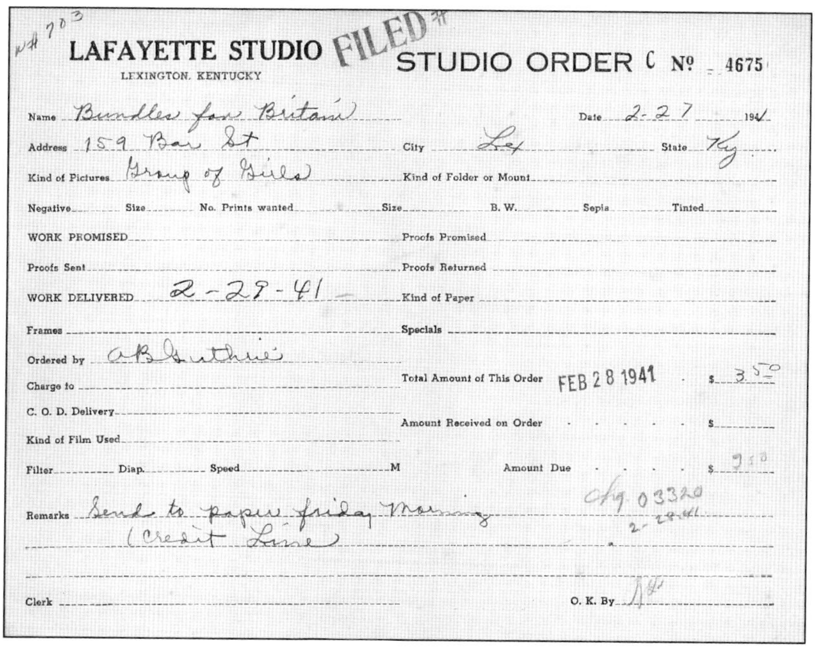

LAFAYETTE STUDIO FILED
LEXINGTON, KENTUCKY
STUDIO ORDER C Nº 4675

Name Bundles for Britain Date 2-27 1941
Address 159 Bar St City Lex State Ky
Kind of Pictures Group of Girls Kind of Folder or Mount
Negative Size No. Prints wanted Size B. W. Sepia Tinted
WORK PROMISED Proofs Promised
Proofs Sent Proofs Returned
WORK DELIVERED 2-28-41 Kind of Paper
Frames Specials
Ordered by A B Guthrie
Charge to Total Amount of This Order FEB 28 1941 $ 3.50
C. O. D. Delivery
Amount Received on Order $
Kind of Film Used
Filter Diap. Speed M Amount Due $
Remarks Send to paper friday Morning (Credit Line)
Clerk O. K. By

Bundles for Britain, February 27, 1941. Each Lafayette Studio order was given an order number and placed in an envelope which detailed the subject of the photograph, the date of the order, photographic details, cost, and the customer's name. This photograph was ordered by A.B. Guthrie Jr., an influential editor of The Lexington Leader, who went on to write critically acclaimed novels about the West. (4675)

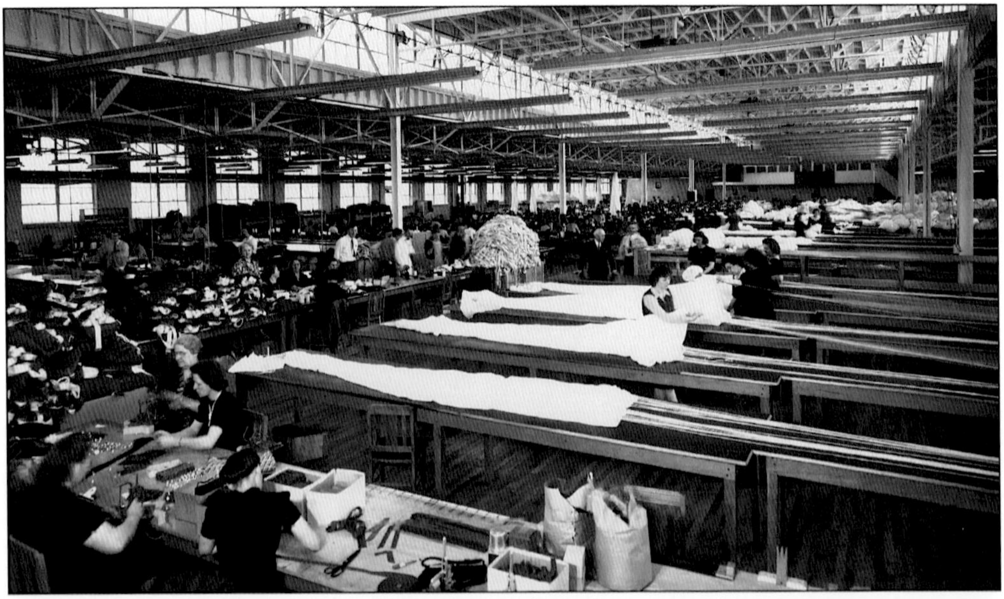

Irving Air Chute Company Inc., April 1943. The Irving Air Chute Company left its location on West Main Street and built a new plant at 1317 Versailles Road in 1942 to meet increased wartime demand for parachutes. This expansion and the shortage of male workers enabled Lexington women to acquire positions at Irving and join the women across the nation who contributed to the war effort through assembly jobs (Wright, John D., p. 191). (5033)

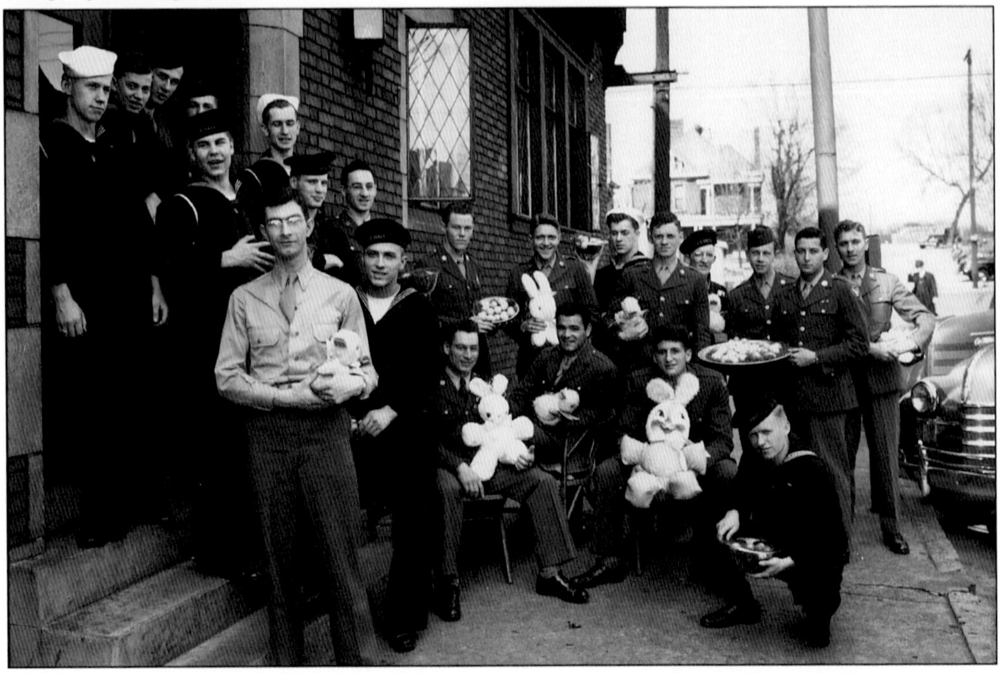

Stop Over Station, April 1944. Stop Over Station opened on February 28, 1942 to provide lodging, meals, and entertainment to military personnel for no cost as they passed through the Blue Grass. The Lexington community's hospitality was especially welcome during the holidays, including this Easter in 1944. After four years of hosting men and women at 109 Esplanade, Stop Over Station closed on January 31, 1946. (5188)

three

Downtown Lexington

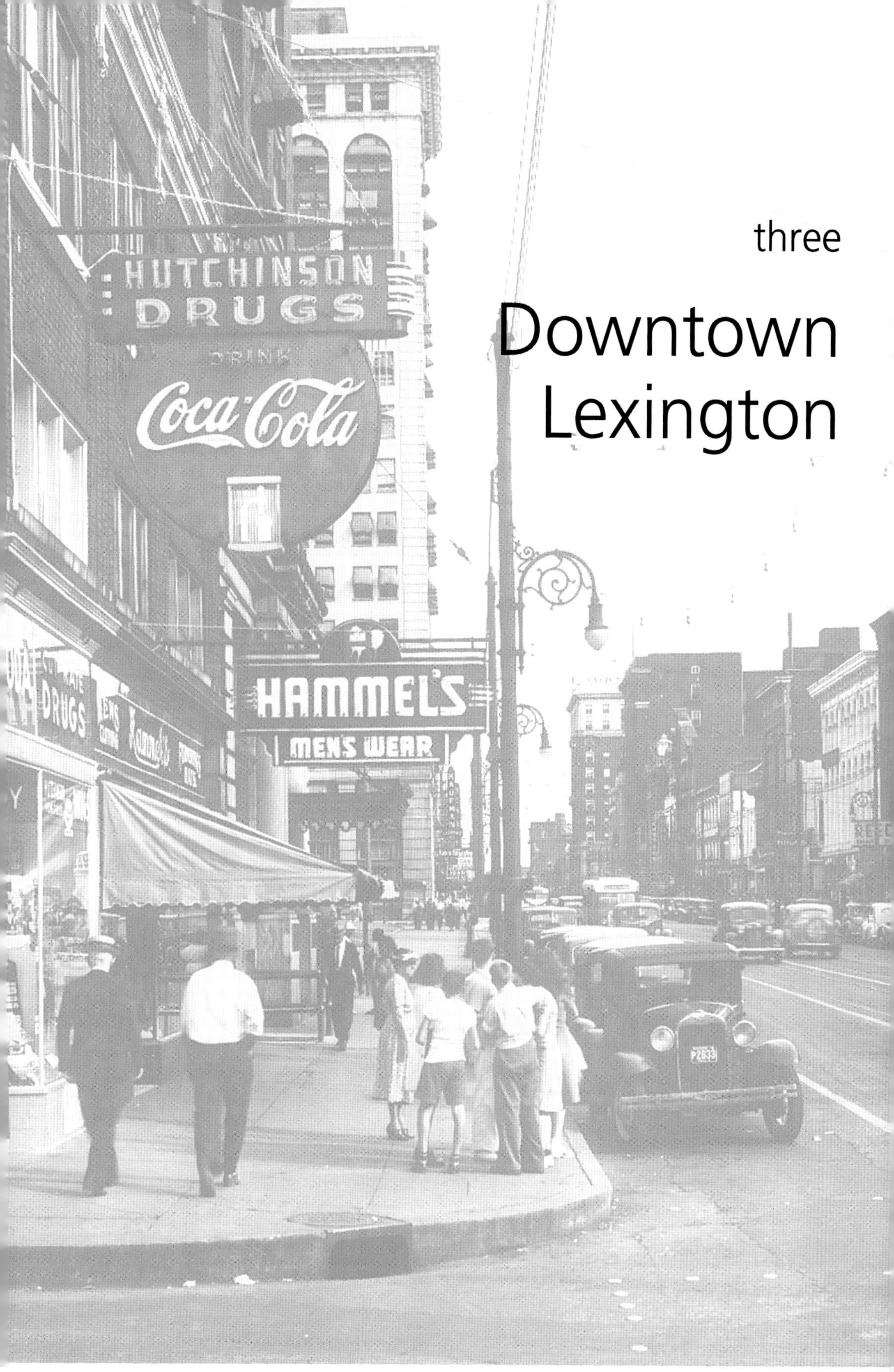

Throughout the 1930s and 1940s, the businesses that lined Lexington's Main Street and clustered on the surrounding side streets were the commercial and entertainment heart of the city. The economic, social, and political changes that took place in the nation and the world were often reflected in the seemingly constant changes in Lexington's downtown business district. Fortunately, Bob Long was there with his camera, and he produced a remarkable visual record of downtown Lexington during this period.

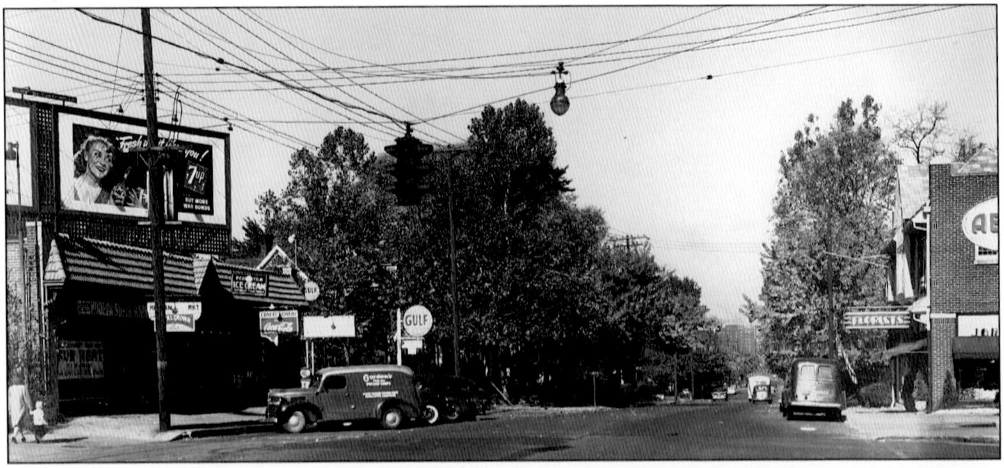

Businesses near the intersection of East Main Street and Walton Avenue, October 1944. These businesses were among the first encountered when entering Lexington's downtown business district by traveling west along Richmond Road, which becomes East Main shortly before this intersection. The florists' shop (right) was opened c. 1941 by Floyd Jordan and Mrs. Ruth L. Logan. Jordan left his former job as a designer for Howard and Heafey Florists to open his own business. By 1944, Ruth Logan had left the business, but Jordan continued to operate it as Jordan Florists until the early 1950s. (5262)

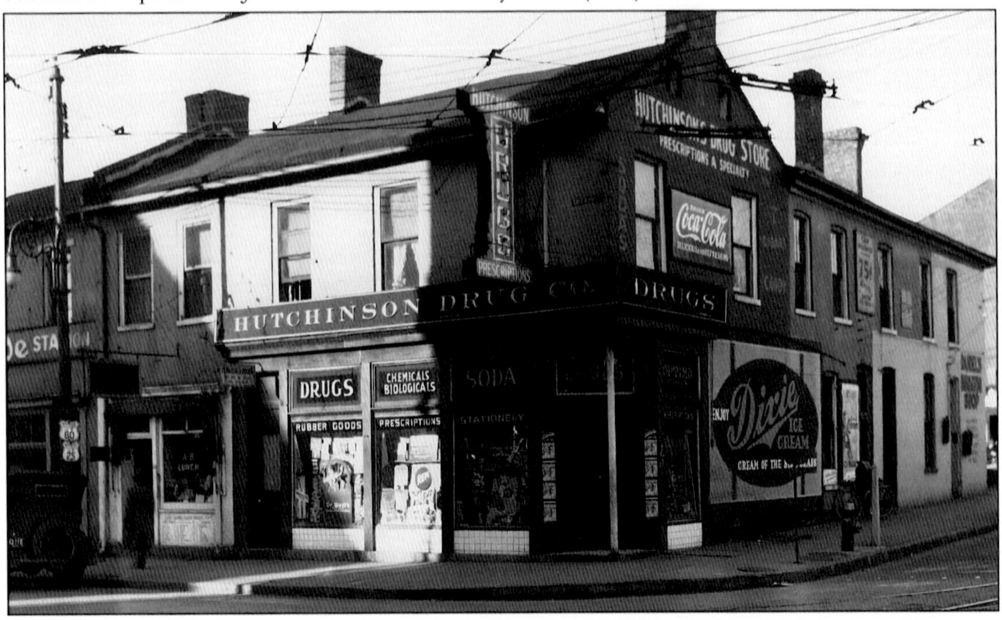

Hutchinson Drug Company, 273 East Main, c. 1935. Around 1925, brothers John W. and Charles E. Hutchinson opened Hutchinson Drugs in this building on the north side of East Main. The building had previously housed Charles W. Curry's drugstore. The Hutchinson brothers operated a drugstore in this location until 1964 when they moved to 376 East Main and this building was torn down. (1511)

Right: Sears Roebuck and Company, south side of East Main Street opposite Hutchinson Drugs, August 1932. Sears Roebuck and Company had operated the smaller store to the right since the late 1920s. Around 1932 Sears expanded into the larger building on the left, the Curry Tunis and Norwood Block. In November of 1934, Sears moved into new quarters at 213-219 East Main. The new store was located on the north side of Main Street a few buildings to the west of those shown in this photograph. (1359)

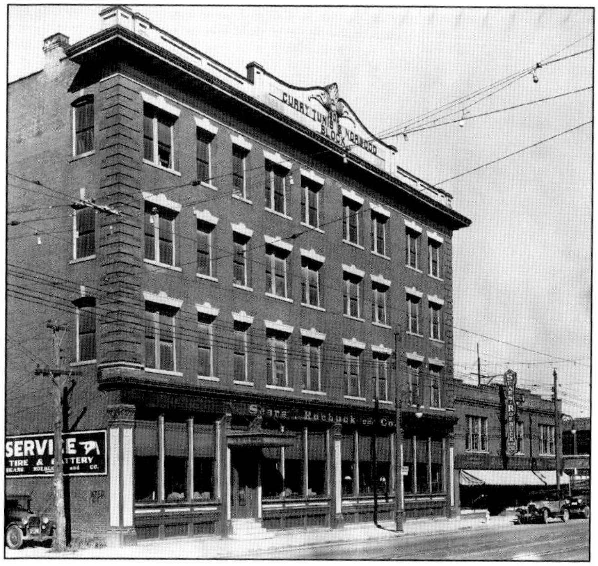

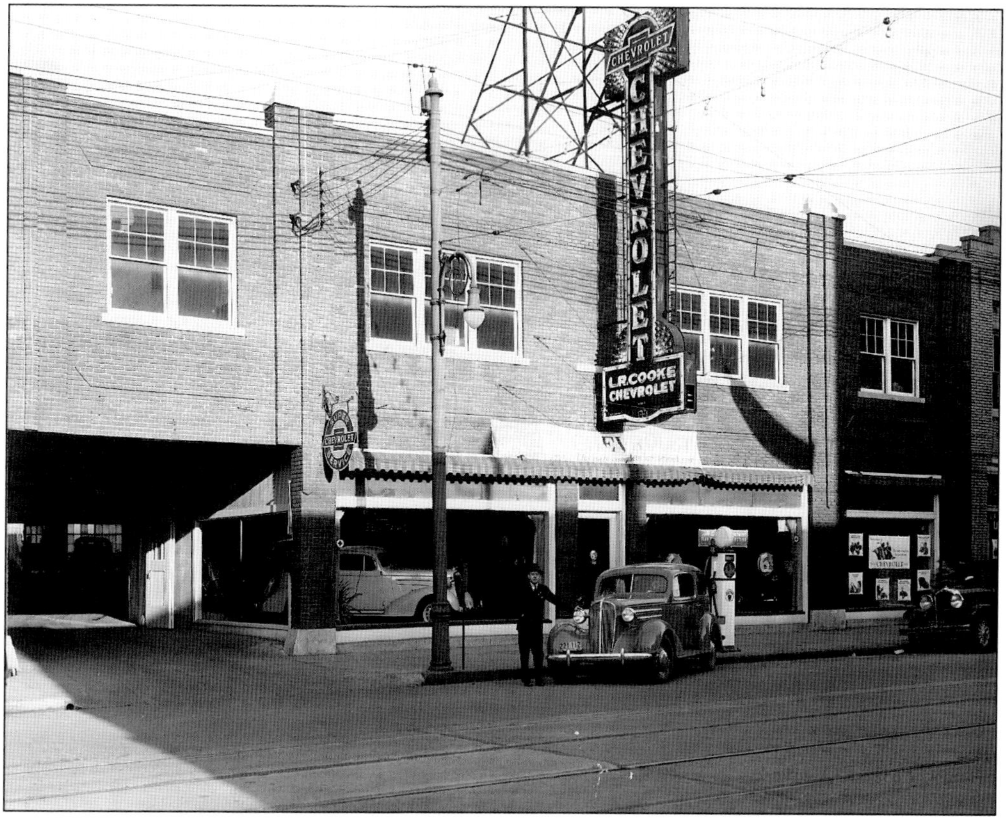

L.R. Cooke Chevrolet Motor Company, 255 East Main, November 1935. The increasing importance of the automobile in the lives of Lexingtonians led to a proliferation of automobile dealerships, garages, gas stations, and tire stores in the downtown area. L.R. Cooke Chevrolet first opened at 255 East Main, the former location of the Fred Bryant Motor Company, in 1935. Cooke Chevrolet moved to 180 East High c. 1945 and was in business on High Street for over 40 years. (3043)

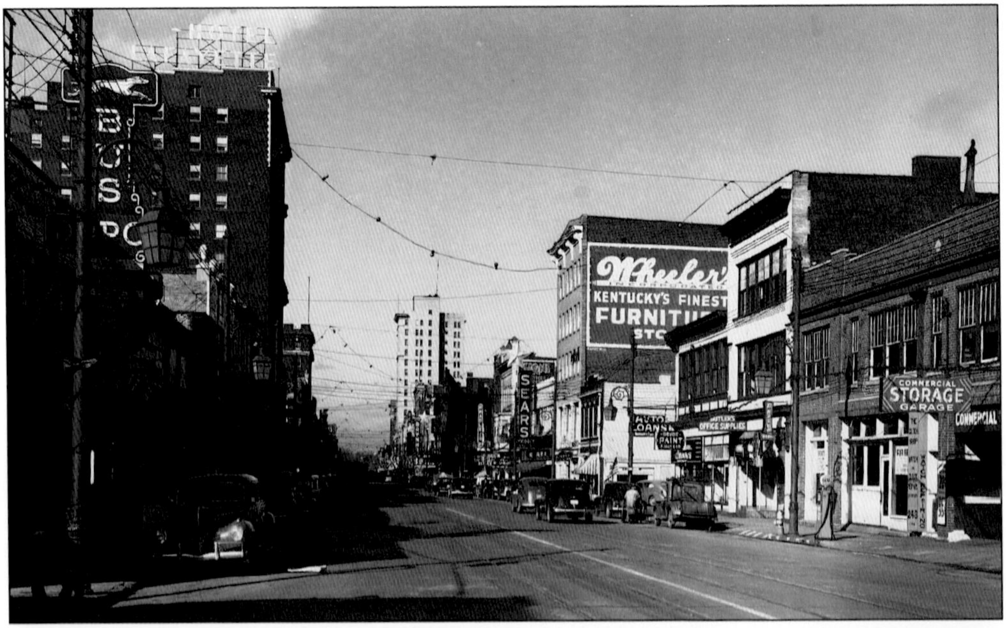

Christmas decorations on Main Street, December 26, 1941. This photograph shows the view looking west along Main Street from near the Greyhound Bus Depot at 242-46 East Main. The depot had been in this location for about six years when this photograph was taken. The A.F. Wheeler Furniture Company opened its store on East Main c. 1925, and Sears moved into the building to the west of Wheeler's in 1934. (4820)

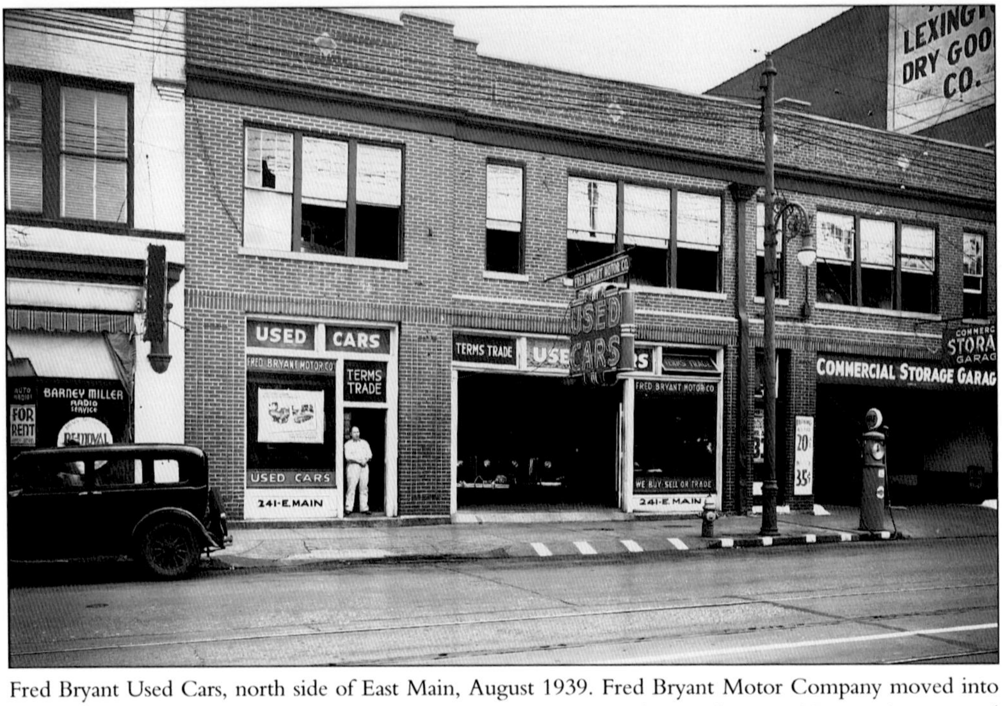

Fred Bryant Used Cars, north side of East Main, August 1939. Fred Bryant Motor Company moved into this building at 241 East Main c. 1935. In 1939, when this photograph was taken, Fred Bryant also operated an Oldsmobile dealership in a building on the east side of the Harrison Avenue Viaduct (now Martin Luther King Boulevard). (4312)

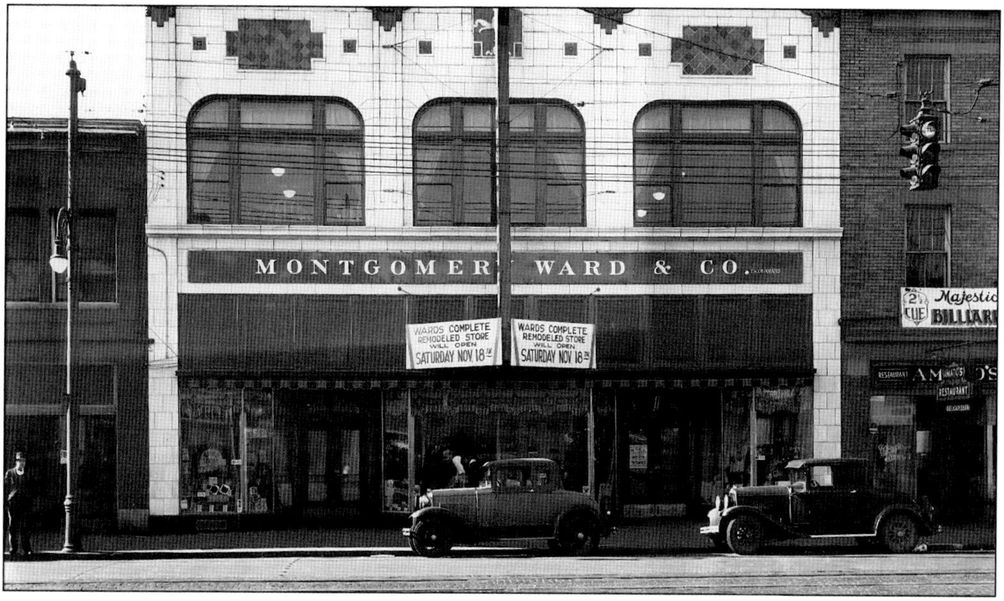

Montgomery Ward & Company, 230-232 East Main, November 1933. This building on the south side of East Main was built in 1929 by W.T. Congleton Company, general contractors, as the first Lexington home of Montgomery Ward and Company. The store opened on October 19, 1929. It was remodeled in 1933 and this photograph was taken a few days before the re-opening, held on November 18, 1933. Around 1938, Montgomery Ward and Company moved from this location to 300 West Main. (1674)

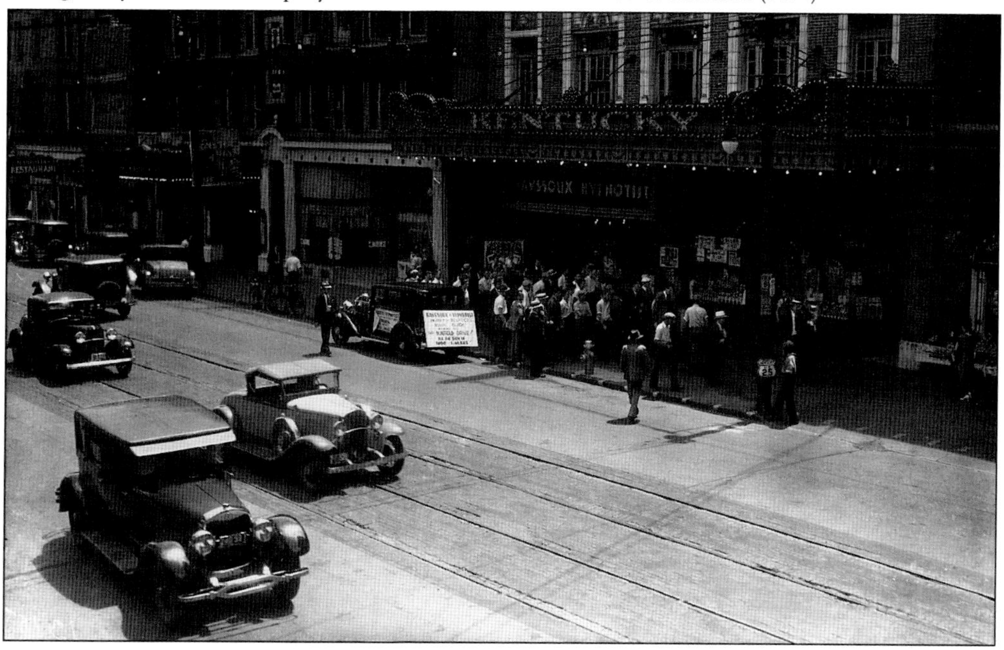

Fayssoux the hypnotist performs at the Kentucky Theater, May 25, 1932. This crowd was gathered outside the Kentucky Theater to watch William Irvine Fayssoux drive a Buick sedan through the streets of Lexington while blindfolded. In addition to this performance, Fayssoux did his hypnotist stage show during a four-night engagement at the Kentucky Theater. The Kentucky Theater opened on October 4, 1922. The Kentucky, an enduring landmark, still draws crowds of moviegoers to downtown Lexington. (1315)

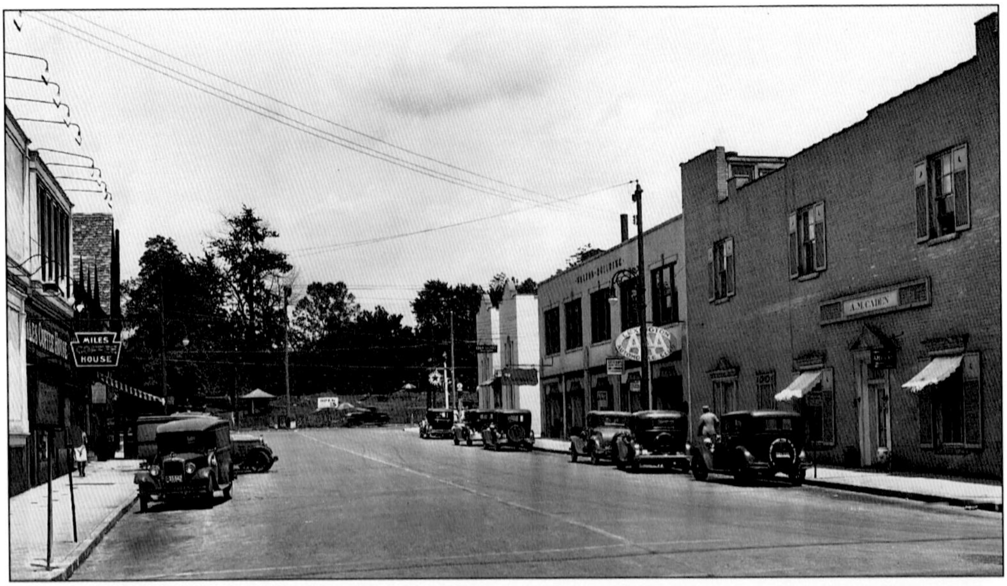

Looking north on Esplanade from Main Street, June 1931. Admission to the miniature golf course on East Short at the Esplanade was 15¢. The Lexington Automobile Club in the center of the block and the Texaco gas station at the end of Esplanade are further evidence of the importance of the automobile to the commercial life of Lexington. (1064)

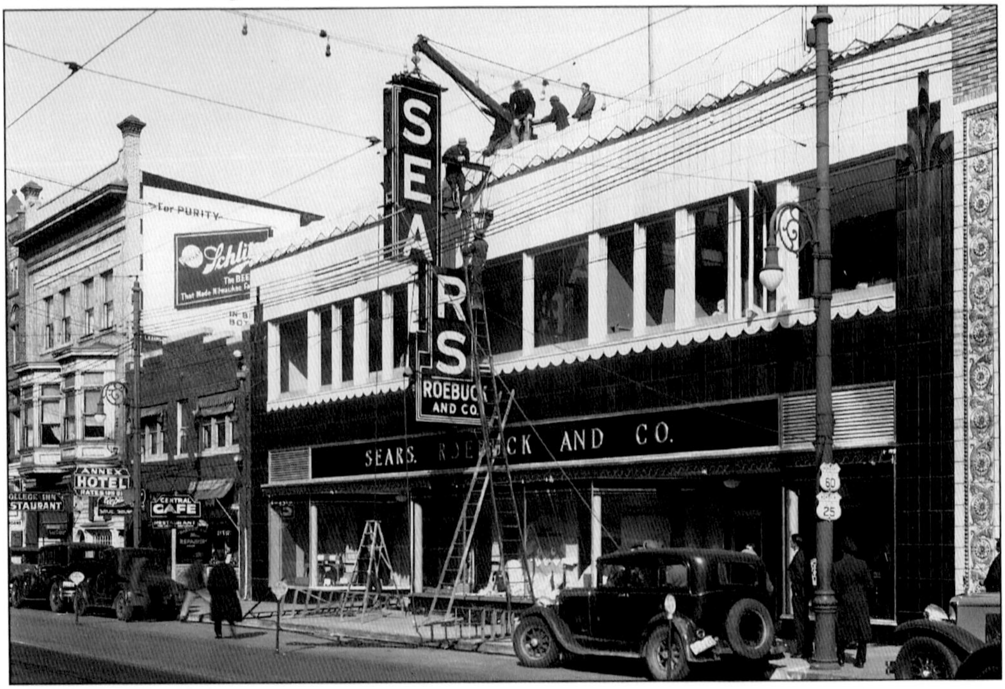

Hanging sign at new location of Sears Roebuck and Company, 213 East Main, November 1934. Sears Roebuck and Company had moved their merchandise from their old location on the south side of East Main into this new building, and the grand opening was scheduled for Saturday, November 17, 1934. Unfortunately, a fire forced the opening to be delayed. The first floor opened on November 19, and the second floor on November 26. (3315)

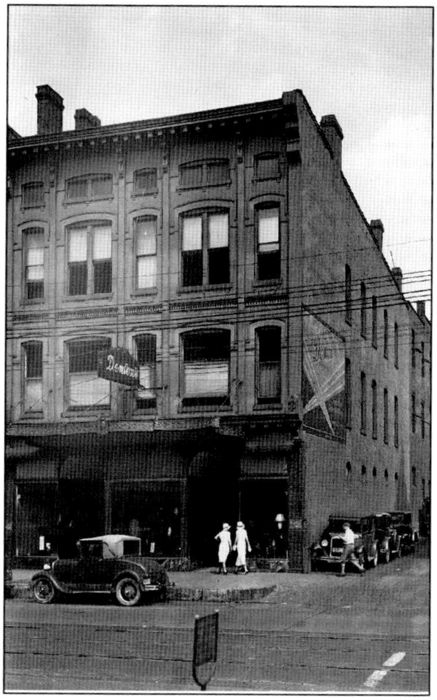

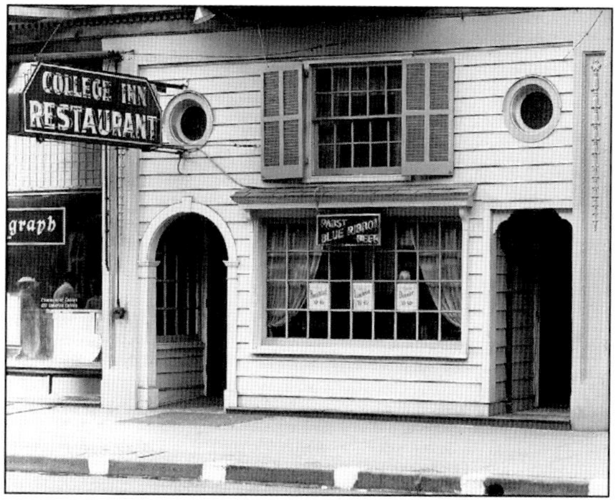

Above: College Inn Restaurant, 207 East Main, July 1936. Around 1928, Leonard B. Rutledge opened the College Inn Restaurant at 161 East Main. He closed the restaurant about four years later. By 1934, Vola Tate, the former manager of the Canary Cottage restaurant, located at 128 East Main, reopened the College Inn in this location, a few doors west of the new Sears and Roebuck store on the north side of East Main Street. (3206)

Above left: Denton's Department Store, northwest corner of Main Street and Ayers Alley, September 1931. The July 13, 1928 flood was the third in Lexington and Fayette Counties in two weeks. At the time of the 1928 floods, this building was the home of Smith Watkins Hardware. Denton's was located farther west at 113-117 East Main and was one of the businesses most severely damaged by the floods. Denton's moved to this location soon after the floods and remained in business here until the late 1930s.

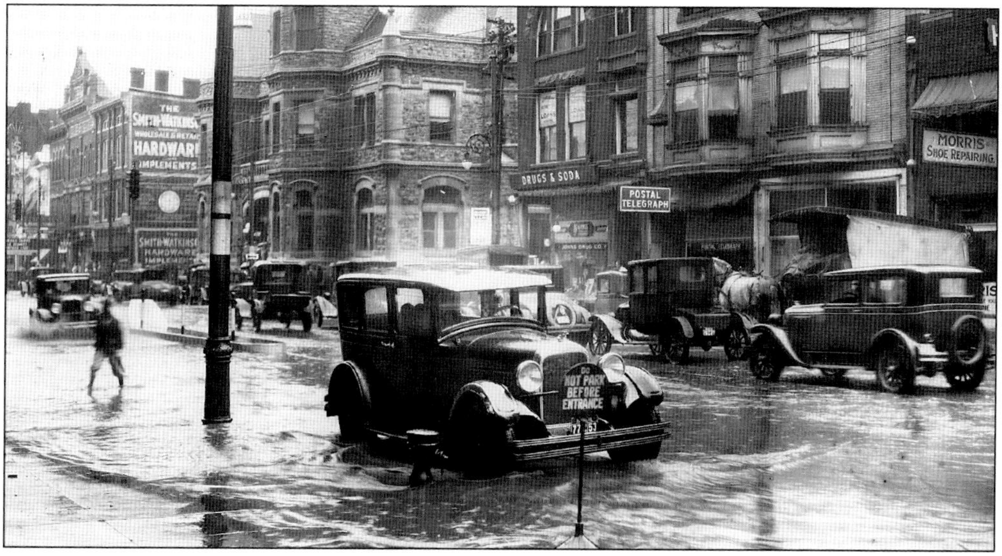

Main Street flood, July 13, 1928. This photograph was taken from a spot on the south side of Main Street near the Kentucky Theater looking toward the north side of East Main at the Walnut Street (now Martin Luther King Boulevard) intersection. The Federal Building was on the northwest corner of Main and Walnut and Johns Drug Store was on the northeast corner. The Federal Building, built 1887–1889, was torn down in 1941. (2063)

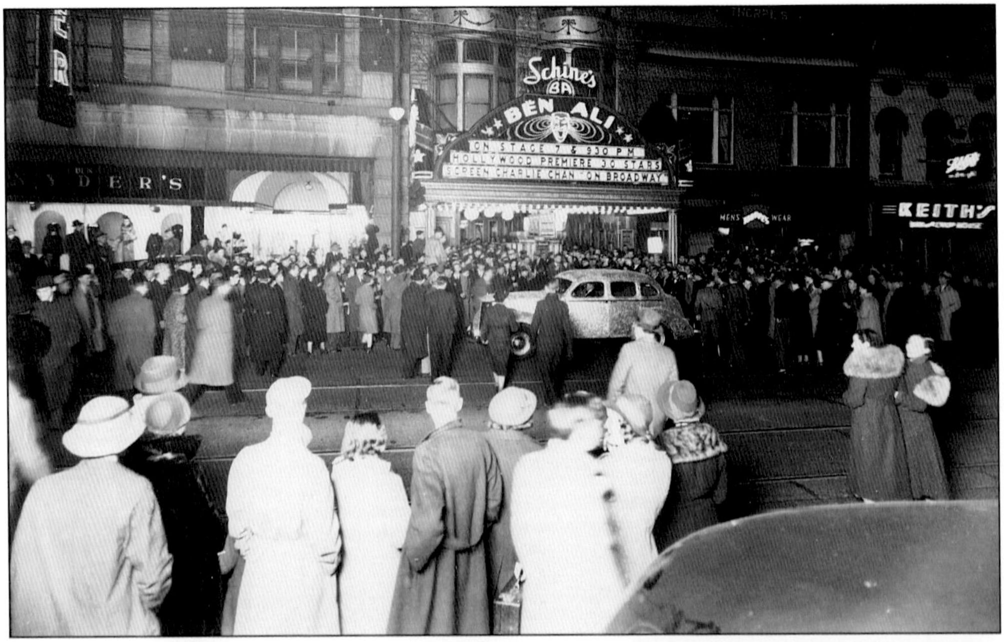

"Hollywood Premier" at the Ben Ali Theater, 121 East Main, October 27, 1937. "Hollywood Premiers" featuring impersonations of "your favorite stars" were popular events at the Ben Ali. Newspaper advertisements boasted, "See your favorite movie star impersonated on our stage. See the gala arrival of the Stars . . . see them drive up in luxurious motor cars." The Ben Ali was located on the north side of East Main opposite the Phoenix Hotel. (3824)

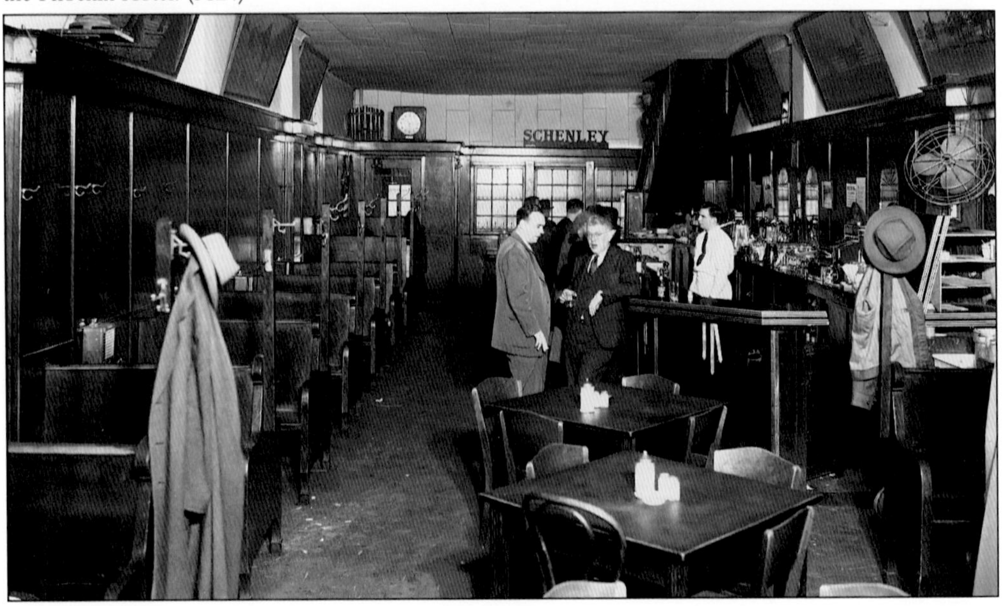

Interior of Keith's restaurant, 129 East Main, January 1946. Keith's Restaurant was on the north side of Main Street opposite the Phoenix Hotel, a few doors east of the Ben Ali Theater. Keith's was opened c. 1937 by William P. Keith, Vaughn W. Mckernon, and Joseph J. Keith. By the time this photograph was taken, Ralph Campbell and Mrs. Mabel W. Campbell were operating the restaurant. A few years later they changed the restaurant's name to the Golden Horseshoe. (5519)

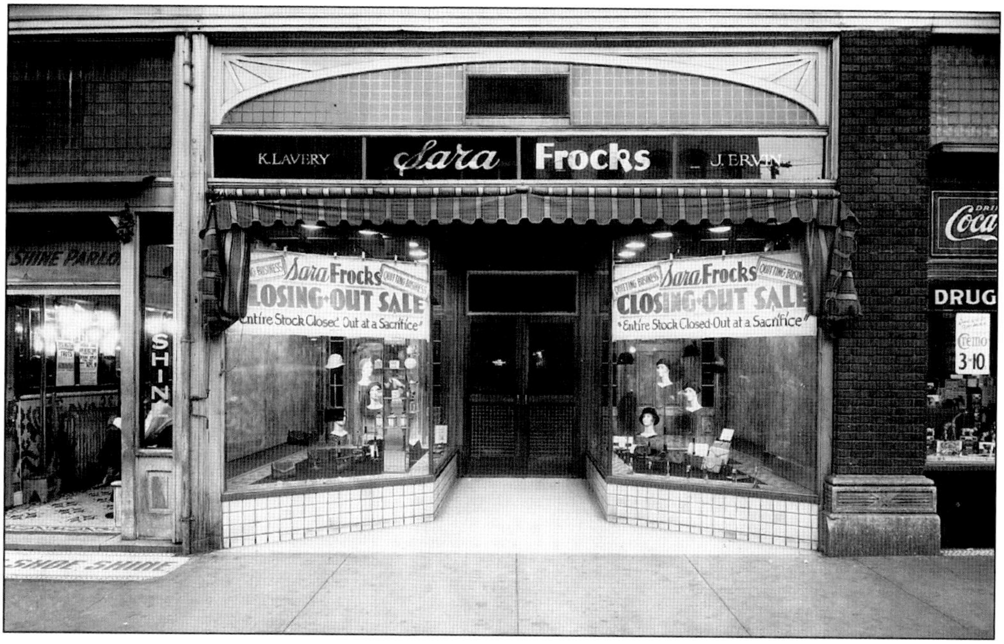

Sara Frocks quitting business sale, September 1932. Around 1930, Katherine Lavery and Josephine Ervine opened Sara Frocks at 104 East Main. Located in the Phoenix block, in a storefront formerly occupied by the Lexington Drug Company, Sara Frocks was one of many businesses that would try to take advantage of the prime retail spaces located on the street level of the Phoenix Hotel. Lavery and Ervine were in business for only a short time before they were forced to close their shop. (1381)

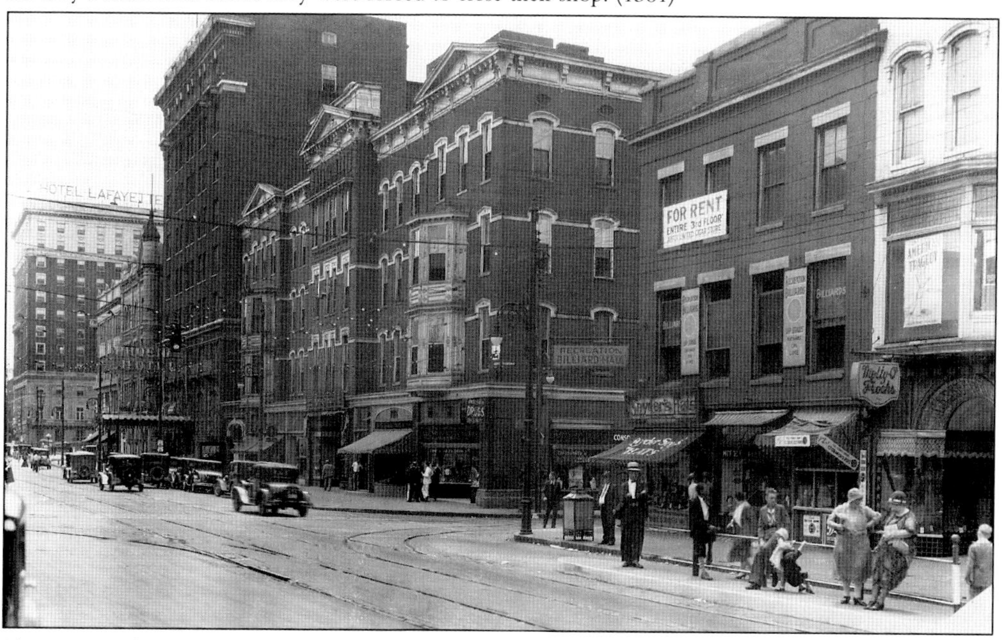

Phoenix Hotel, southeast corner of Main and Limestone Streets, August 1930. For many years the Lafayette Hotel, on the southeast corner of Main Street and the Harrison Avenue Viaduct, and the Phoenix Hotel were the major hotels in Lexington. A hotel operated at the southeast corner of Main and Limestone Streets for over 175 years. The Phoenix Hotel was torn down in 1982. (1790)

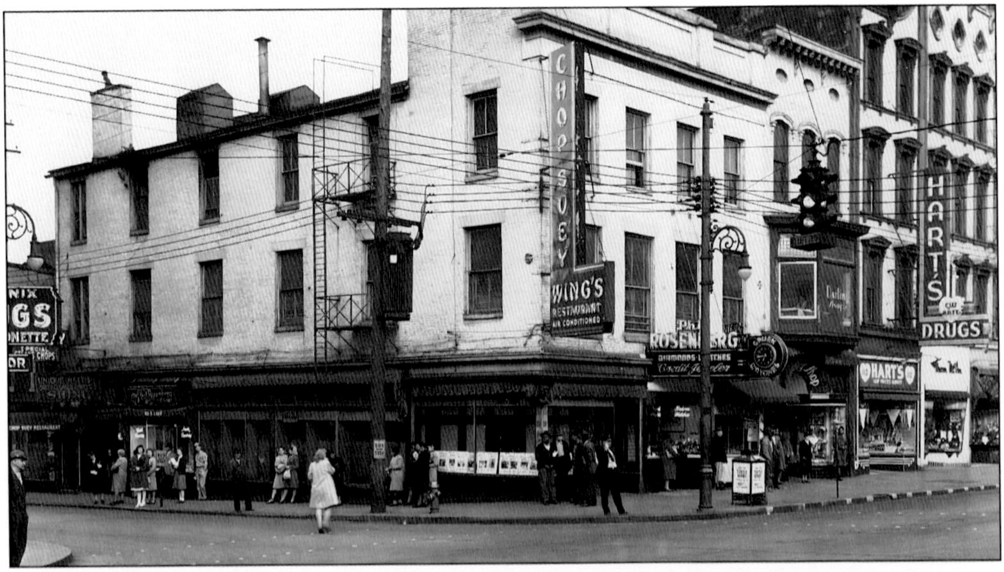

Southwest corner of Main and Limestone Streets, April 1944. Across Limestone Street from the Phoenix Hotel, this building is located at what was one of Lexington's busiest intersections. By 1944, Phil Rosenberg had been in the jewelry business for over 30 years. He opened this jewelry store at 102 West Main c. 1933. In April of 1944, the corner storefront adjacent to Rosenberg's was being prepared for the August opening of the Leed's women's wear store. (5197)

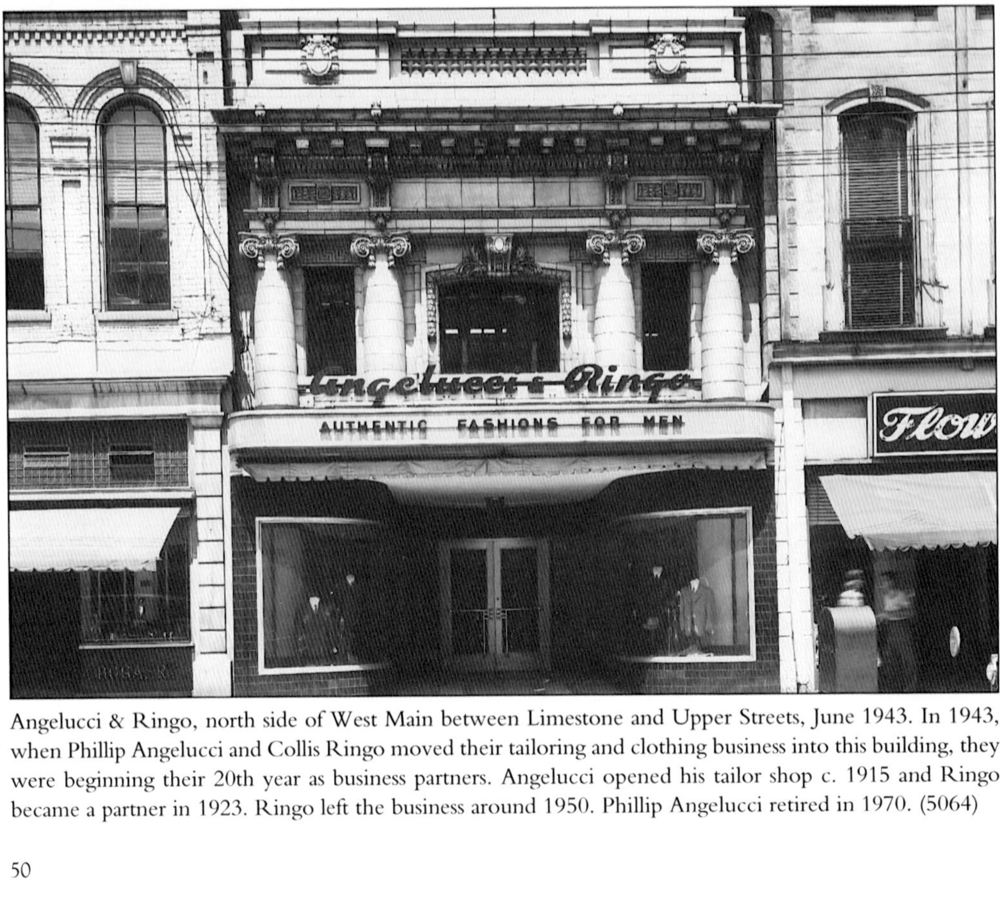

Angelucci & Ringo, north side of West Main between Limestone and Upper Streets, June 1943. In 1943, when Phillip Angelucci and Collis Ringo moved their tailoring and clothing business into this building, they were beginning their 20th year as business partners. Angelucci opened his tailor shop c. 1915 and Ringo became a partner in 1923. Ringo left the business around 1950. Phillip Angelucci retired in 1970. (5064)

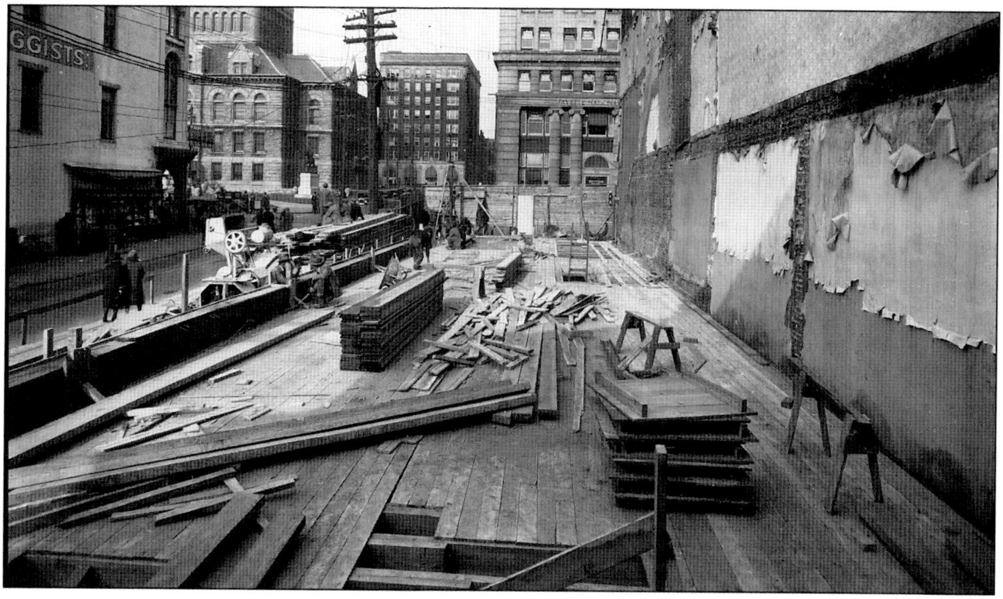

Construction site, southeast corner of Main and Upper Streets, c. 1930. In this unusual view, looking north along Upper Street from the southeast corner of Main and Upper Streets, a portion of Lexington's fifth courthouse is visible at left. At right, on the northeast corner of Main and Upper, a portion of the Fayette National Bank building can be seen. (638)

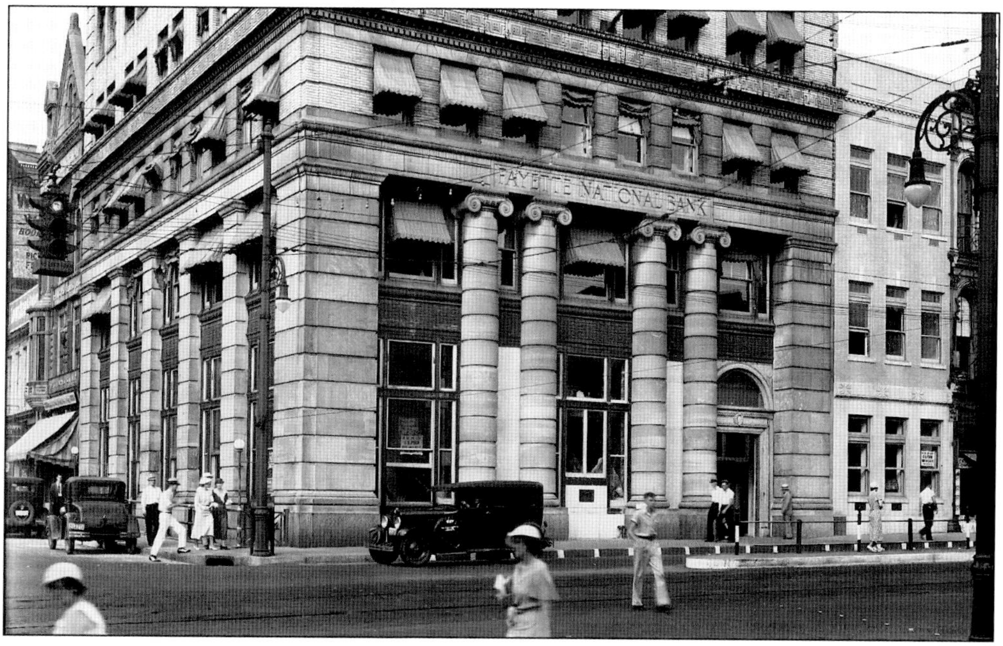

Fayette National Bank building, northeast corner of Main and Upper Streets, June 1934. Completed in 1914, this 15-story building was Lexington's tallest for nearly 60 years. Fayette National Bank fell victim to the deepening effects of the Depression and closed in 1931. That same year, the First National Bank and Trust Company moved its offices to the first floor of the building. Kentucky Utilities Company occupied the second, third, and fourth floors. The remaining 11 floors provided office space for a variety of other businesses. (1618)

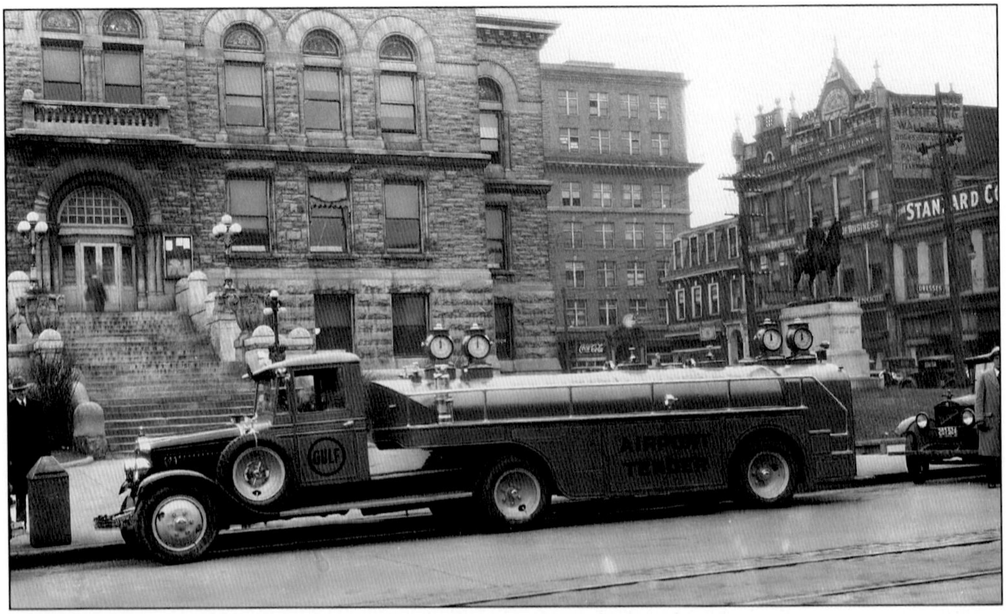

Airport tender in front of courthouse, March 1931. This airport tender was on a tour of central Kentucky when it made a stop in Lexington to promote the services and products of the Gulf Refining Company. Lexington's fifth courthouse was completed in 1900. Visible at right, on the east lawn of the courthouse, is the Pompeo Coppini statue of Confederate Brigadier General John Hunt Morgan. (938)

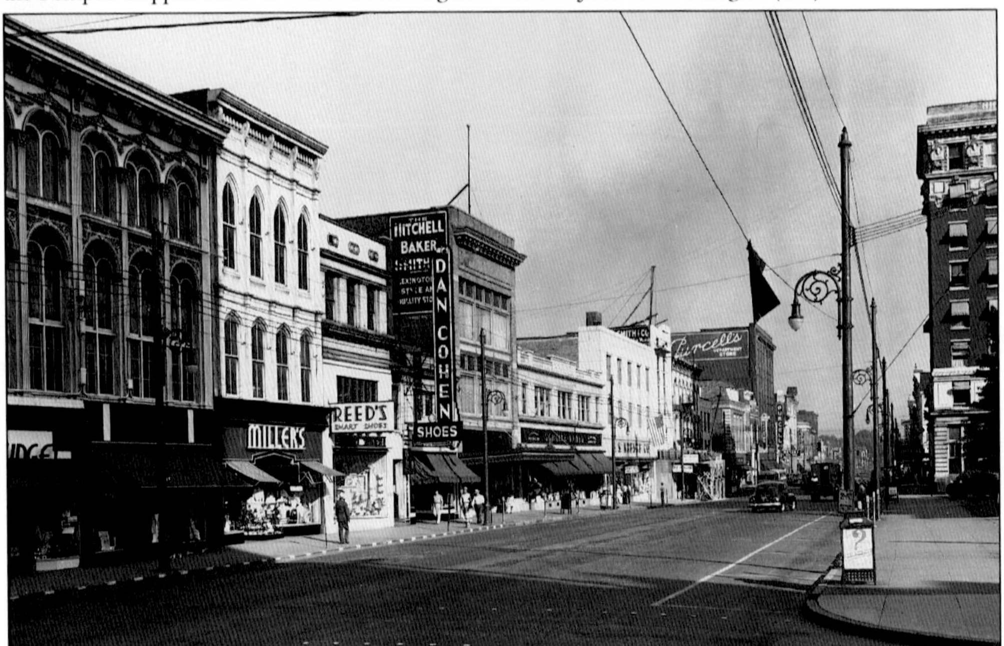

South side of Main Street between Upper and Mill Streets, July 25, 1947. This photograph was taken the day of the grand opening of the new S.S. Kresge's store (with American flag). The old Kresge's store, which opened in 1912, was torn down and this new store constructed on the same site in 1946 and 1947. Around 1942, Dan Cohen Shoes moved from its previous location, farther west in the same block, to the location shown above. (5850)

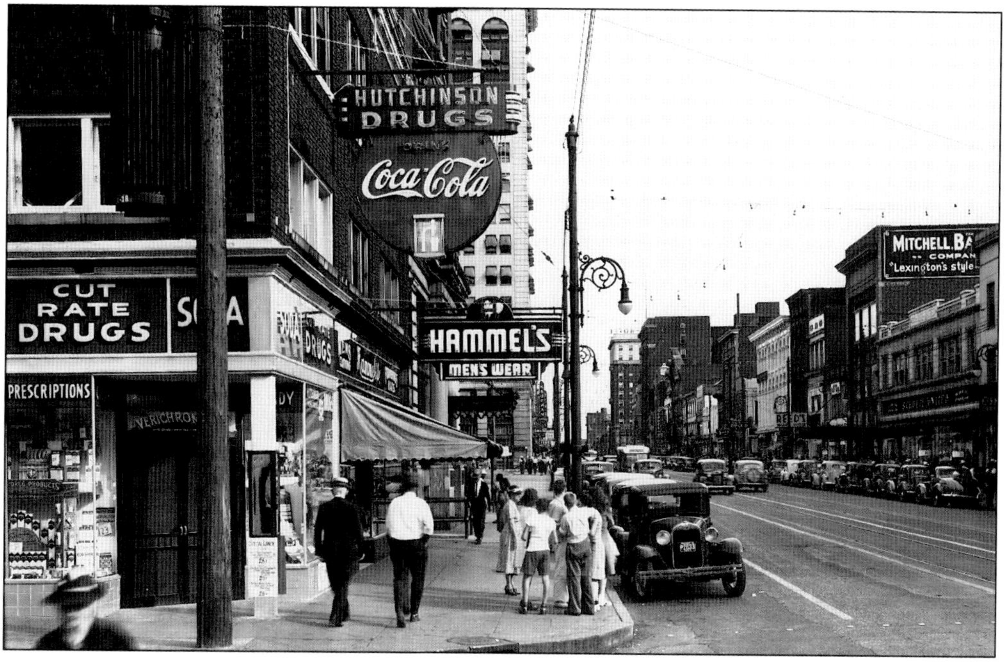

Hutchinson Drugs, 273 West Main, September 1939. For a few years, starting c. 1939, brothers John W. and Charles E. Hutchinson, who owned Hutchinson Drugs at 273 East Main, operated a second drugstore at 273 West Main, on the northeast corner of Main and Mill Streets. In this view, looking east along Main Street, the Phoenix Hotel and the Lafayette Hotel can be seen in the distant center on the south side of Main. (4320)

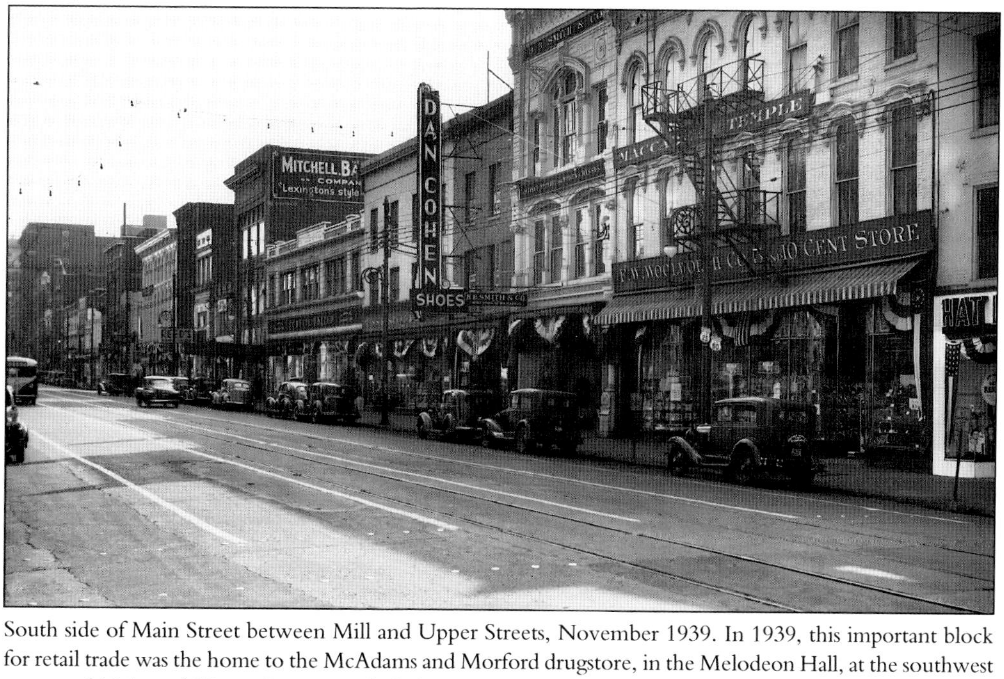

South side of Main Street between Mill and Upper Streets, November 1939. In 1939, this important block for retail trade was the home to the McAdams and Morford drugstore, in the Melodeon Hall, at the southwest corner of Main and Upper Streets. Included among the other businesses on the block were six women's clothing stores, four department stores, a milliners, two shoe stores, and a china shop. (4358)

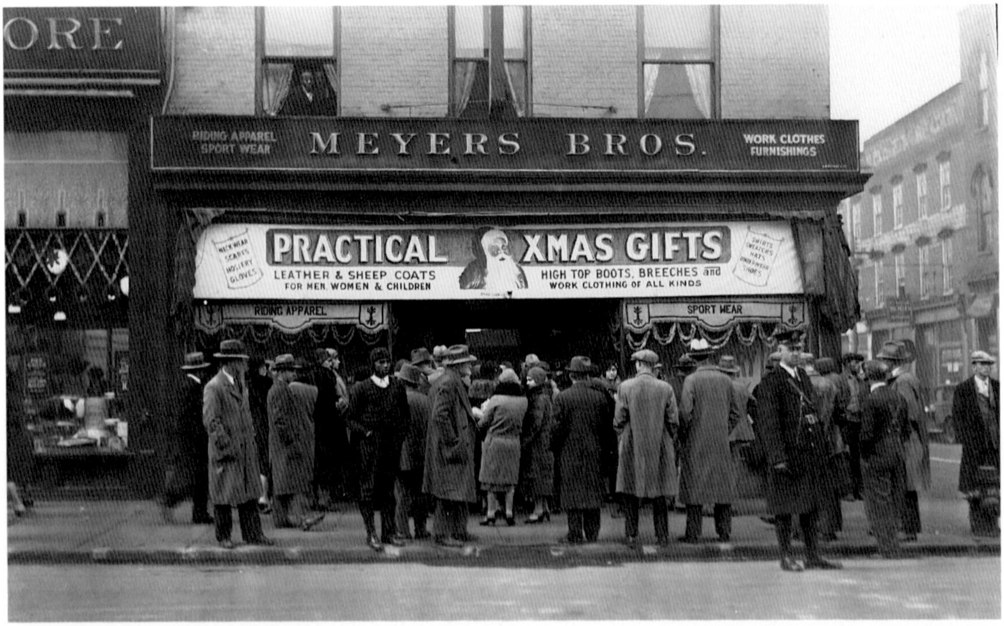

Meyers Brothers at the southeast corner of Main and Mill, December 1930. In 1920, brothers Emanuel and Edward J. Meyers moved from Louisville to Lexington and opened an army surplus clothing store. Later they began manufacturing and selling riding apparel and sportswear. In 1937, the Meyers brothers, in association with Milton Baer of Louisville, opened an expanded riding apparel and sportswear factory in the Market House. (952)

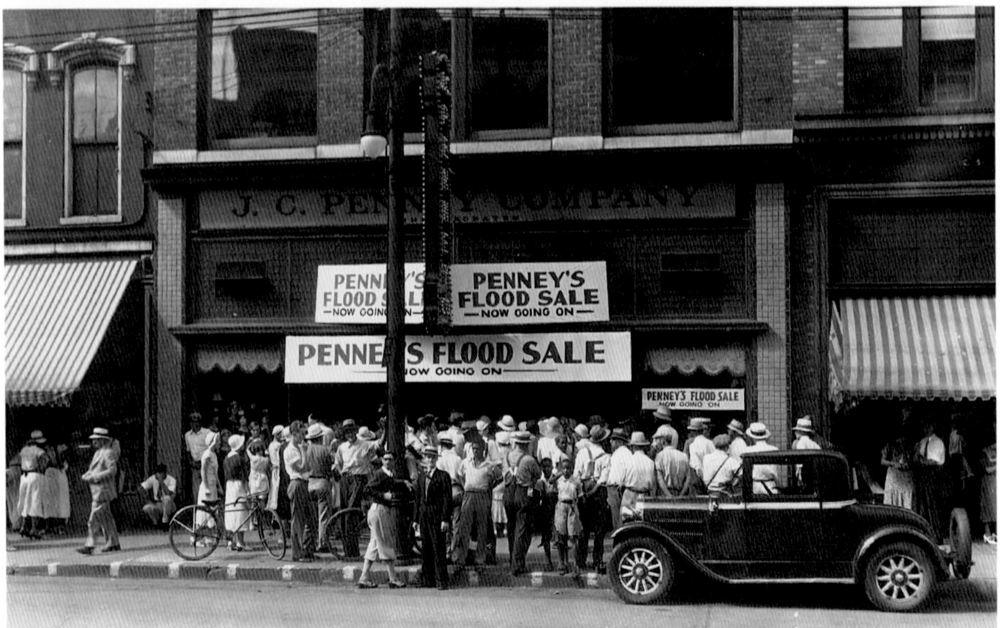

Penney's flood sale, 314 West Main, August 1932. This sale followed the August 2, 1932 flood. Until the completion of the P.W.A. storm sewer project, flood sales were an all-too-common occurrence at businesses in downtown Lexington. This J.C. Penney's store opened in 1929 and closed in January of 1946. (1365)

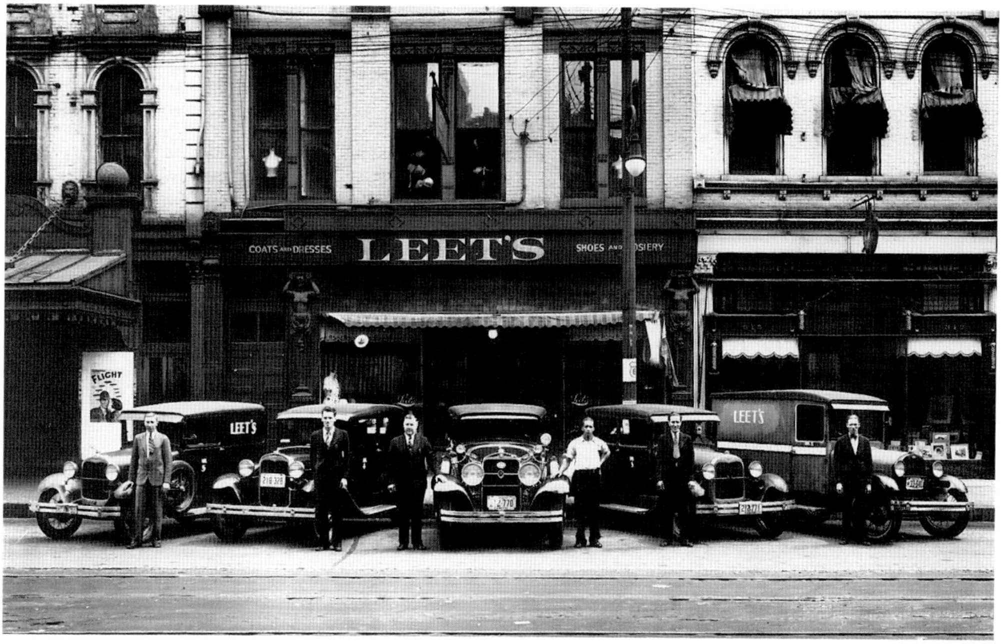

Leet's Ready-To-Wear, 317-319 West Main, c. 1930. In the mid-1920s, Lucy Mabel Leet and her husband, Simeon, opened a ladies furnishings store at 347 West Main. Around 1930 they moved their business to this location adjacent to the Ada Meade Theater on the north side of West Main. This was formerly the home of the New York Wholesale Millinery Company. (U-474)

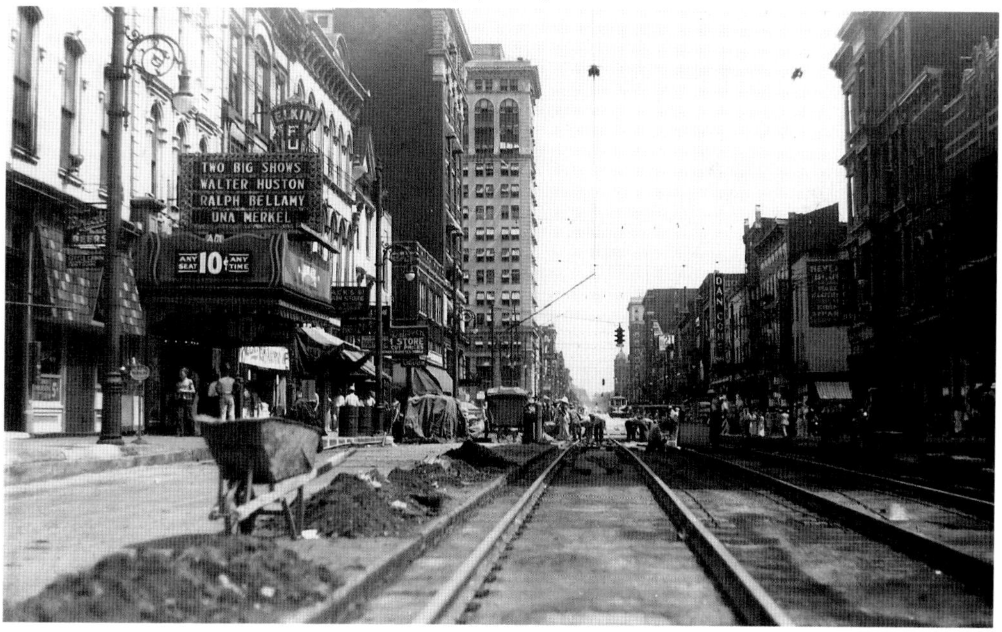

Construction work on streetcar tracks, West Main Street, August 7, 1935. Looking east along Main Street, the Ada Meade Theater can be seen at left and the Carty building, on the southwest corner of Main and Mill Streets, can be seen at right. It is the four-story building to the left of J.C. Penney Company. Completed in 1872 and torn down in 1938 to make way for the construction of a new Montgomery Ward Store, the Carty building has been called the first "tall" building in Lexington. (3246)

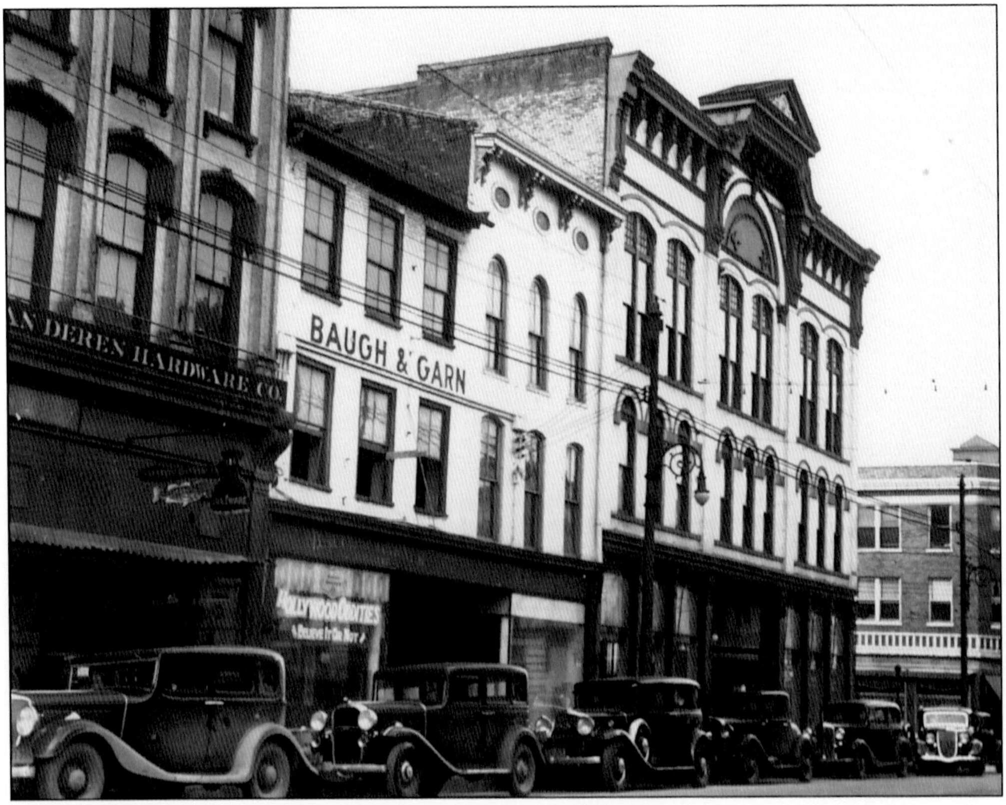

Van Deren Hardware and Baugh and Garner, November 1935. Farther west, on the south side of Main Street, Van Deren Hardware and Baugh and Garner furniture store were located in the same block with the Carty building and J.C. Penney Company. C.F. Brower Furniture Company was in the building at the end of the block, at the southeast corner of Main and Broadway. (3054)

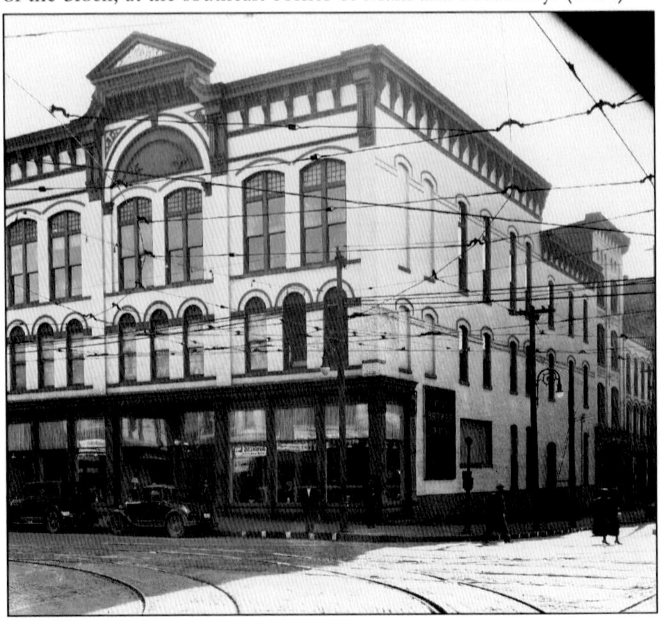

C.F. Brower Furniture Company, *c.* 1934. C.F. Brower Furniture Company was located in this building on the southeast corner of Main and Broadway from the 1890s until c. 1940 when the Southern Bedding company moved their retail store, Sleepy Head House, from 415-419 West Main into the Brower building. Sleepy Head House remained at this location until 1979, when the Brower building was turned over to its new owner, Kentucky Central Life Insurance Company. (U-128)

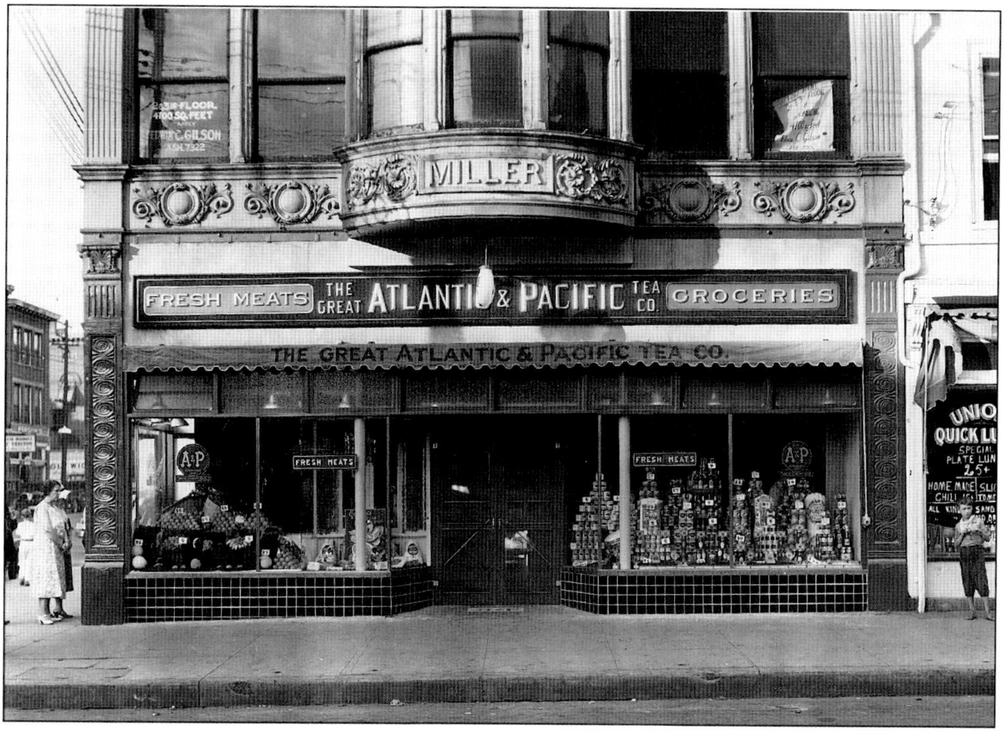

The Great Atlantic & Pacific Tea Company, northeast corner of West Main and Broadway, *c.* 1931. The Miller building, located across Main Street from the C.F. Brower Furniture Company, was built in 1892. The Great Atlantic & Pacific Tea Company opened this grocery store on the first floor of the Miller building in August of 1931. By 1941, this store had closed, but A & P still operated seven other stores in Lexington including one at 440 East Main and one at 540 West Main. (1101)

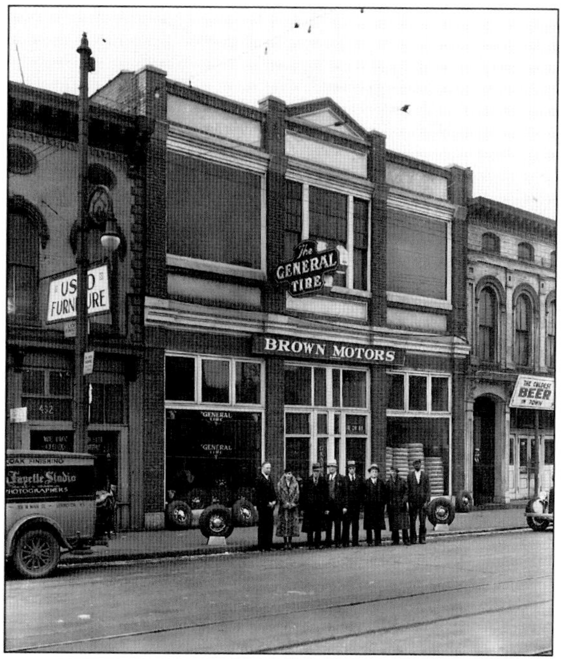

Brown Motor Company, February 1934. William B. Brown opened this tire store at 436-438 West Main Street c. 1933. By 1937, Brown Motor Company had moved to 508-516 West Main, formerly the location of the Purcell Garage where William Brown had worked before opening his own business. By 1939, Brown Motors had moved to Church Street where it remained until c. 1955 when Mr. Brown became vice president of the World-Wide Tobacco Company Inc. (1844)

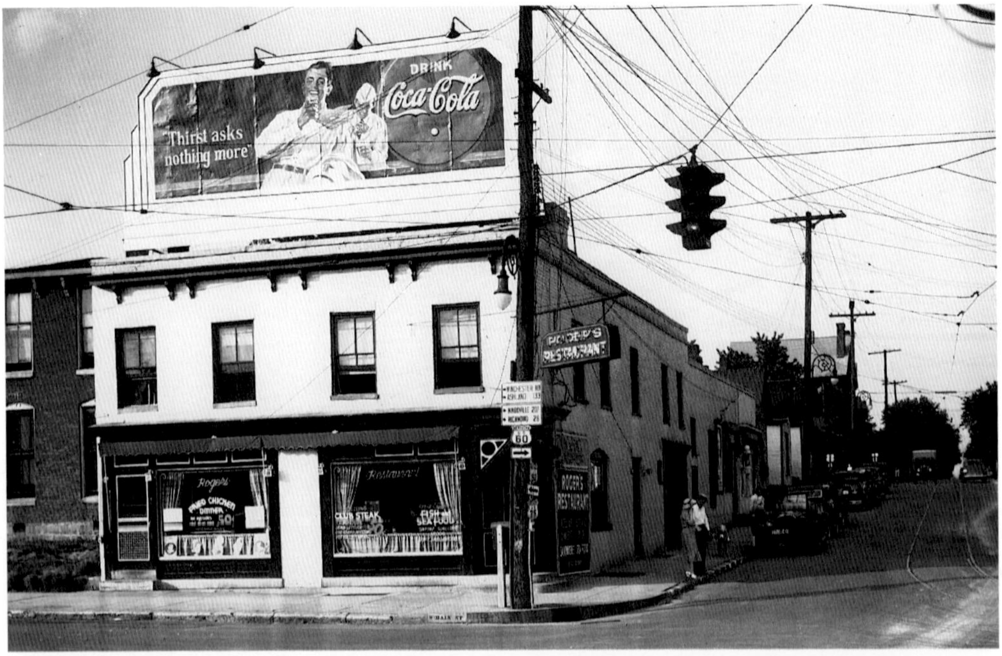

Rogers Restaurant, 601 West Main, July 1938. In 1923, George Rogers purchased the confectionery business located on the northeast corner of Main and Jefferson Streets and opened Rogers Restaurant. Famous for its chili, Rogers Restaurant remained at this location until 1965 when it moved to 808 South Broadway where it is still in business today. (4018)

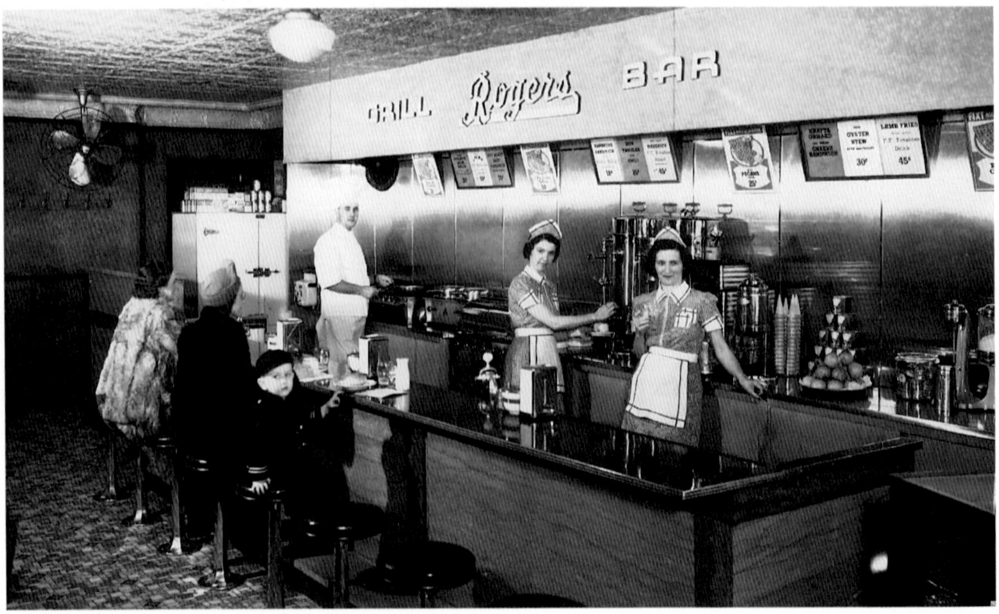

Interior of Rogers Restaurant, March 1941. In operation for over 75 years, Rogers Restaurant was opened with $100 that George Rogers borrowed from his grandmother. In the late 1930s and early 1940s the original Rogers Restaurant at 601 West Main had become so popular that George Rogers opened branch restaurants at 708 East Main, on North Limestone Street at Carlisle, and at 333 West Short Street. By the mid-1940s the branch restaurants had closed. (4684)

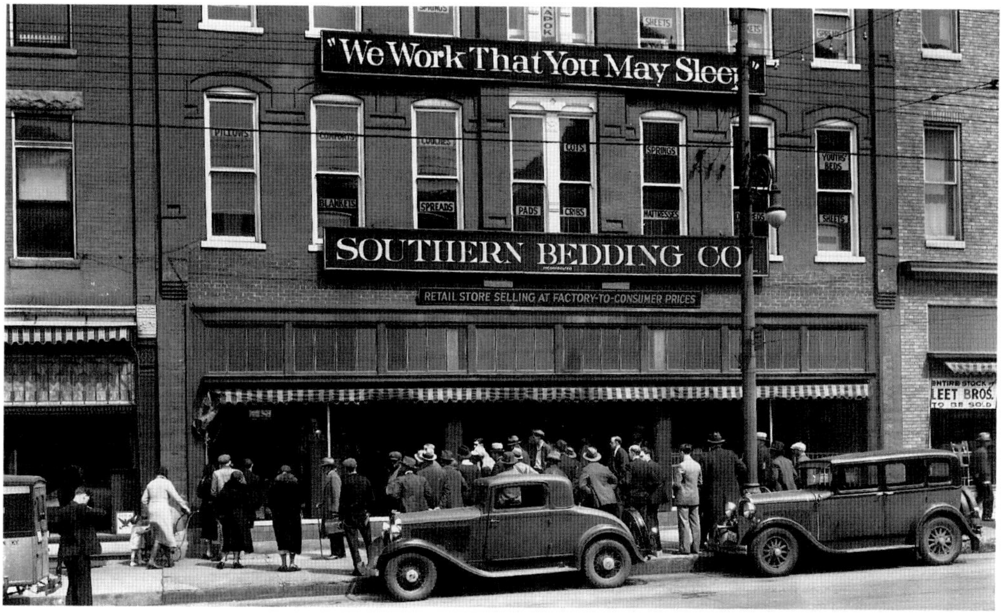

Radio broadcast from window of Sleepy Head House, 415 West Main Street, March 1934. Sleepy Head House, the retail branch of the Southern Bedding Company had been in business at this location on the north side of West Main Street for three years when this photo was taken. Southern Bedding Company was using WLAP, Lexington's first licensed radio station, to advertise their products. WLAP had been on the air for just over a year when this photograph was taken. (1887)

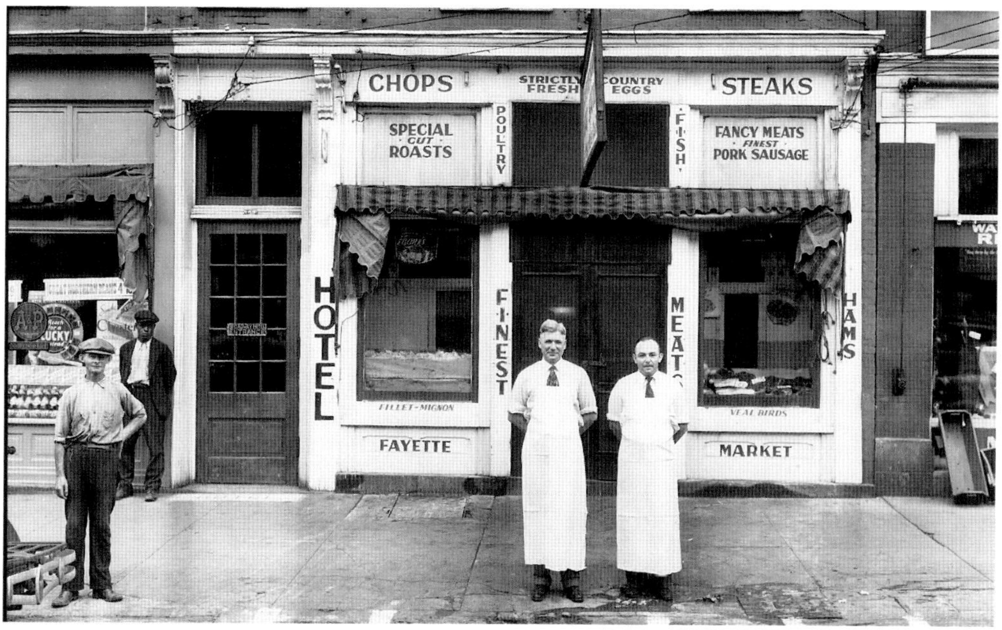

Fayette Meat Market, 129 North Broadway, c. 1931. The Fayette Meat Market was located on the west side of Broadway in the first block north of Main Street. Around 1937, the Raybould family that ran the Fayette Meat Market during most of the 1930s opened a second butcher shop on Merino Street. Under various owners, the Fayette Meat Market was in operation at this location from the early 1930s until c. 1942. (1099)

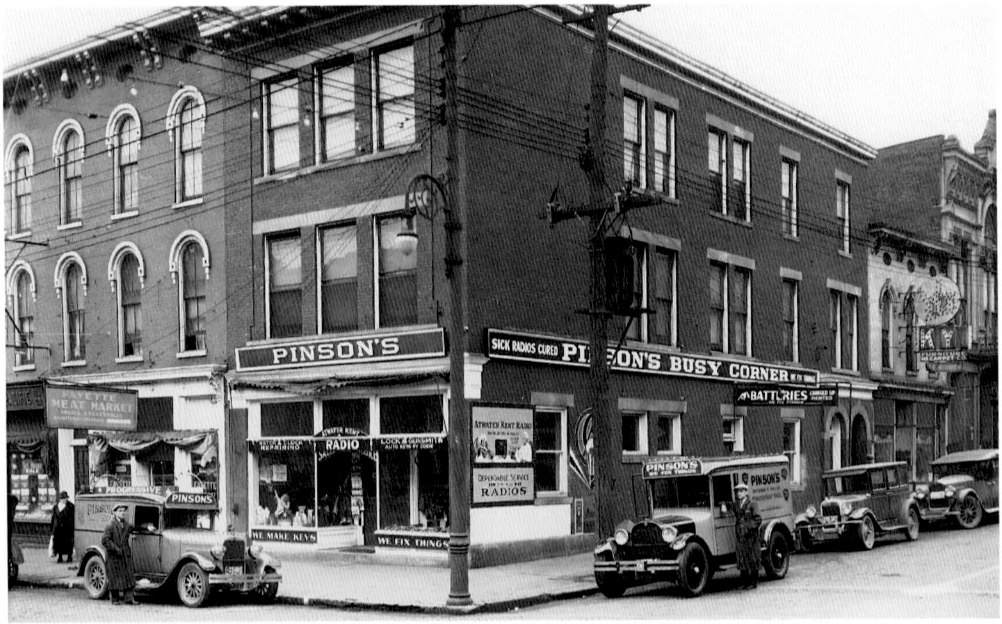

Pinson's Radio Service, 131 North Broadway, on the southwest corner of Short and Broadway, January 1931. Originally opened by Harry M. Pinson c. 1927 at 147 North Mill Street, Pinson Radio Service moved to this location c. 1930. By 1941, Pinson Radio Service had become Pinkston's Service, and was being run by Haldon R. Pinkston. He expanded the business to include leather and turf goods, and Pinkston Hardware would operate at this location until the early 1980s. (840)

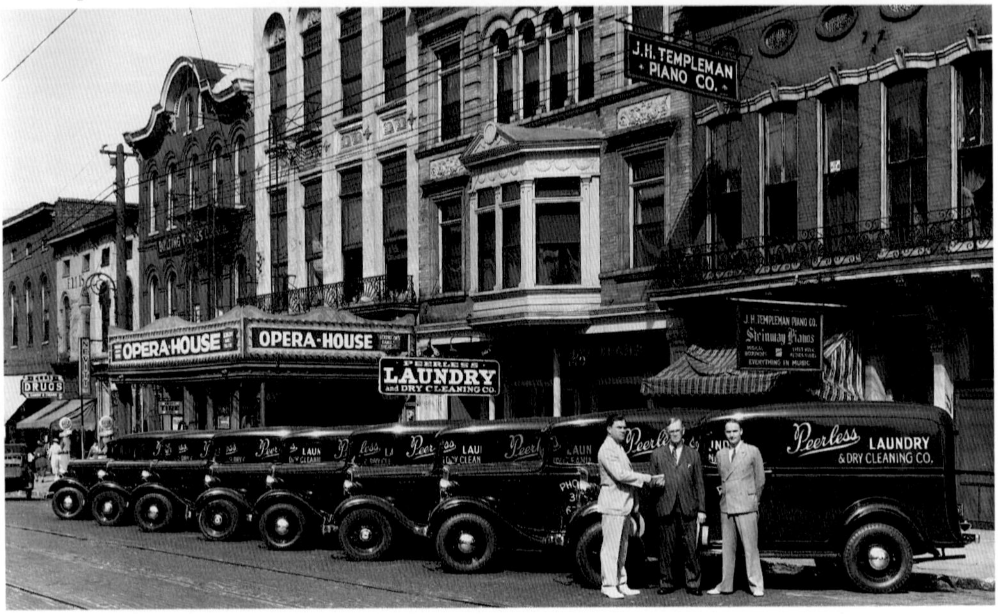

Peerless Laundry fleet of trucks on North Broadway, June 1935. Peerless Laundry opened c. 1911 at 227 West Short Street. By 1919, it had moved to this location on the west side of Broadway, next to the Lexington Opera House. The Opera House opened on July 19, 1887. Designed by Herman L. Rowe, this opera house was built to replace the one located at the southeast corner of Main and Broadway which burned on January 15, 1886. (3467)

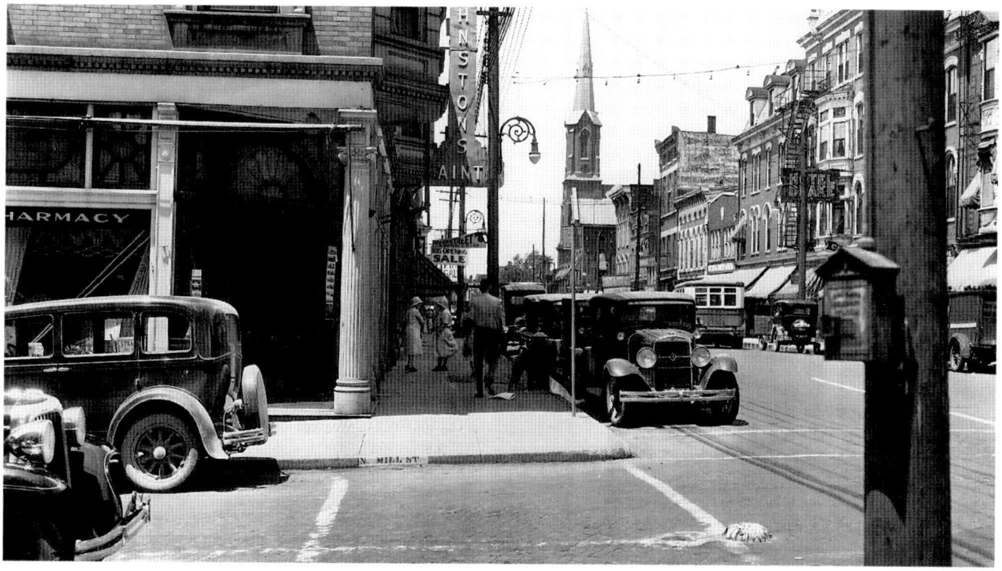

Southwest corner of Short and Mill Streets, July 1931. This photograph was taken soon after Eugene Sageser opened this pharmacy at 127 North Mill. The Drake Hotel is visible to the right, on the north side of Short between Mill and Broadway. The steeple of Saint Paul's Catholic Church, located across Broadway on the north side of Short Street between Broadway and Saunier Avenue, is also visible. (1075)

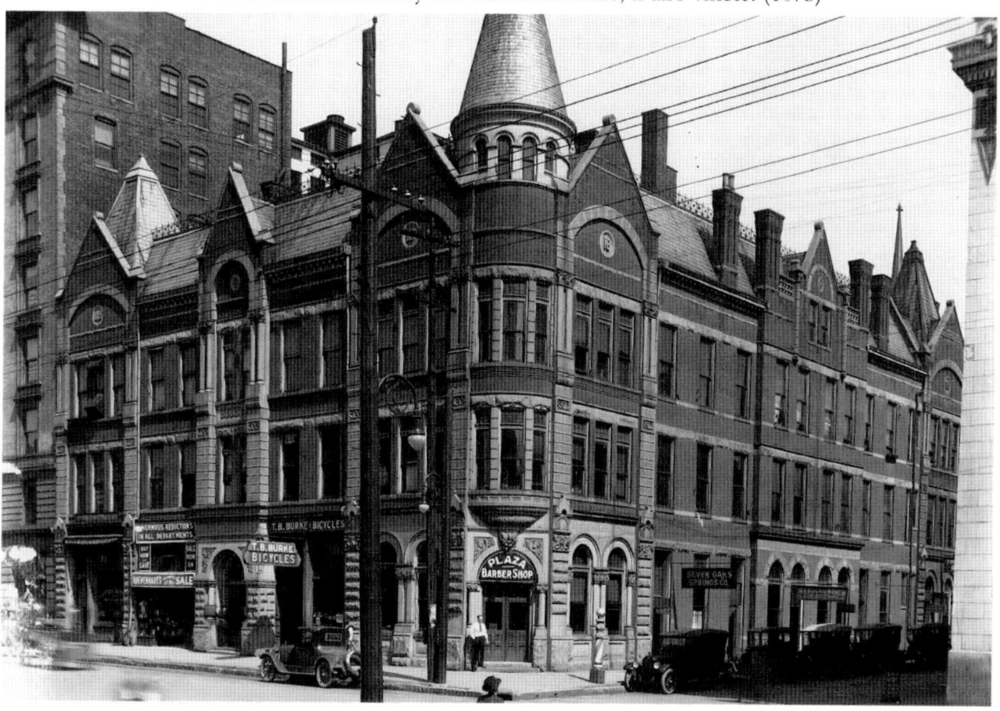

Northern Bank Building, northwest corner of Short and Market Streets, c. 1921. The Northern Bank building, constructed in 1889, is still standing at the northern end of Cheapside, although the turret and conical roof have been removed. Until October 26, 1921, when Court Days were made illegal, the merchants who occupied space in the Northern Bank building were well positioned to benefit from the monthly gatherings on Cheapside. (699)

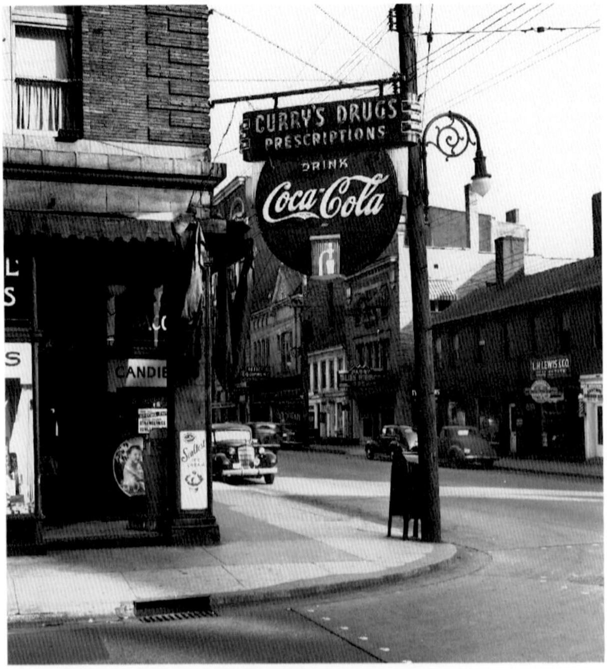

Curry's Drug Store, 167 West Short Street, June 1940. As early as 1923, Charles W. Curry was running a drugstore on Main Street, first at 273 East Main and later at 101 West Main. Around 1936, he moved to this location on the ground floor of the McClelland Building at the northeast corner of North Upper and West Short Streets. About 1944, he opened Curry's Apothecary in the Doctor's Building at 200 West Second. (4507)

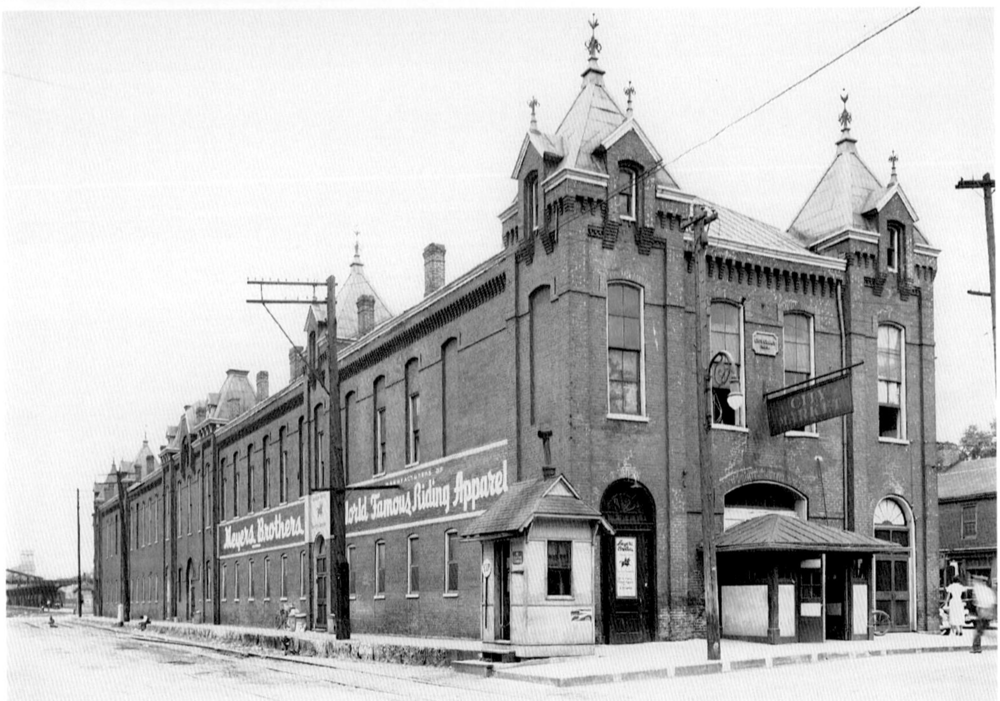

City Market, June 1937. The market house covered the entire block bordered by Limestone and Upper Streets and Water and Vine Streets. Built in 1879, the building was torn down in 1941. This photograph was taken soon after the Meyers brothers and Milton Baer opened their riding apparel and sportswear manufacturing facility on part of the second floor. A Lexington Herald article announcing the plans to open the manufacturing facility indicated that it would employ between 75 and 100 people. (3762)

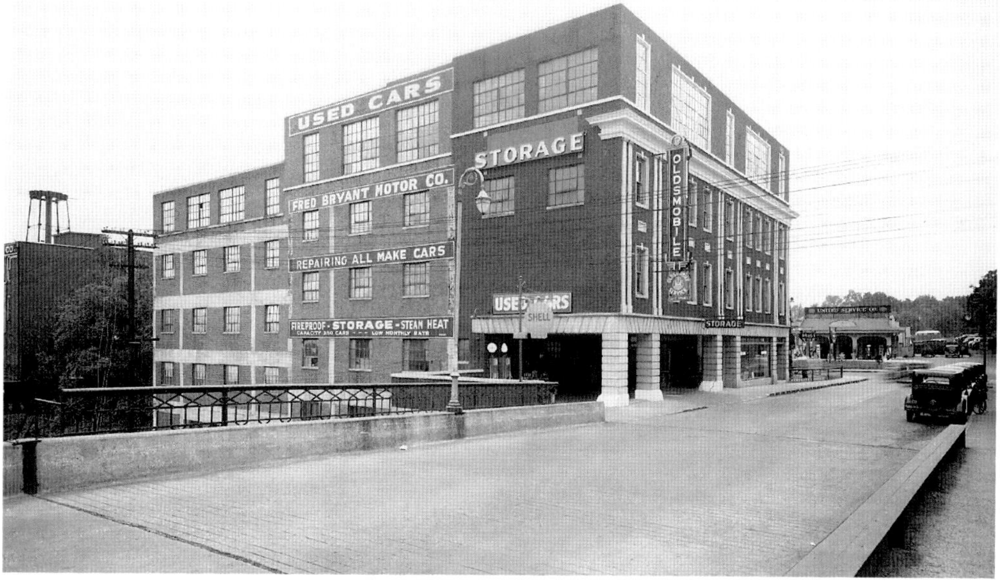

Fred Bryant Motor Company, Harrison Street viaduct (now the Martin Luther King Boulevard), August 1936. Fred Bryant, a native of Jackson, Kentucky, came to Lexington in 1914. Bryant acquired a Chevrolet agency and started Fred Bryant Motor Company in 1924. In 1936, he sold the Chevrolet agency to L.R. Cooke and began selling Oldsmobiles. Bryant operated the Oldsmobile dealership at this location until he sold the business in 1964. (3235)

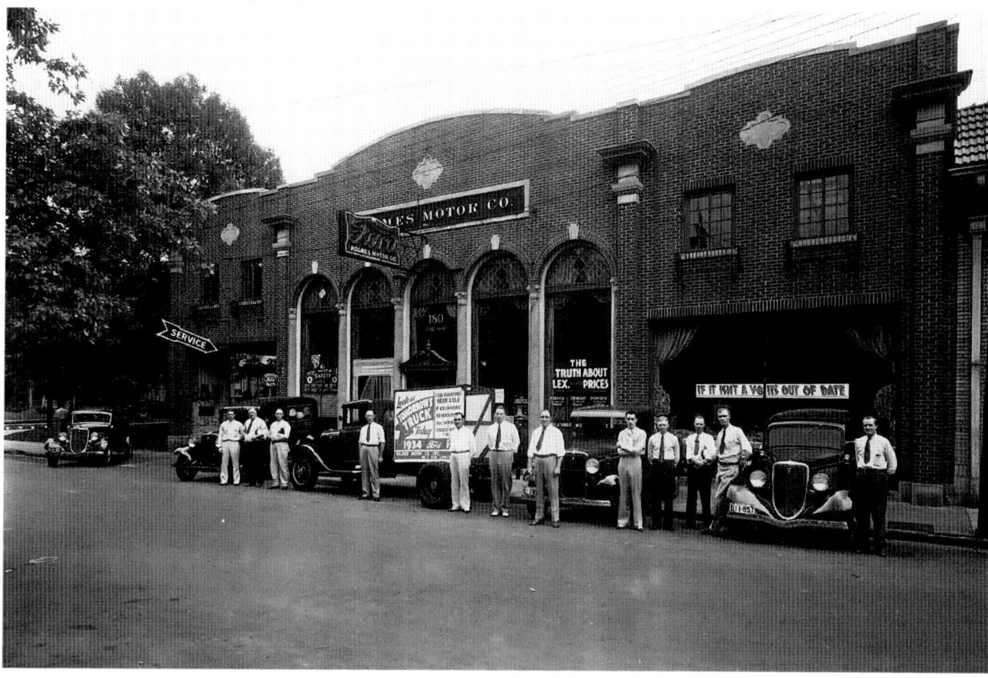

Holmes Motor Company, 180 East High Street, July 1934. This photograph was taken shortly after Jack Holmes took over operation of the Ford dealership from J.W. Frazer at this location on High Street adjacent to the United Service Company. By 1945, this was the site of L.R. Cooke Chevrolet. (1588)

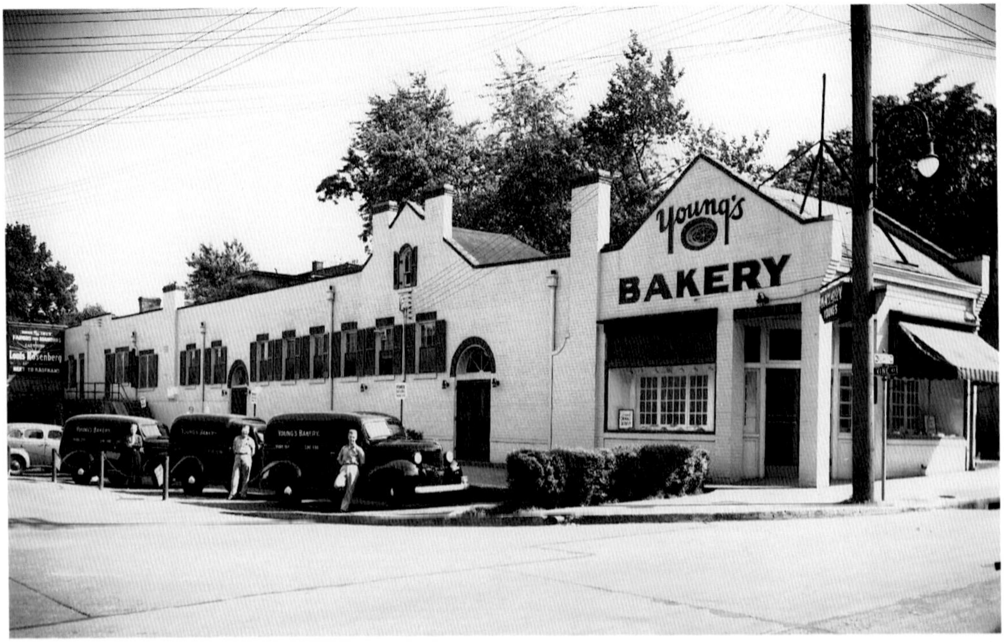

Young's Bakery, May 1939. In May of 1939, George E. Young moved his bakery business from 115 North Broadway to 148 South Limestone, on the east side of South Limestone, between Vine and High Streets. Customers were invited to an informal opening for free tea, cakes, cookies, and a loaf of "our fast-becoming-famous butter and egg bread." By 1945, George E. Young had sold Young's Bakery and was president of Lexington Flying Service, Inc. (4269)

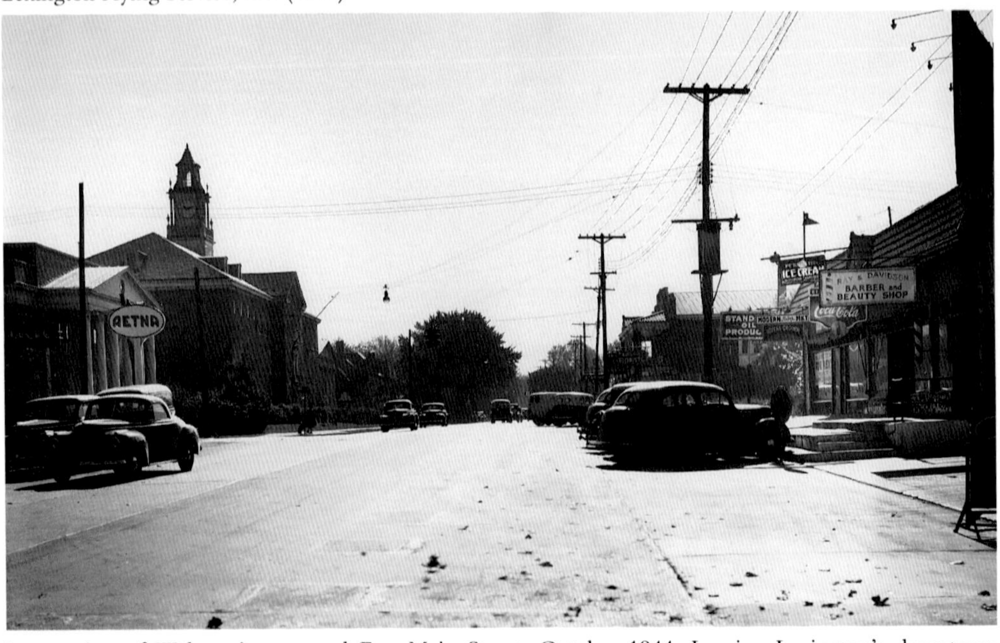

Intersection of Walton Avenue and East Main Street, October 1944. Leaving Lexington's downtown business district by traveling east along Main Street toward Richmond Road, the original Henry Clay High School, built in 1928, is on the left, on the northeast corner of Walton Avenue and East Main Street. In the fall of 1970, a new Henry Clay High School opened at 2100 Fontaine Road. (5262)

four

Lexington at Play

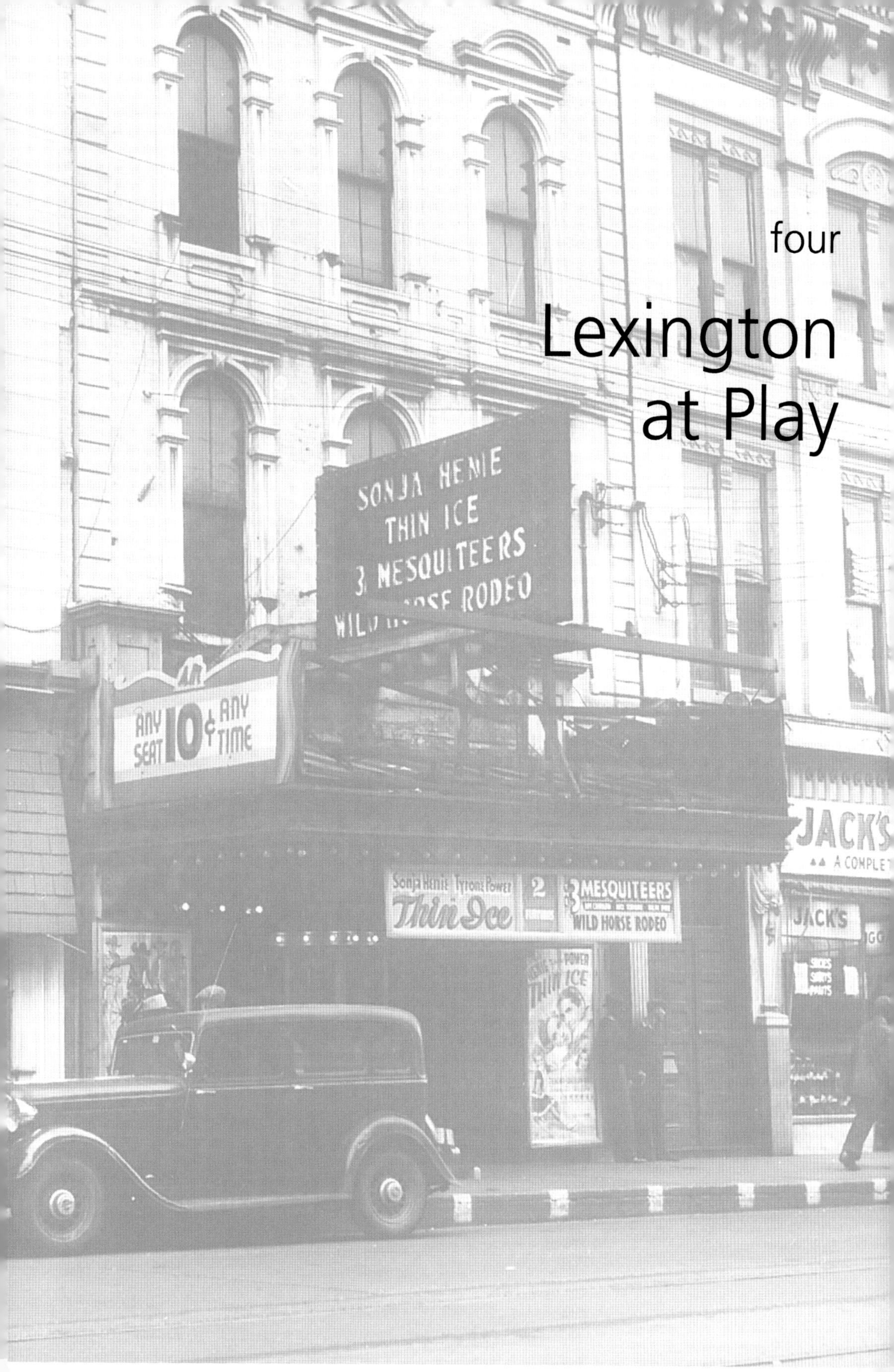

In the 1930s and 1940s, the citizens of Lexington were fortunate to be able to choose from a wide variety of entertainments, pastimes, and diversions. City parks, dance clubs, commercial amusement parks, live theater and musical performances, vaudeville shows, horse races, radio programs, and the thriving motion picture business, were just some of the options open to someone trying to decide how to spend his free time. Bob and Ida Long had worked in "show business." That they retained their affection for the entertainment industry is made evident by the number of photographs they took documenting that aspect of life in Lexington.

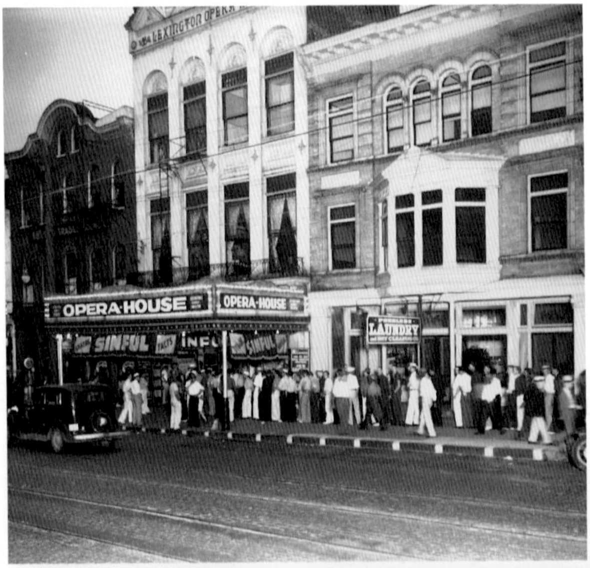

Left: Sinful at the Lexington Opera House, July 1937. The Lexington Opera House had been in operation for almost 50 years when this photo was taken. Sinful was one of the more popular movies to show at the Opera House in the late 1930s. Because of the "delicate subject" of Sinful, matinees were open only to women and evening shows only to men. A July 15, 1937 Lexington Herald article reported that "Spectators passing the theater said the scene reminded them of the time when the Opera House was the site of the one-night stands of famous stage stars. Persons were lined up three abreast from the box office on North Broadway all the way to Second Street and also Short Street." (3773)

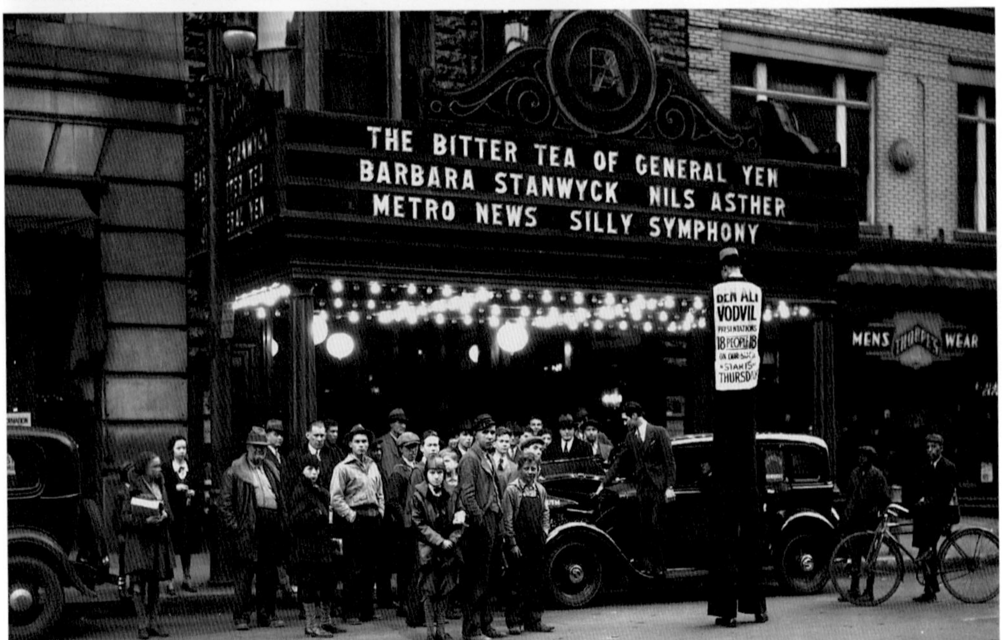

"Vodvil" at the Ben Ali Theater, c. 1933. In an effort to attract audiences, the Ben Ali combined movies and live stage shows. The Ben Ali, located on the north side of East Main opposite the Phoenix Hotel, was named for multi-millionaire horseman James Ben Ali Haggin. (1482)

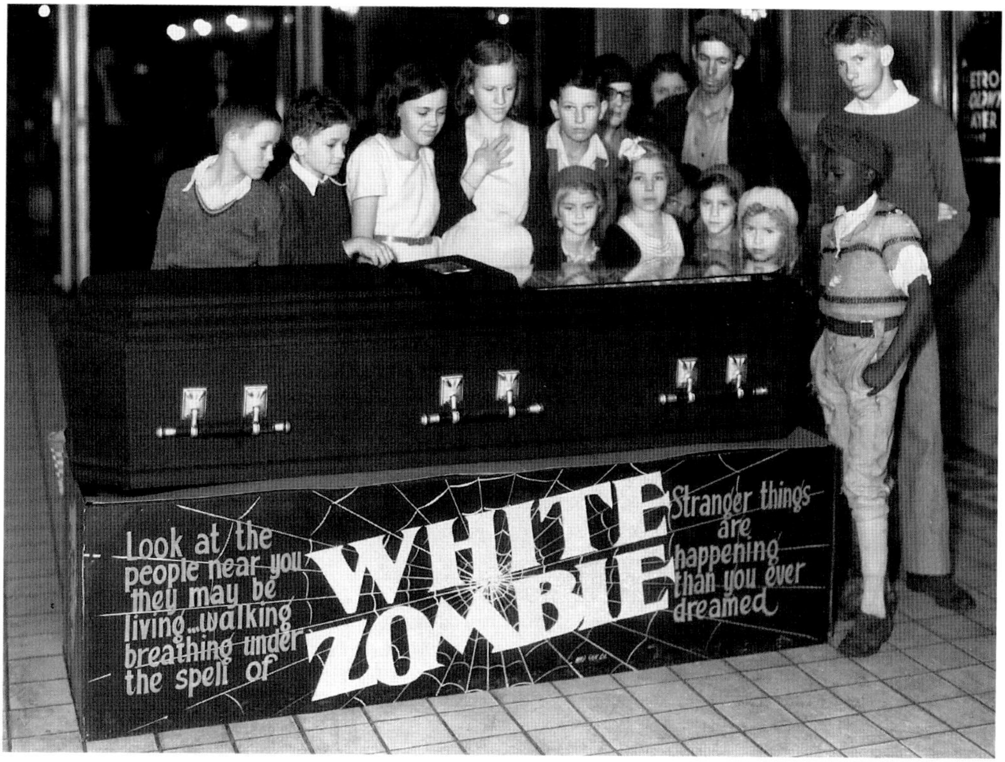

Above: White Zombie at the Ben Ali, September 1932. Elaborate lobby displays and other advertising gimmicks were common during the 1930s as Lexington's theaters competed for audiences. Even though African Americans and whites mingled in the lobby of the Ben Ali, African-American moviegoers were still relegated to seats in the second balcony. (1394)

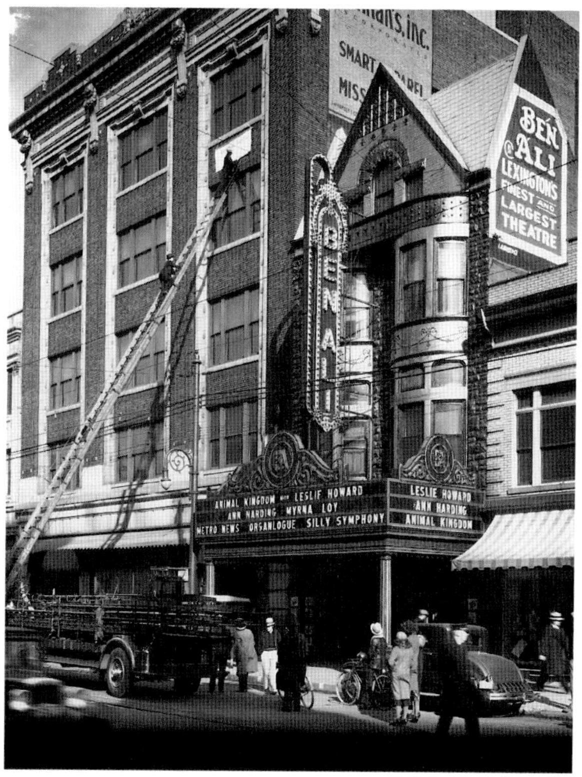

Right: Ben Ali Theater, c. 1933. The Ben Ali Theater opened on September 23, 1913. The theater was damaged by fire on January 11, 1916. This fire truck, however, was not there to put out a fire. The men on the ladder are hanging a sign to promote a membership drive for Lexington's Man O' War post of the American Legion. The Ben Ali was torn down in 1965. (1471)

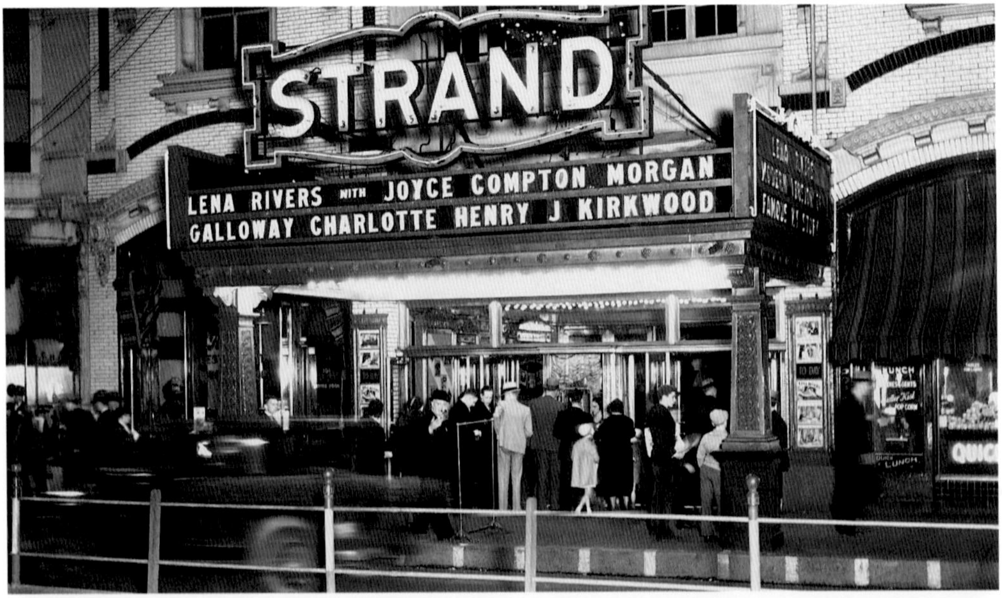

Lena Rivers showing at the Strand, April 1932. Former Lexington resident Joyce Compton had one of the leading roles in Lena Rivers. Bowling Green, Kentucky native Morgan Galloway was also featured in the film. Built and originally operated by the Phoenix Amusement Company, the Strand, at 153 East Main Street across from the Phoenix Hotel and Union Station, opened on October 12, 1915. The last film was shown at the Strand in 1973, and it was torn down in 1979. (1264)

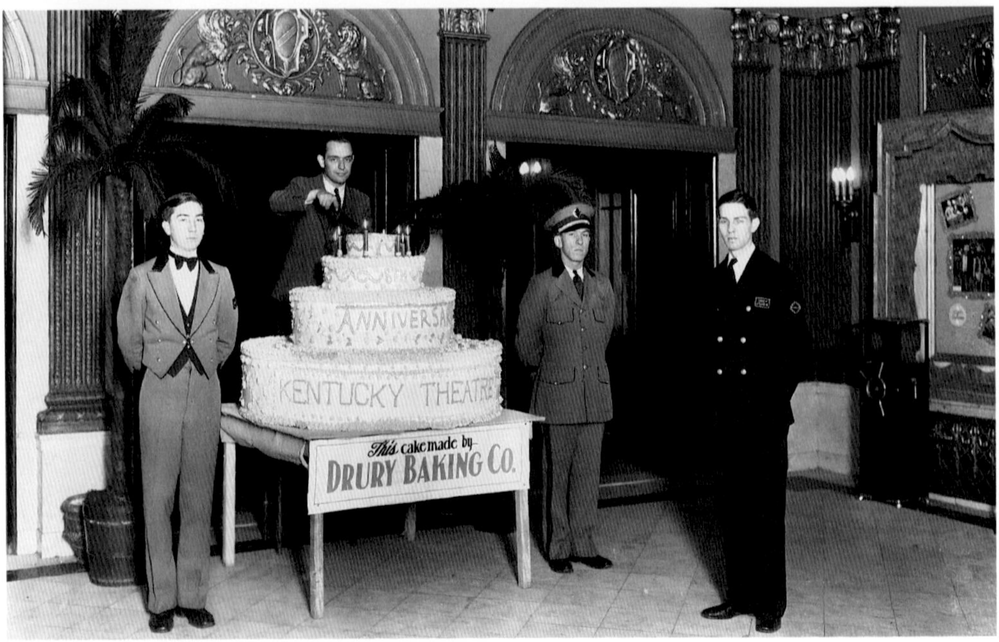

Eighth anniversary celebration at the Kentucky Theater, October 1930. The Lafayette Amusement Company, which at the time also operated the Ada Meade Theater, opened the Kentucky Theater on October 4, 1922. During the week of October 19, 1930, the Kentucky Theater celebrated its eighth anniversary and the first anniversary of its purchase by the Publix Theater Corporation. Lexington's Drury Baking Company, in business since 1914, baked the cake for the celebration. (991)

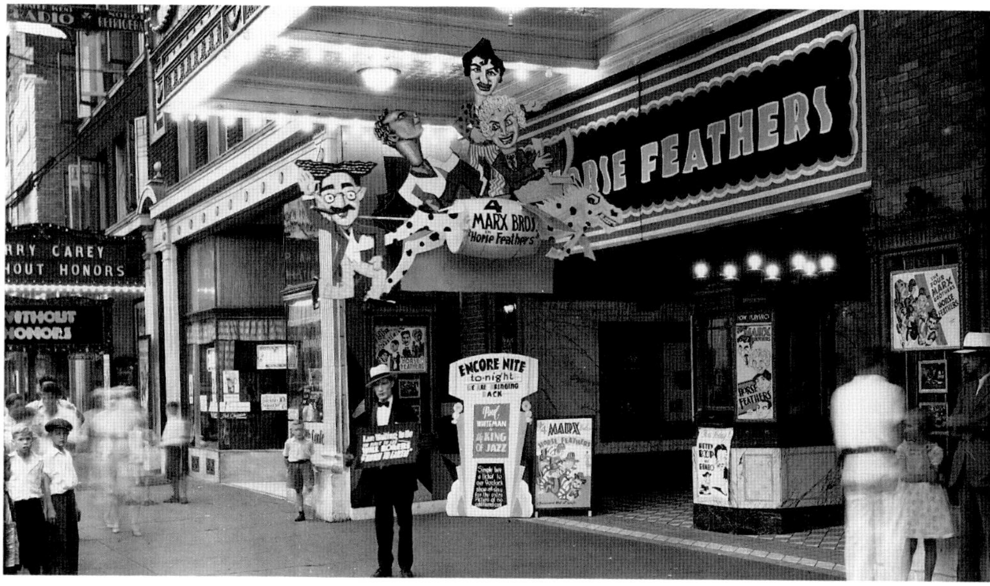

Horse Feathers at the Kentucky Theater, August 1932. *Horse Feathers*, starring the four Marx Brothers, Groucho, Harpo, Chico, and Zeppo, played at the Kentucky during August of 1932. The sign held by the man standing in front of the theater reads, "I am waiting to be the first to see Will Rogers in Down to Earth." *Down to Earth* would be the next film featured at the Kentucky after *Horse Feathers* completed its run. This sort of publicity stunt was common during the early 1930s. (1372)

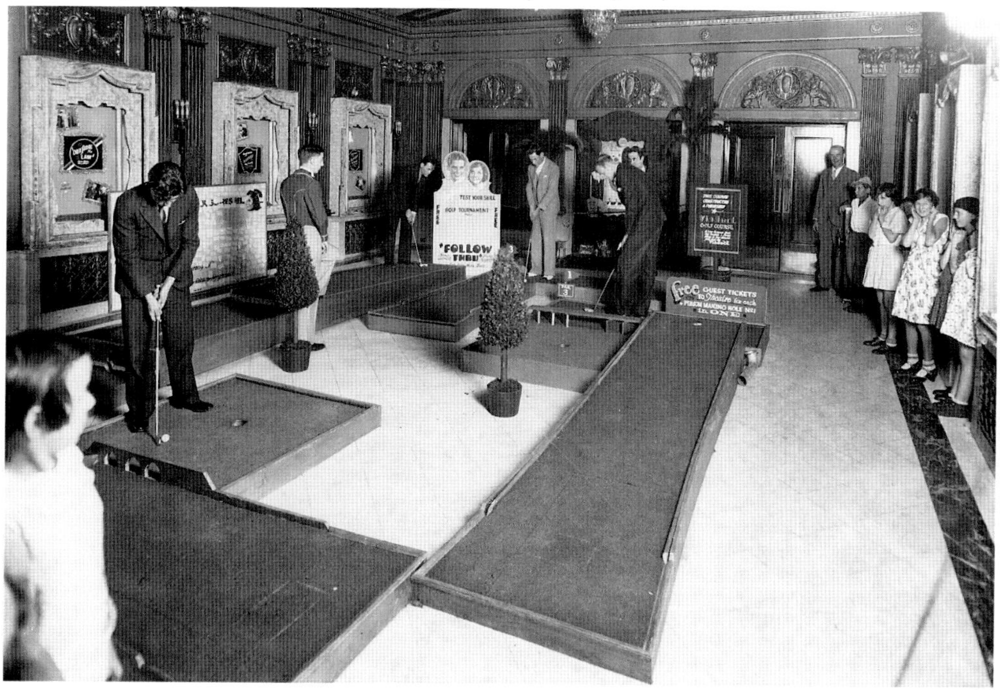

Indoor Miniature Golf Course in the Lobby of the Kentucky Theater, September 1930. This indoor miniature golf course was set up in the lobby of the Kentucky Theater to promote the musical comedy Follow Thru, starring Charles Rogers and Nancy Carroll. There are more photographs of the Kentucky Theater in the Lafayette Studio collection than any other building or business in Lexington. (794)

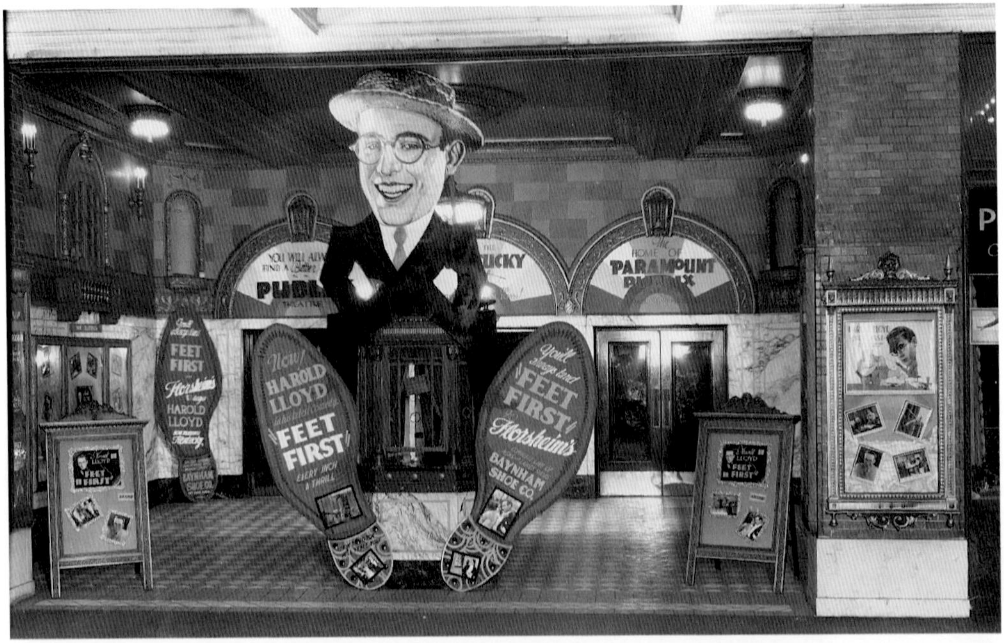

Harold Lloyd's *Feet First* at the Kentucky Theater, November 1930. Lexington's theaters used various methods to attract audiences. Some offered lower admission prices, others paired live stage shows with movies. Elaborate facades, usually done by the Byrd Sign company, seemed to be the favorite method of advertising at the Kentucky while it was a Paramount Publix Theater. Many of the Lafayette Studio photographs of the Kentucky Theater were commissioned during the time the Kentucky was part of the Paramount Publix chain. (972)

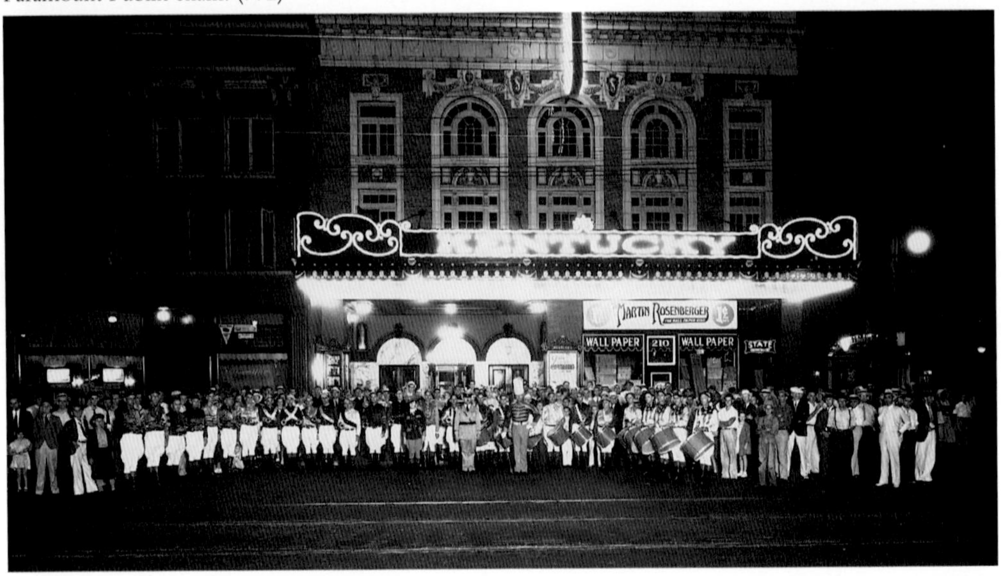

Kentucky Theater opening night, August 19, 1933. The Phoenix Amusement Company acquired the Kentucky Theater and the State Theater in 1933. This "opening night" was held to present the refurbished Kentucky Theater to the public. Among other improvements, the Phoenix Amusement Company had installed new sound equipment, repainted, recovered the seats, and raised the floor to minimize future flood damage. In 1933, the Phoenix Amusement Company also owned the Strand and the Ben Ali. (1719)

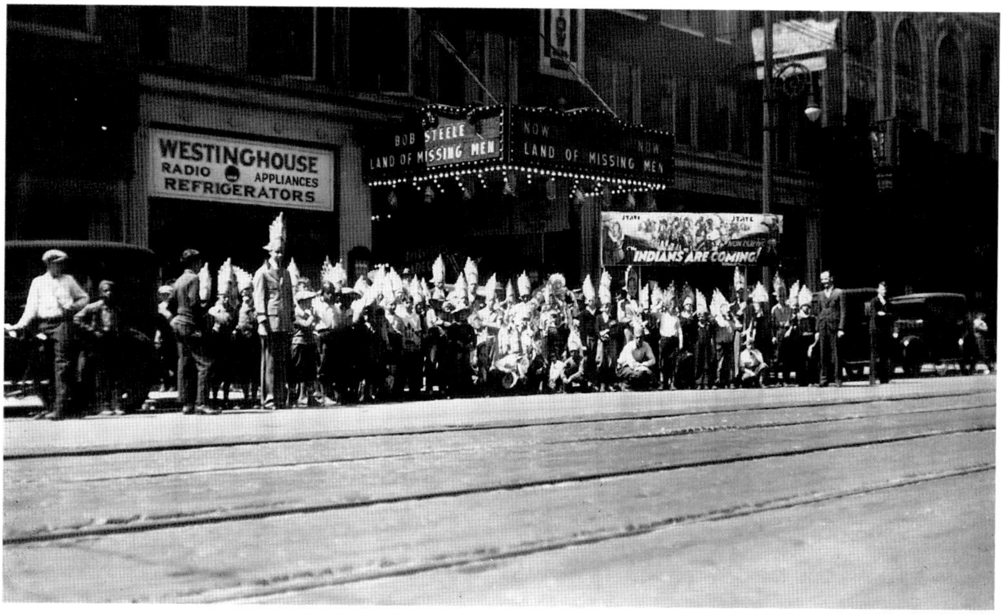

The Indians Are Coming at the State Theater, April 1931. As a promotion for the 12-part Tim McCoy serial, *The Indians Are Coming*, the State Theater held an "Indian Parade." The first 100 children to sign up for the parade received a free ticket to the first show and an "Indian hat." The child with the best cowboy or Indian makeup received a free ticket to all 12 chapters of the serial. (879)

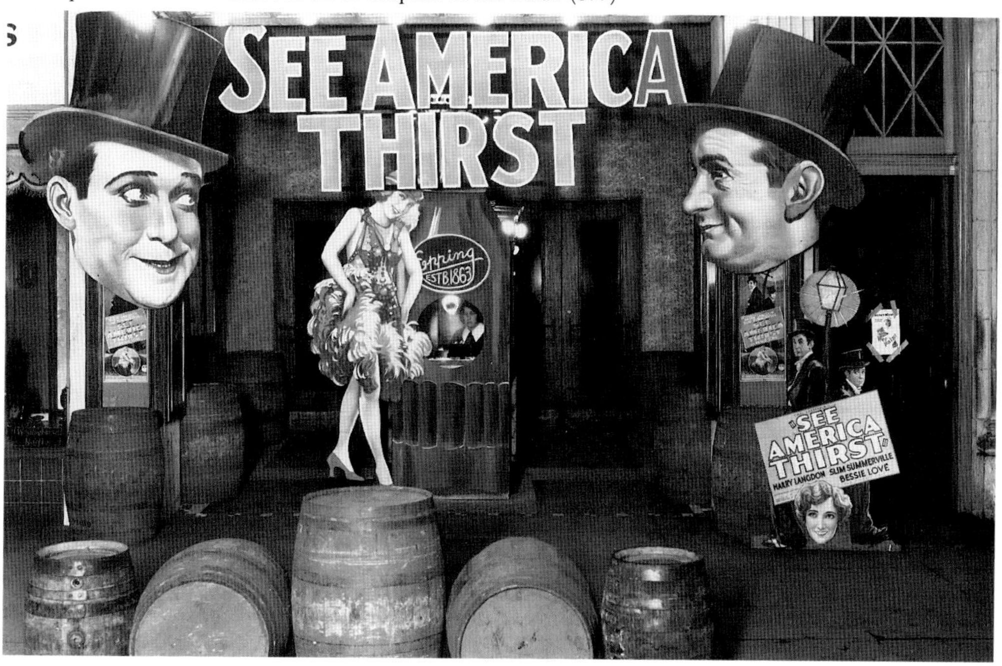

See America Thirst at the State Theater, January 1931. The Epping Bottling Works sign was a prominent part of this display advertising See America Thirst. This comedy, with prohibition and gangster themes, was Harry Langdon's first feature length sound film. Eppings produced such soft drinks as Kentucky Club Ginger Ale and 7-Up. Eppings was also a distributor of Falls City Beer after the repeal of prohibition in December of 1933. (838)

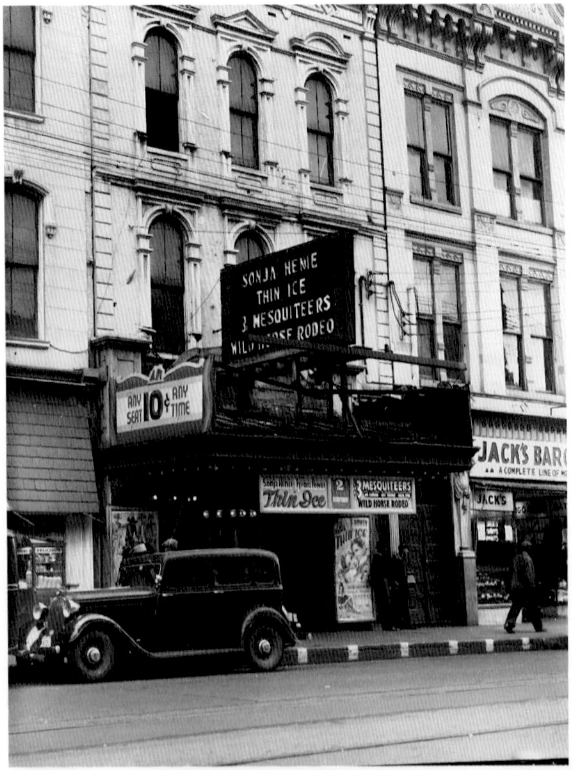

Left: Ten cent admission at the Ada Meade, November 1938. As early as 1934, the Ada Meade Theater had offered 10¢ admission prices during some summer months. By 1938, the Ada Meade advertised 10¢ admission for any time and any seat. Other Lexington theaters regularly charged from 15¢ to 25¢. (4094)

Below: National Recovery Administration Labor Day parade, September 4, 1933. Parades were also popular diversions. The September 5, 1933 Lexington Herald reported that the "two mile long column of marchers, floats, and decorated motor cars" took 40 minutes to complete the parade route down Main Street from Ashland Avenue to Broadway. The crowd, said to be the largest that had ever gathered in Lexington, was estimated at 30,000. (1709)

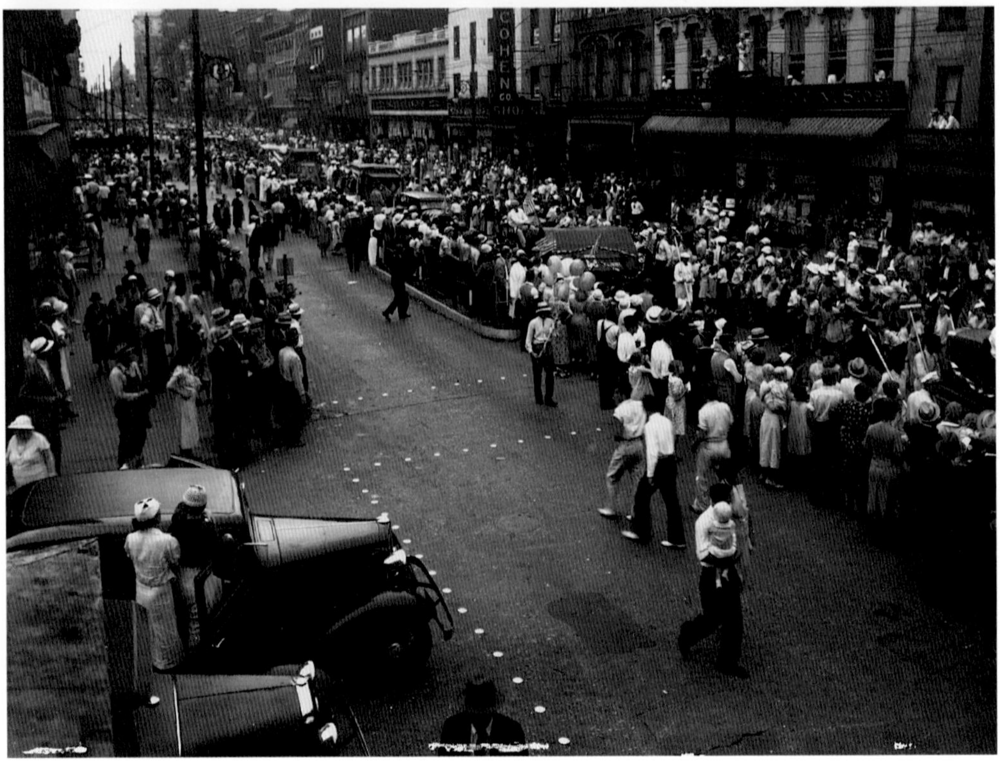

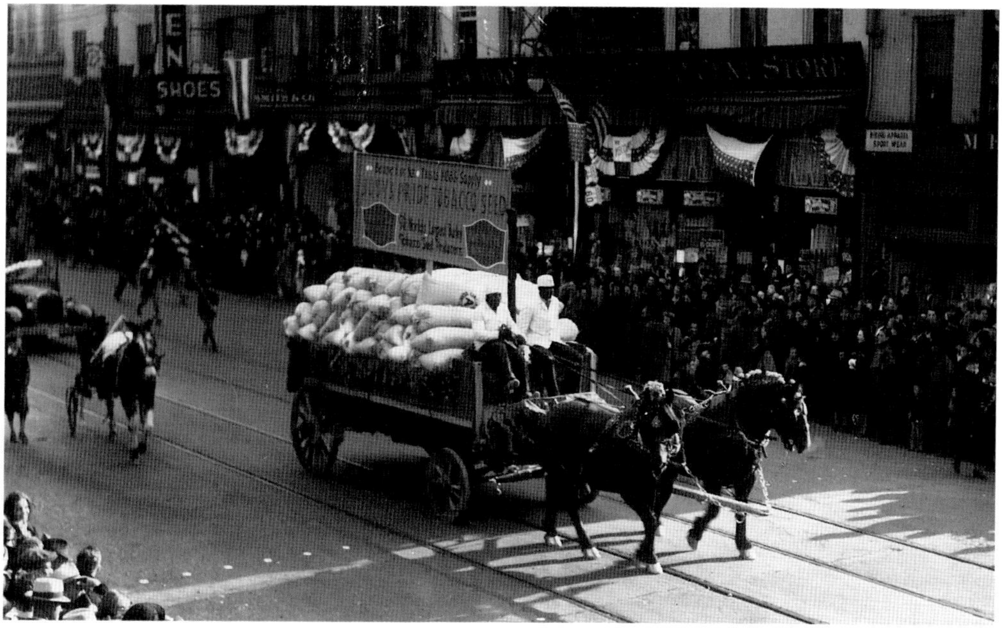

Tobacco Carnival Parade, November 9, 1938. Five years after the NRA Labor Day parade, Lexington's first Tobacco Carnival was held. The three-day carnival began on November 8, with a parade in the afternoon and the governor's banquet in the evening. Speakers at the banquet included Governor A.B. "Happy" Chandler and Thomas Rust Underwood, Lexington Herald editor, and future congressman and senator. Chandler closed the governor's banquet by leading the crowd in singing "My Old Kentucky Home." (4102)

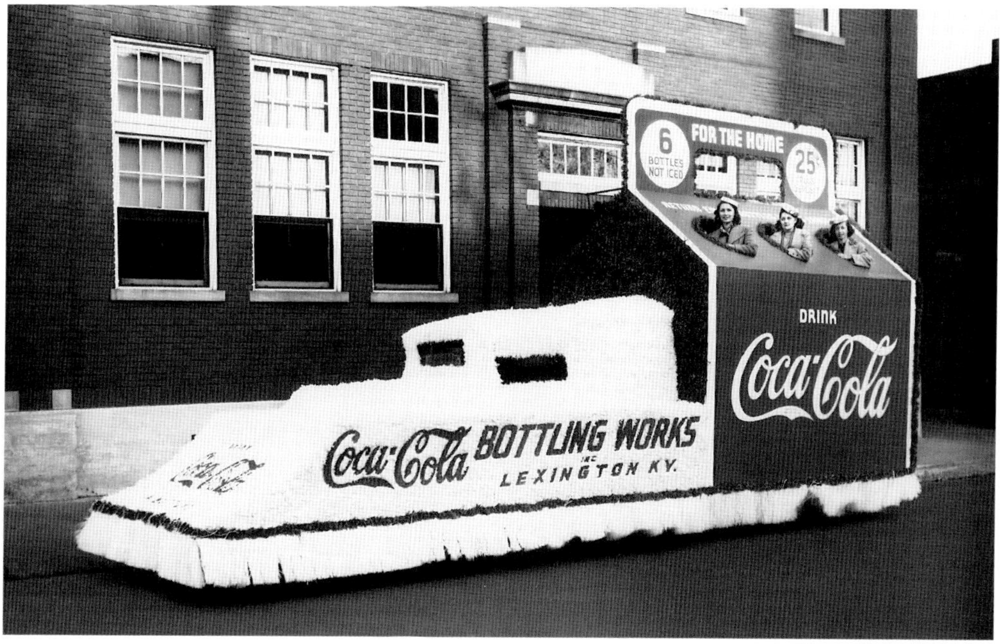

Coca-Cola Bottling Works Float Ready for Tobacco Carnival Parade, November 9, 1938. It was estimated that from 15,000 to 25,000 people lined the streets to watch the parade which included the Henry Clay High School marching band, and floats such as this one, sponsored by the Coca-Cola Bottling Company, and the Lexington Utilities Company float, shown below. (4101)

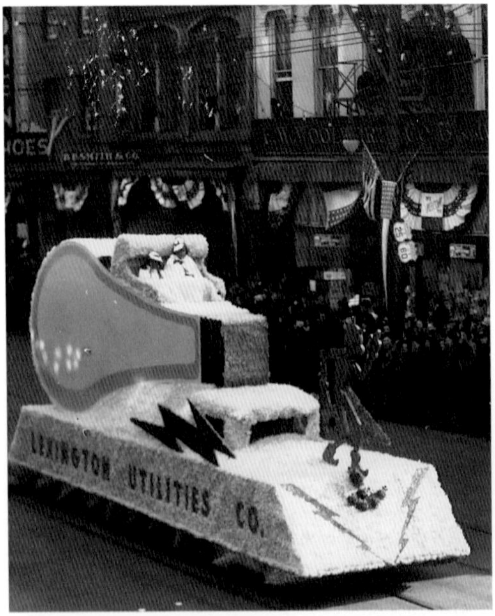

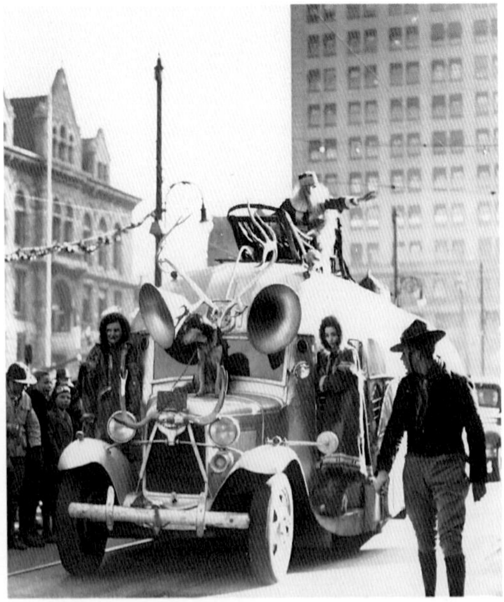

Above left: Lexington Utilities Company float, Tobacco Carnival parade, November 9, 1938. In addition to the parade and the governor's banquet, the Tobacco Carnival also included a contest to select a Tobacco Queen, and a tobacco exposition at the Tattersall warehouse on South Broadway. Martha Kathryn Lamkin, of Magnolia, Kentucky, was selected as the 1938 Tobacco Queen. (4102)

Above right: Christmas parade, November 30, 1935. Newspaper reports of the 1935 Christmas parade were very subdued compared to those from two years earlier. The reports seemed to indicate that the 1935 parade was much less elaborate and drew much smaller crowds that the 1933 parade. The year 1933 seems to have been the year that parades reached the height of their popularity in Lexington. The 1933 Christmas parade drew over 30,000 people, breaking the record set two months earlier by the N.R.A. Labor Day Parade. (3086)

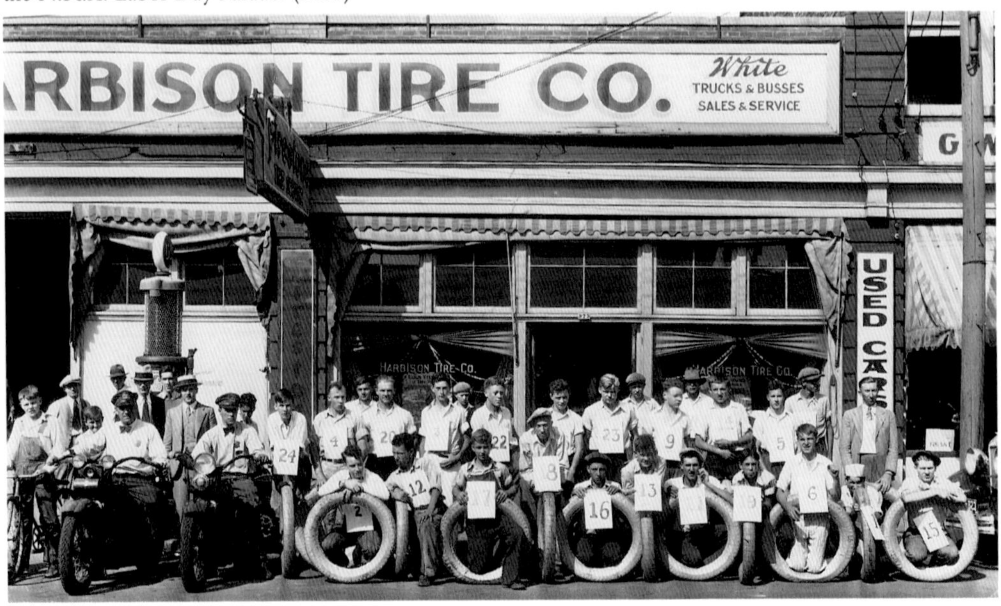

Right: B&F Electric Company bowling team, April 1949. Business-sponsored bowling and softball leagues were popular during the late 1940s. Lexington's first bowling alley opened in the late 1890s. Throughout most of the 1940s, three bowling alleys operated in the downtown area along with eight or nine pool halls. By 1949, the number of bowling alleys had dropped to two, one on East Main and one on Euclid Avenue. (6086)

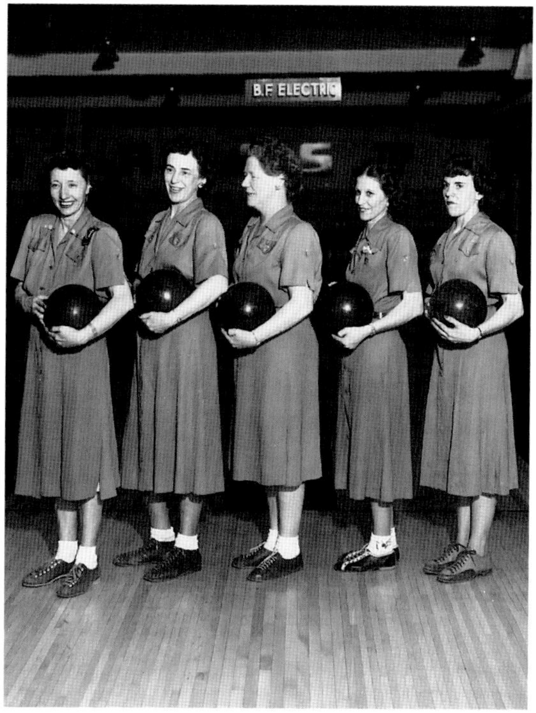

Below: 1941 Triple Crown winner Whirlaway with tour group at Calumet Farm, May 1947. After his father's death in 1931, Warren Wright inherited Calumet Farm on Lexington's Versailles Road. Under the ownership of Wright's father, Calumet had been a standardbred farm. Warren Wright took Calumet into the thoroughbred business, and under his leadership it became one of the leading thoroughbred farms in the country. Trained by Ben A. Jones, Whirlaway was Calumet's first champion. He won 32 races and set a record for career winnings. (5794)

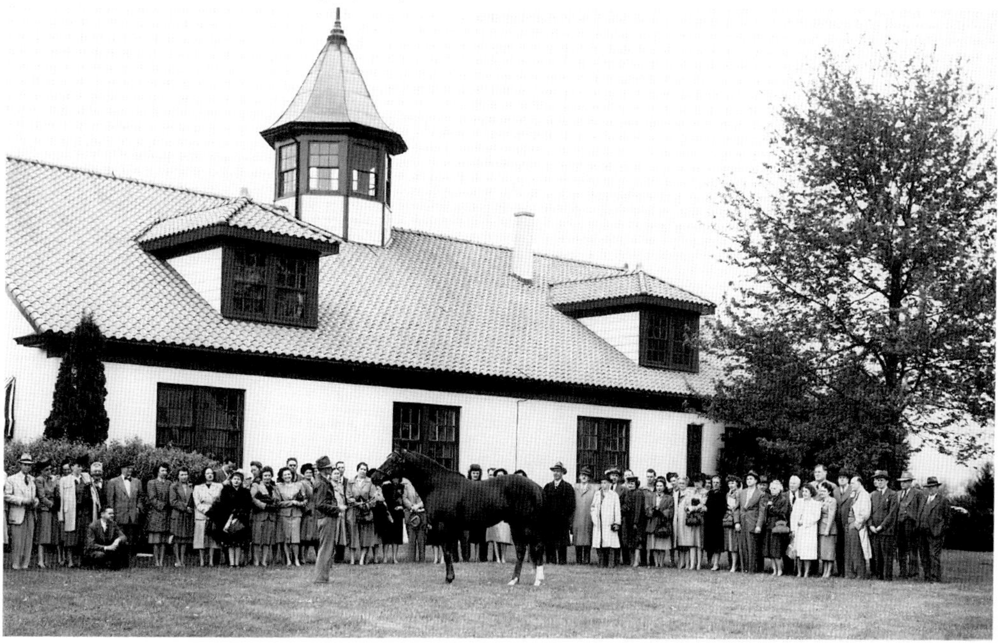

Opposite below: Blue Grass Day Roll-A-Tire Race Contestants, August 1931. The Lexington Board of Commerce organized Blue Grass Day, a city-wide sale designed to attract shoppers from surrounding counties. Buses and the interurban railway offered reduced round-trip fares from surrounding towns. Lexington streetcars, taxis, and buses offered free rides into downtown. The crowds and safety concerns forced the delay of the Roll-A-Tire Race, but when it was finally run, William Waits of Lexington won the $15 first place prize. (1744)

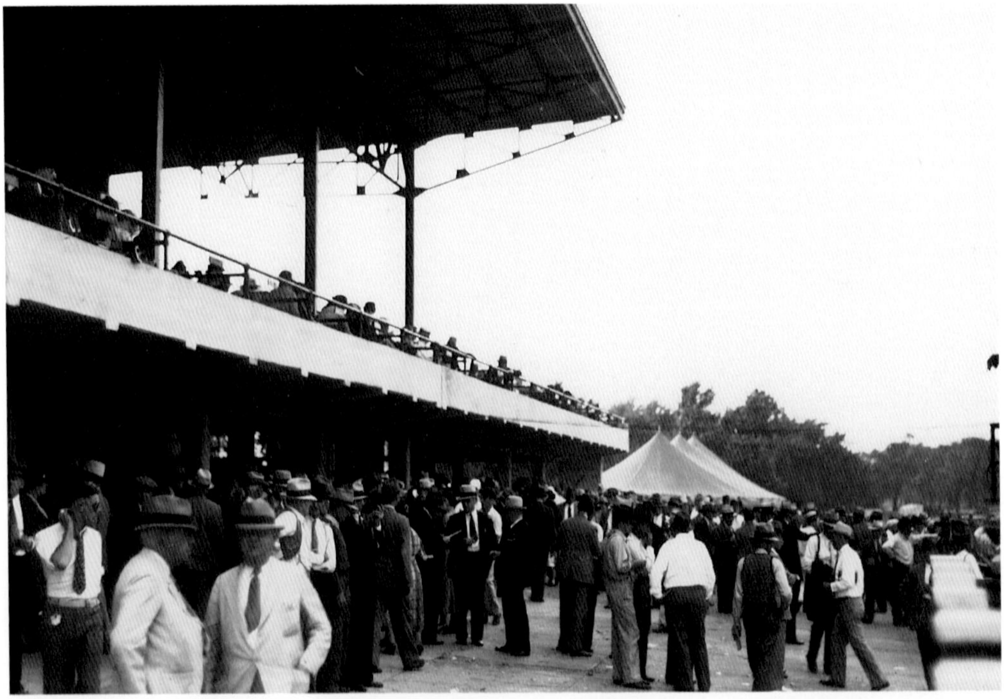

Crowds at the trotting track, c. 1935. Both thoroughbred and harness racing have long been popular in Lexington. Since 1875, the Red Mile has drawn large crowds for harness races, and Keeneland Race Course, which opened in 1936, continues to draw crowds of thoroughbred racing fans. Until 1933, thoroughbred races were held at the Kentucky Association track at Fifth and Rose Streets. (3011)

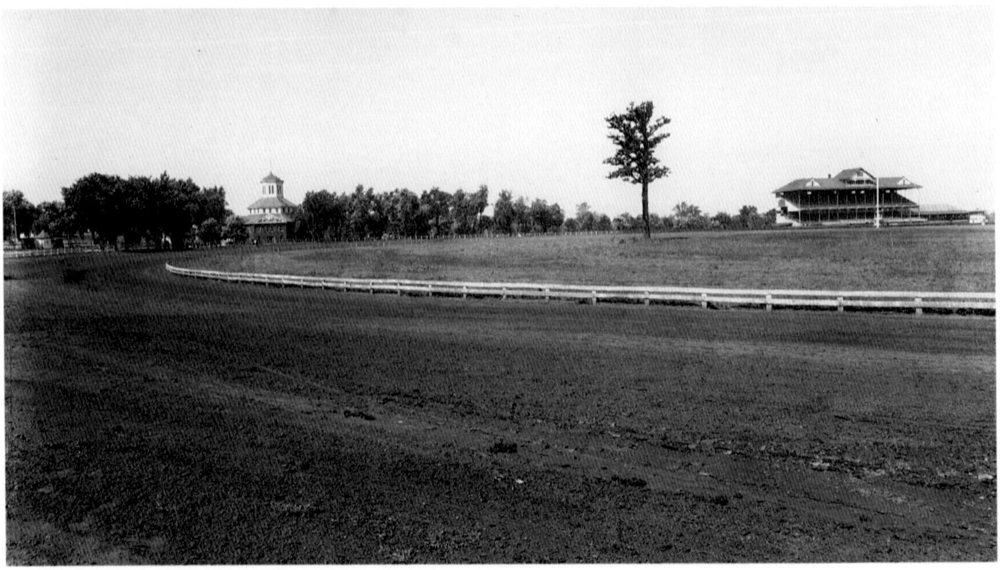

Kentucky Trotting Horse Breeders Association track, August 1930. Racing began at the track now known as the Red Mile in 1875. The round barn at left was designed by John McMurtry. Originally designed to house floral exhibits, it was built in 1880 and is still standing. The grandstand at right, built in 1893 to replace the previous grandstand which had collapsed the year before, was destroyed by fire in 1931, the year after this photograph was taken. (1157)

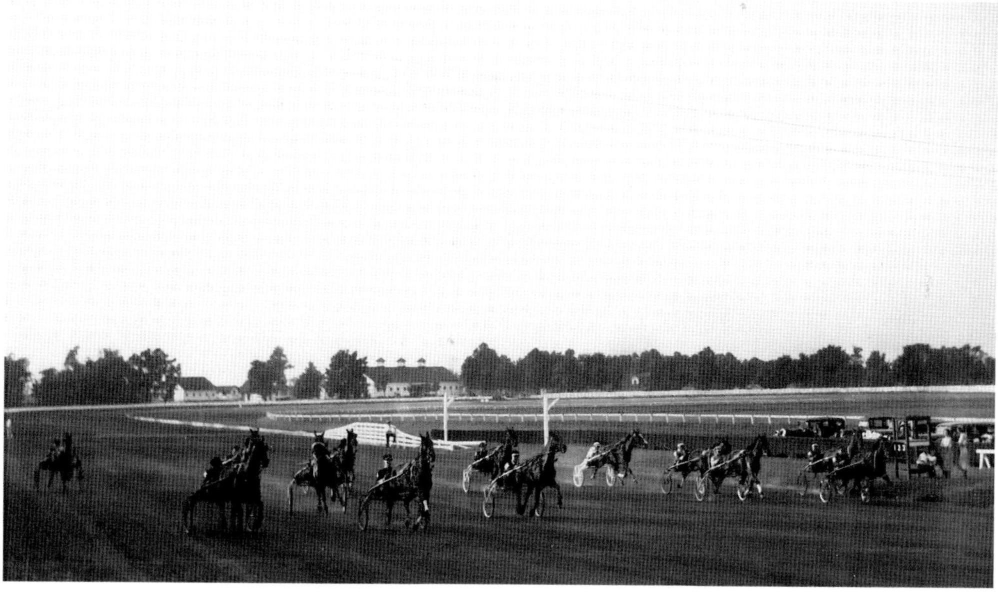

Harness races at the trotting track, c. 1935. From 1875 to the early 1940s, the track was operated by the Kentucky Trotting Horse Breeders Association. In 1945, the Lexington Trots Breeders Association took over and continues to operate the track now known as the Red Mile. On September 28, 1875, Odd Fellow won the first race held at the track under the auspices of the Kentucky Trotting Horse Breeders Association. (3081)

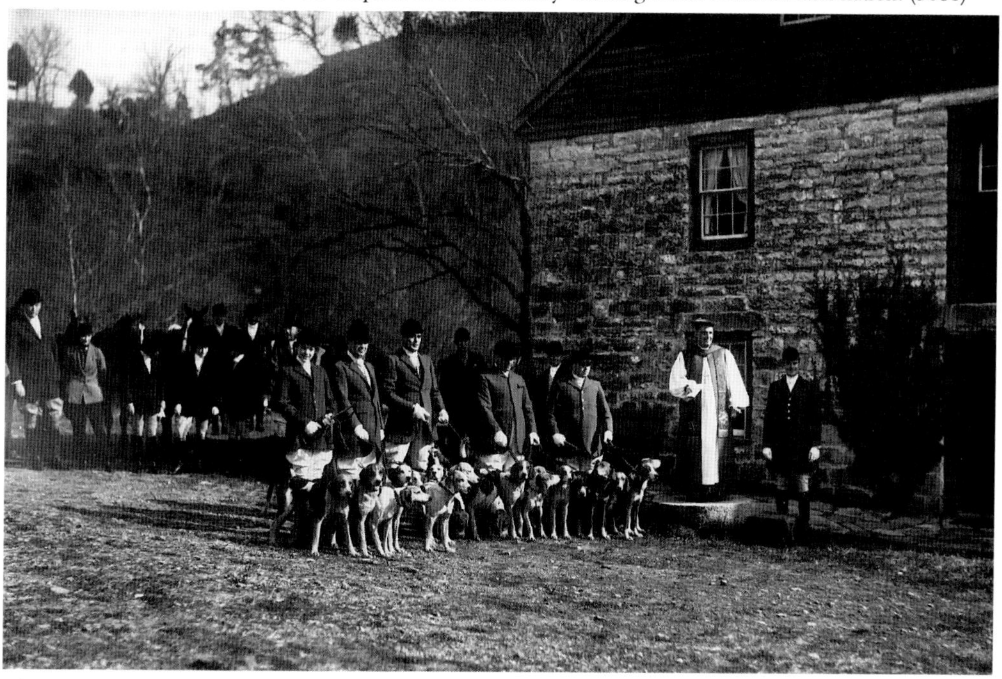

Blessing of the Hounds at Grimes Mill, November 18, 1933. The Iroquois Hunt and Polo Club opened its hunting season with the Blessing of the Hounds Ceremony. In 1933, the ceremony was conducted by the Rt. Rev. H.P. Almon Abbott, bishop of the Lexington Episcopal diocese, who had officiated at the Club's inaugural Blessing of the Hounds ceremony the previous year. Named for Iroquois, the first American horse to win the English Derby, the Iroquois Hunt Club was founded in the early 1880s. (1670)

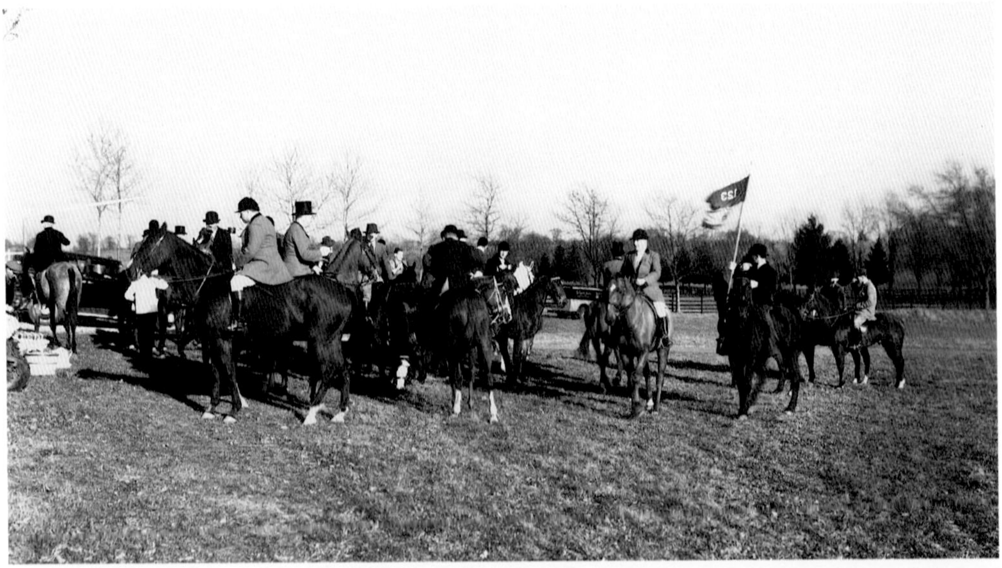

Iroquois Hunt Group, c. 1935. In addition to fox hunts, the club also held an annual horse show and barbecue. In 1931, the Hunt Club joined with the newly formed Elkhorn Polo Club to form the Iroquois Hunt and Polo Club. Polo matches grew in popularity in the early 1930s, drawing thousands of spectators to the matches held at Hamburg Place, the farm of John E. Madden. By 1934, the club also had a women's team, a girl's team, and a children's Shetland pony team. (1666)

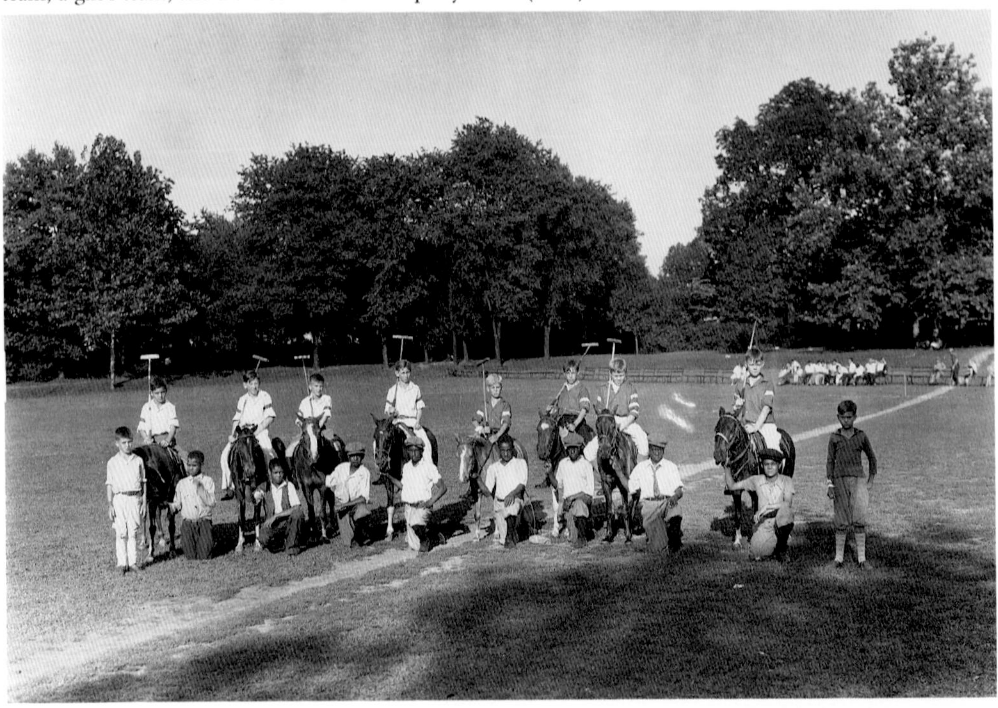

Iroquois Hunt and Polo Club's red and white Shetland pony polo teams, 1931. The July 25, 1931 Lexington Leader reported that a crowd of 1,500 witnessed the polo match between the Red and White teams. The match, the first ever held at Woodland park, was for the junior championship of Kentucky. Members of the winning Red team were presented loving cups, donated by the city playgrounds and recreation board. (1106)

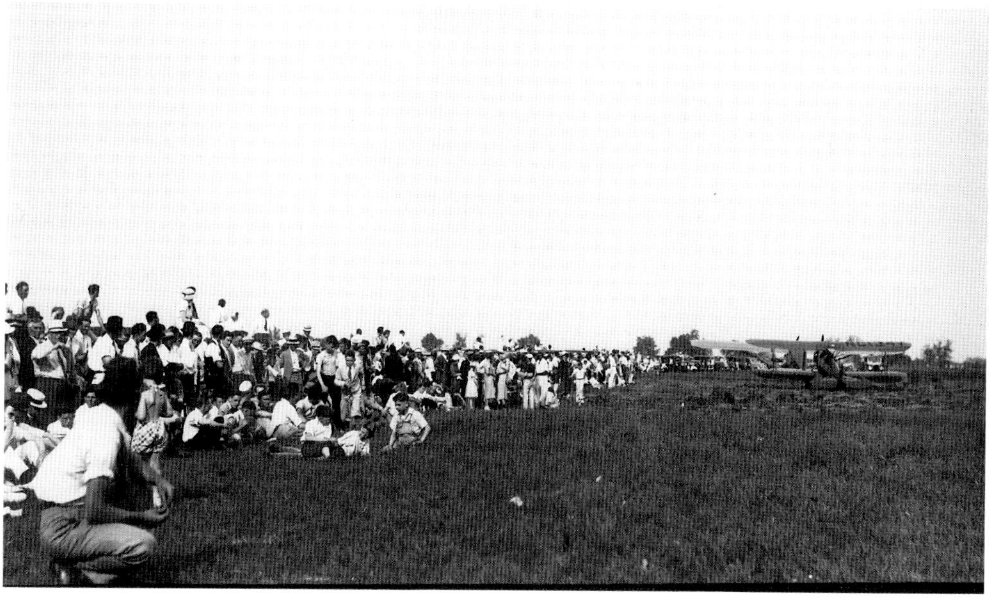

Air show at Cool Meadow Airfield, c. 1936. The exact date of this airshow is not known, but it was held at Cool Meadow airfield located on Newtown Pike. In 1930, the city leased 250 acres from James Blythe Anderson and built the Cool Meadow airfield on the land that had been part of Anderson's Glengarry Farm. Cool Meadow was built to replace the smaller Halley Field located on Leestown Road. (3223)

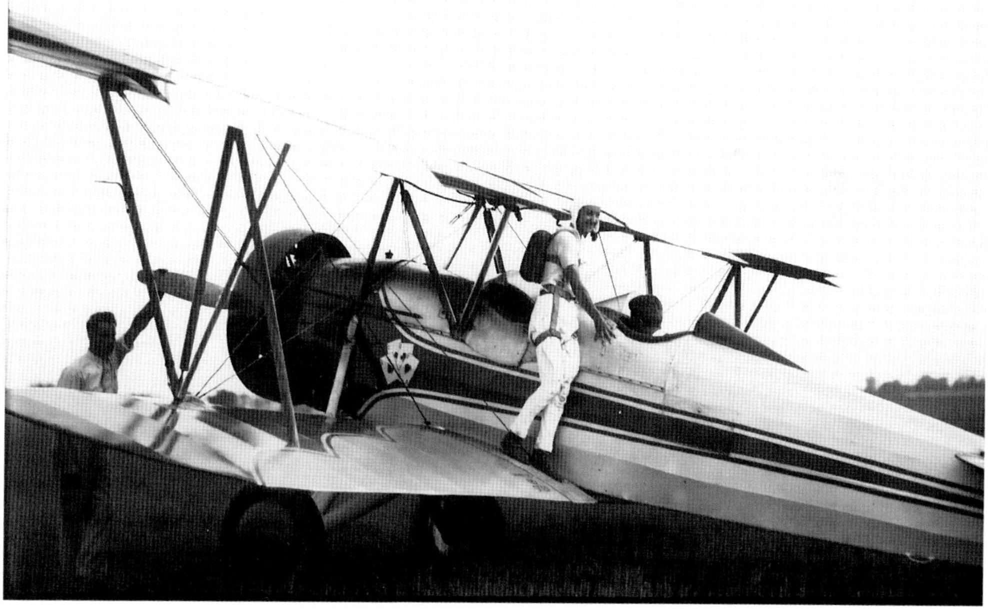

Unidentified air show performer at Cool Meadow Airfield, c. 1936. Charles Lindbergh landed at Halley Field in 1928 when he stopped in Lexington to visit Dr. Scott D. Breckinridge. According to a March 29, 1928 Lexington Leader article, Lindbergh had trouble finding Halley Field when he arrived and then barely cleared trees at the end of the runway on takeoff. Lindbergh's visit certainly helped convince the airport committee of the Board of Commerce that Lexington needed a new airport. (3223)

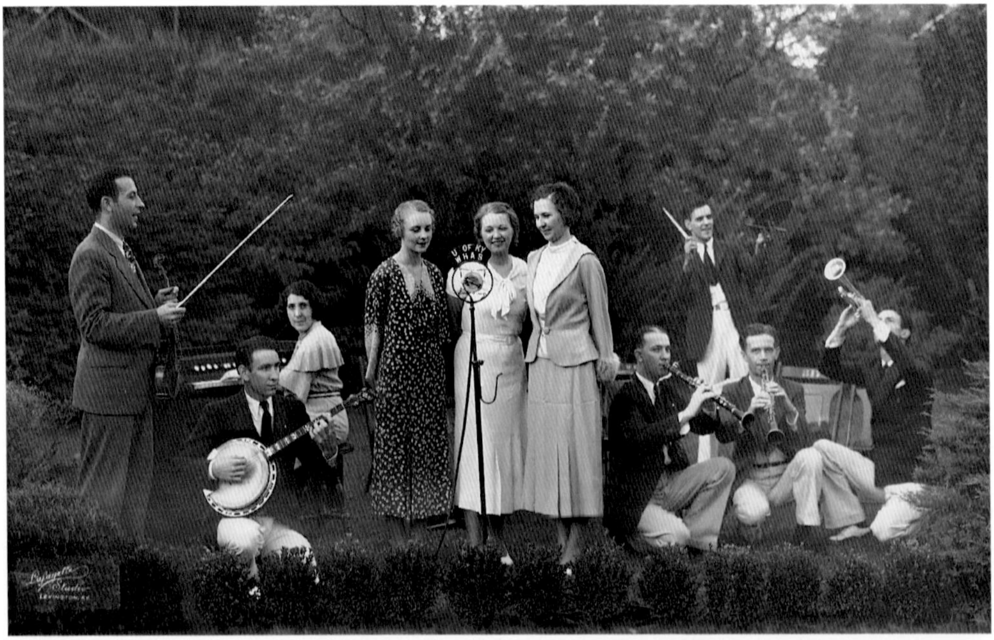

University of Kentucky musical performance broadcast over WHAS Radio, July 1933. In April of 1929, the University of Kentucky began broadcasting educational programs over Louisville's WHAS radio station. Kentucky's first licensed radio station, WHAS went on the air on July 18, 1922. Throughout the 1930s and 1940s, radio played an increasingly important role in the lives of Lexingtonians as a source of both entertainment and news. (1986)

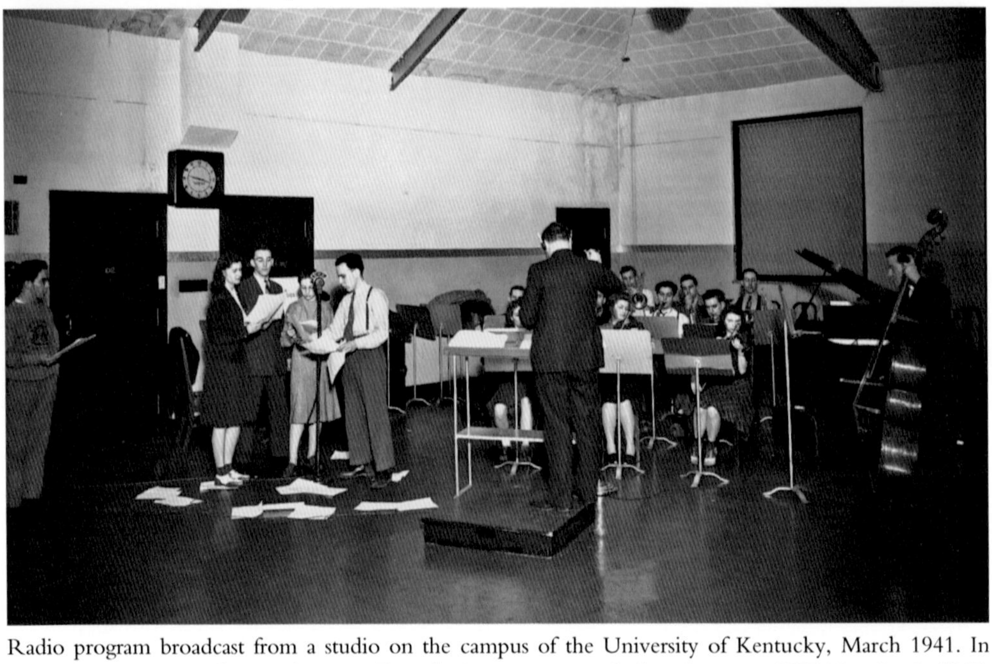

Radio program broadcast from a studio on the campus of the University of Kentucky, March 1941. In 1941, the University of Kentucky was still producing programs to be broadcast over WHAS radio. In 1947, WBKY, the university's non-commercial educational radio station, went on the air. The oldest university-owned FM radio station in the country, WBKY now operates under the call letters WUKY. (4679)

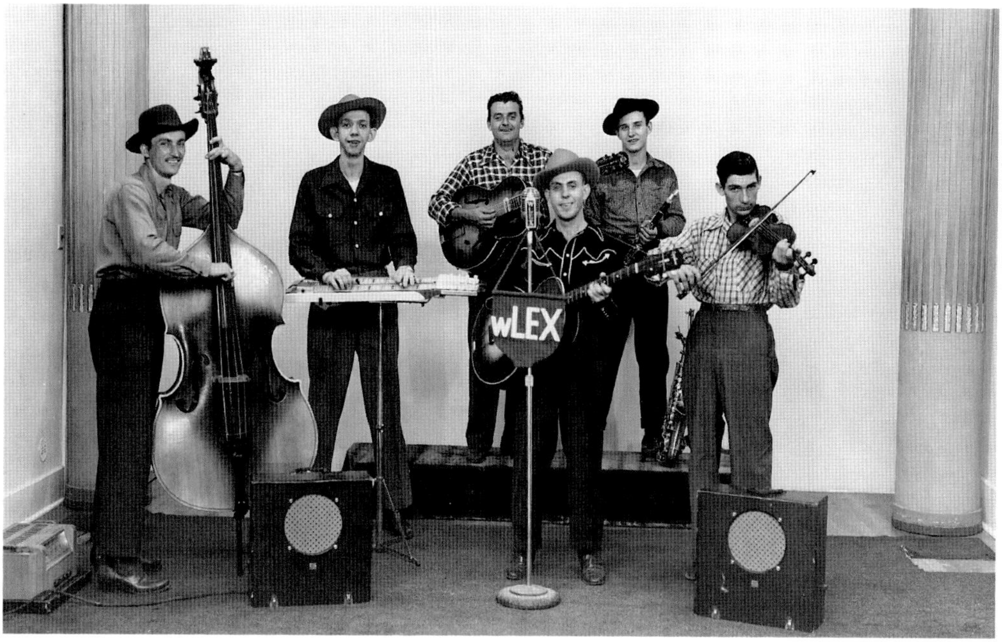

The Blue Grass Troubadours, October 1947. In addition to network programs, Lexington radio stations broadcast live performances by local musicians such as the Blue Grass Troubadours. In December of 1933, a radio station began broadcasting under the call letters WLEX. This unlicensed temporary station went on the air as part of a contest being held at the Joyland Park Casino. It was not until 1946 that a licensed radio station with the call letters WLEX went on the air. (5696)

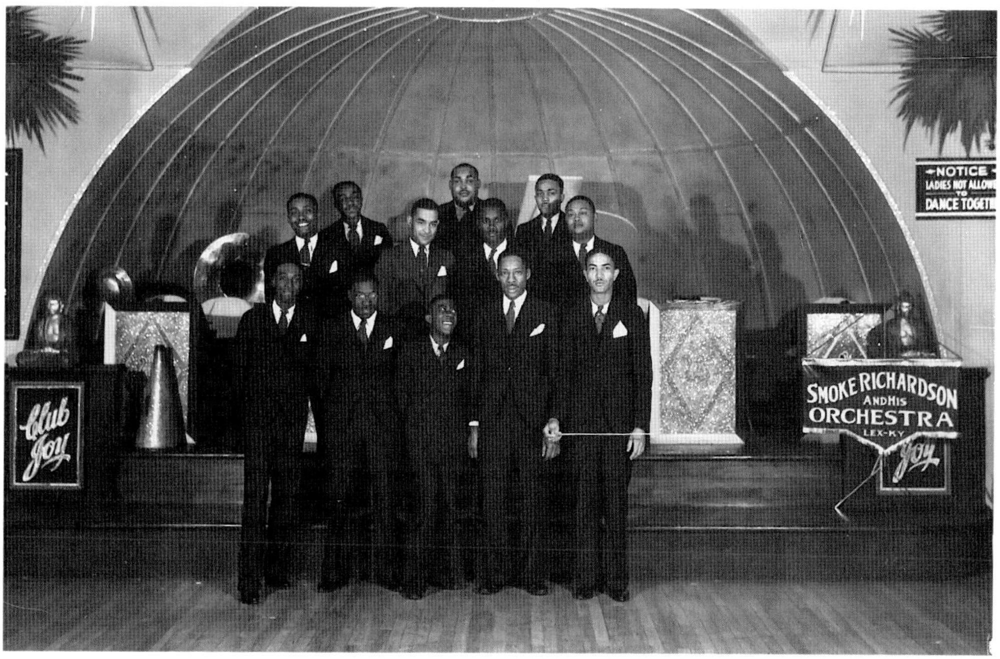

Smoke Richardson and his Orchestra at Club Joy, April 1934. For those who wanted live entertainment and dancing, Club Joy and, in the summer, the Joyland Dance Casino at Joyland Park, presented a variety of local and regional performers such as Smoke Richardson and his Orchestra. (1890)

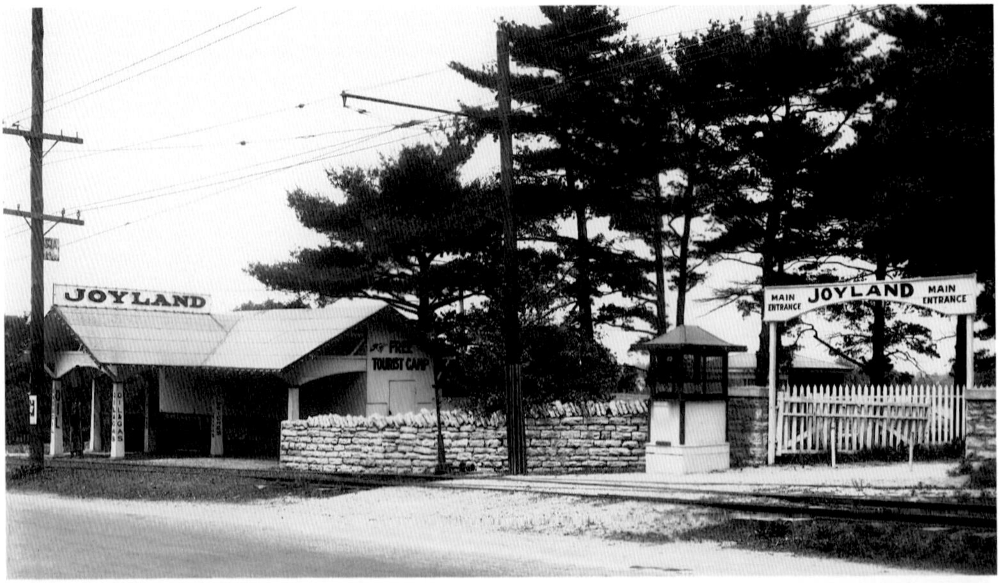

Joyland Park entrance, c. 1930. Joyland Park, situated on 25 acres 2 miles north of Lexington on the Paris Pike, held its official opening on May 30, 1923. It offered parking space for 5,000 cars and was also on the interurban rail line and bus routes. Joyland Park was owned by Frank Brandt and brothers John W. and F. Keller Sauer (Waller, p. 227). The Sauer brothers managed the park and A.M. James managed the Joyland Dance Casino. (694)

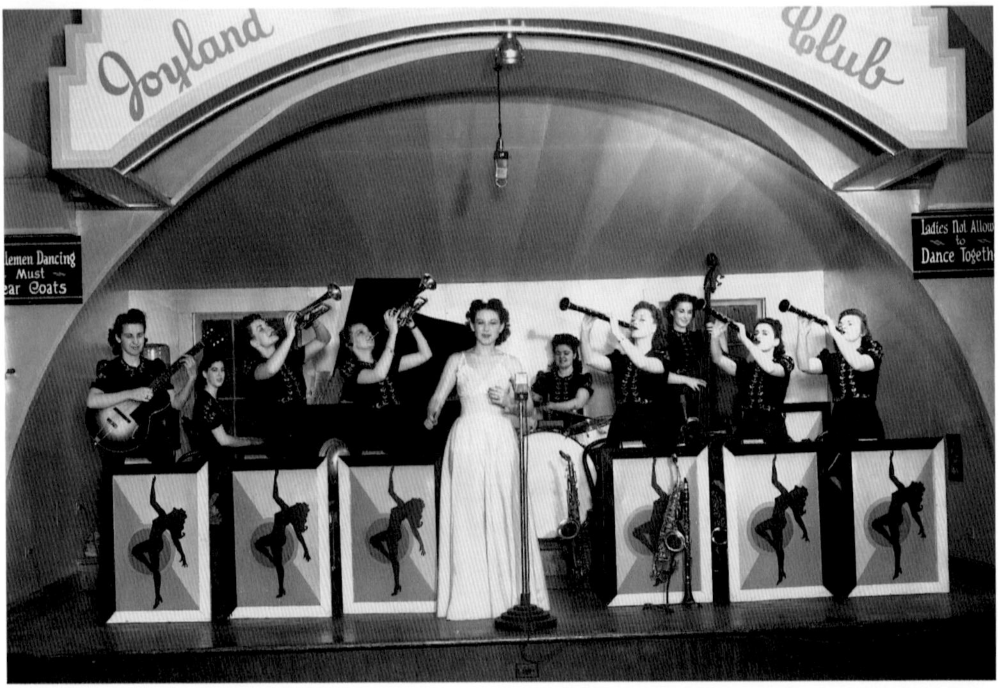

Betty Coed and the Debs at Club Joy, February 1940. Local performers such as Betty Coed and the Debs often performed at Club Joy during the winter months. When Joyland Park opened for the summer season, A.M. James was able to bring star attractions to the Joyland Dance Casino. Duke Ellington and his orchestra played at Joyland on August 13, 1937 as did Arte Shaw and his orchestra on August 31, 1938. (4446)

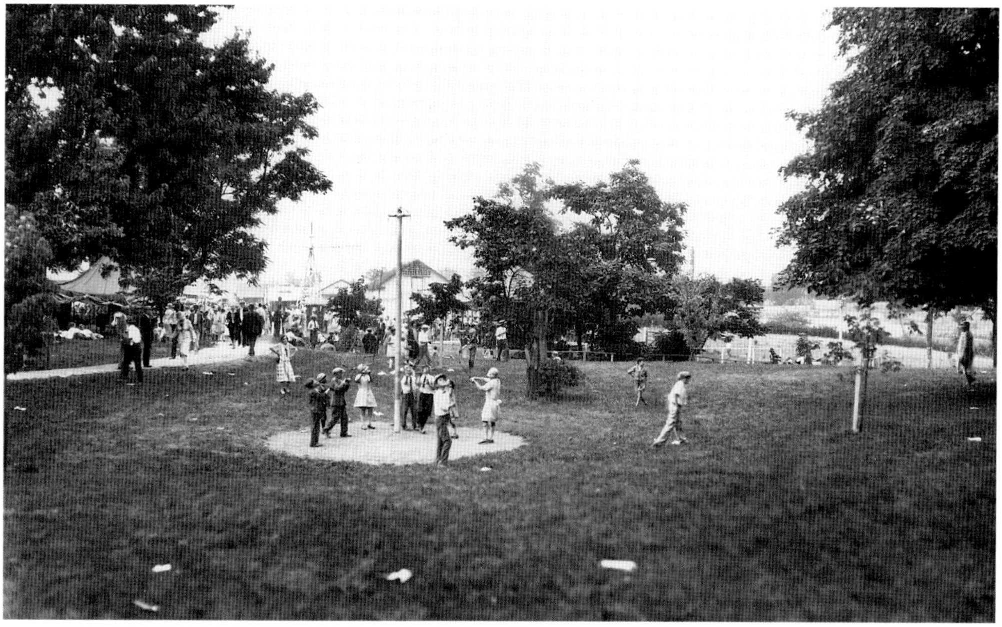

Joyland Park playground, c. 1930. In addition to the entertainment at Club Joy and the Joyland Dance Casino, the park offered a variety of other amusements designed to appeal to the entire family including a playground, a midway, picnic grounds, a swimming pool, pony rides, and a pool parlor. (2120)

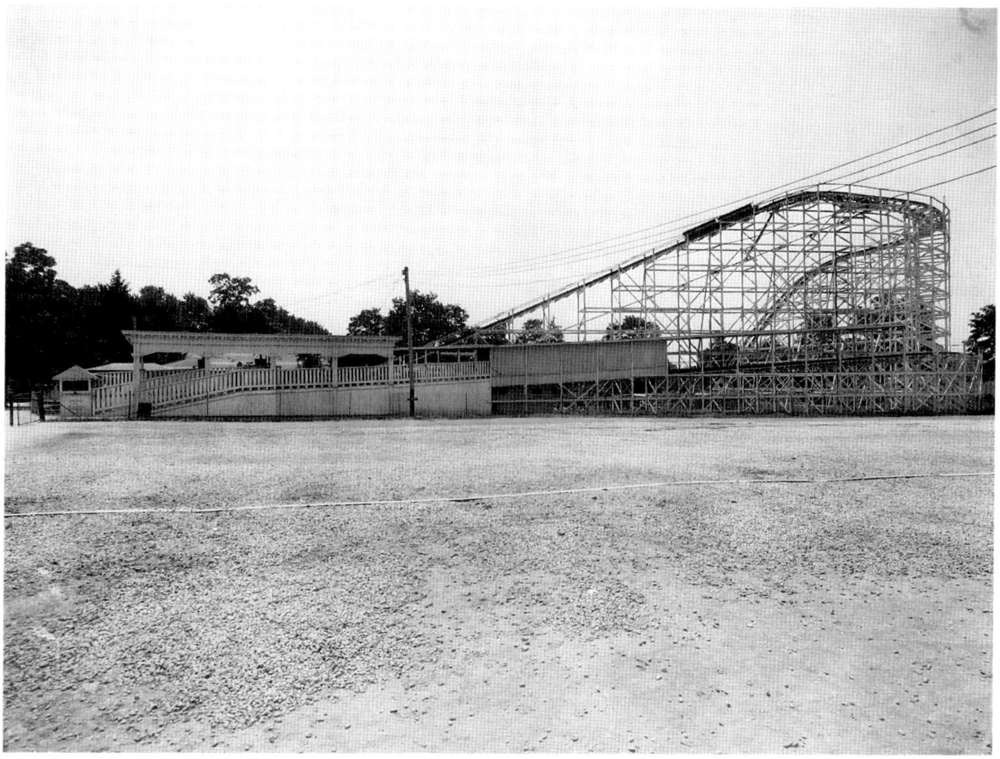

Rollercoaster at Joyland Park, c. 1930. In the late 1920s, the Sauers continued to make improvements to Joyland Park by adding new rides such as this rollercoaster, the Wildcat. (2120)

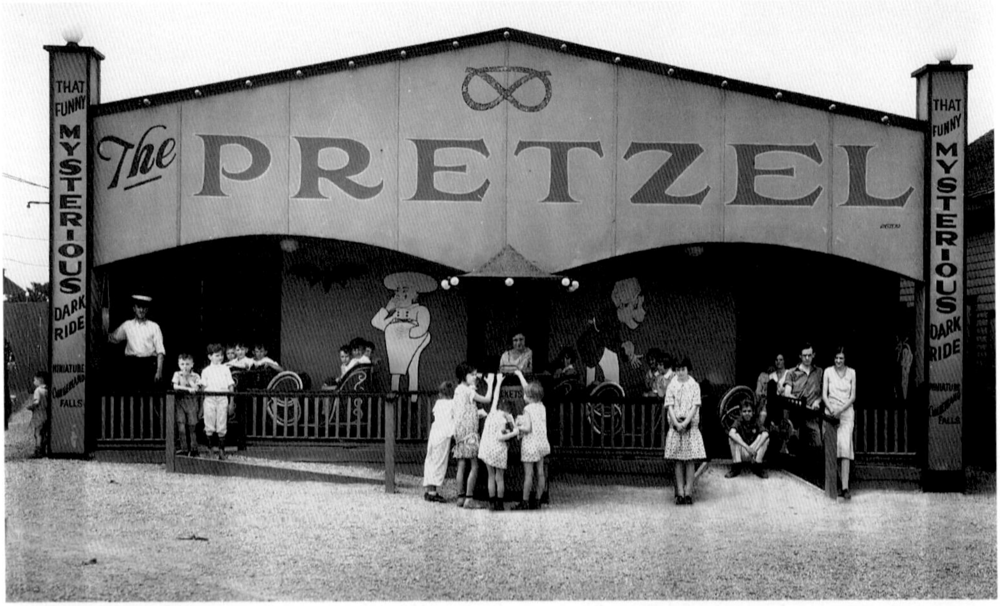

The Pretzel at Joyland Park, June 1930. Among other rides, the midway featured the Pretzel, "that funny mysterious dark ride." (669)

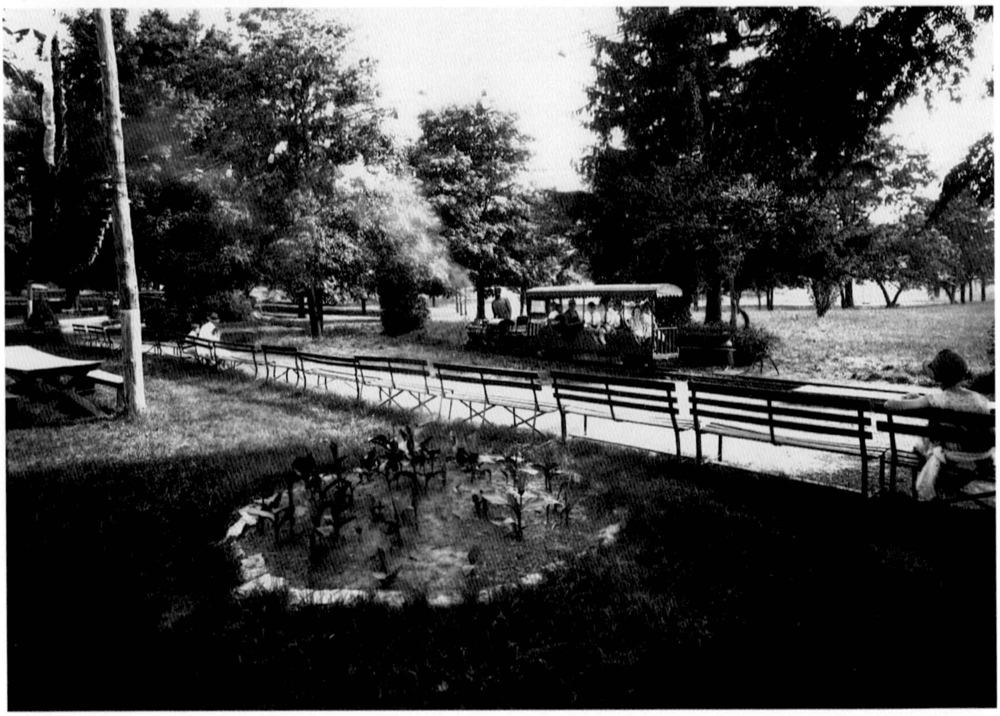

Scenic railroad at Joyland Park, c. 1930. On July 7, 1942, Joyland Park was sold at auction for $54,000. M.C. Haddix, Carl King, and Garvice Kincaid bought the park, but the sale did not include this Scenic Railroad, which was owned by the Fayette Amusement Company. Joyland Park continued in operation until the mid-1960s when two separate fires destroyed the casino, and the dressing rooms and grandstand at the pool. (669)

five

Selling Lexington

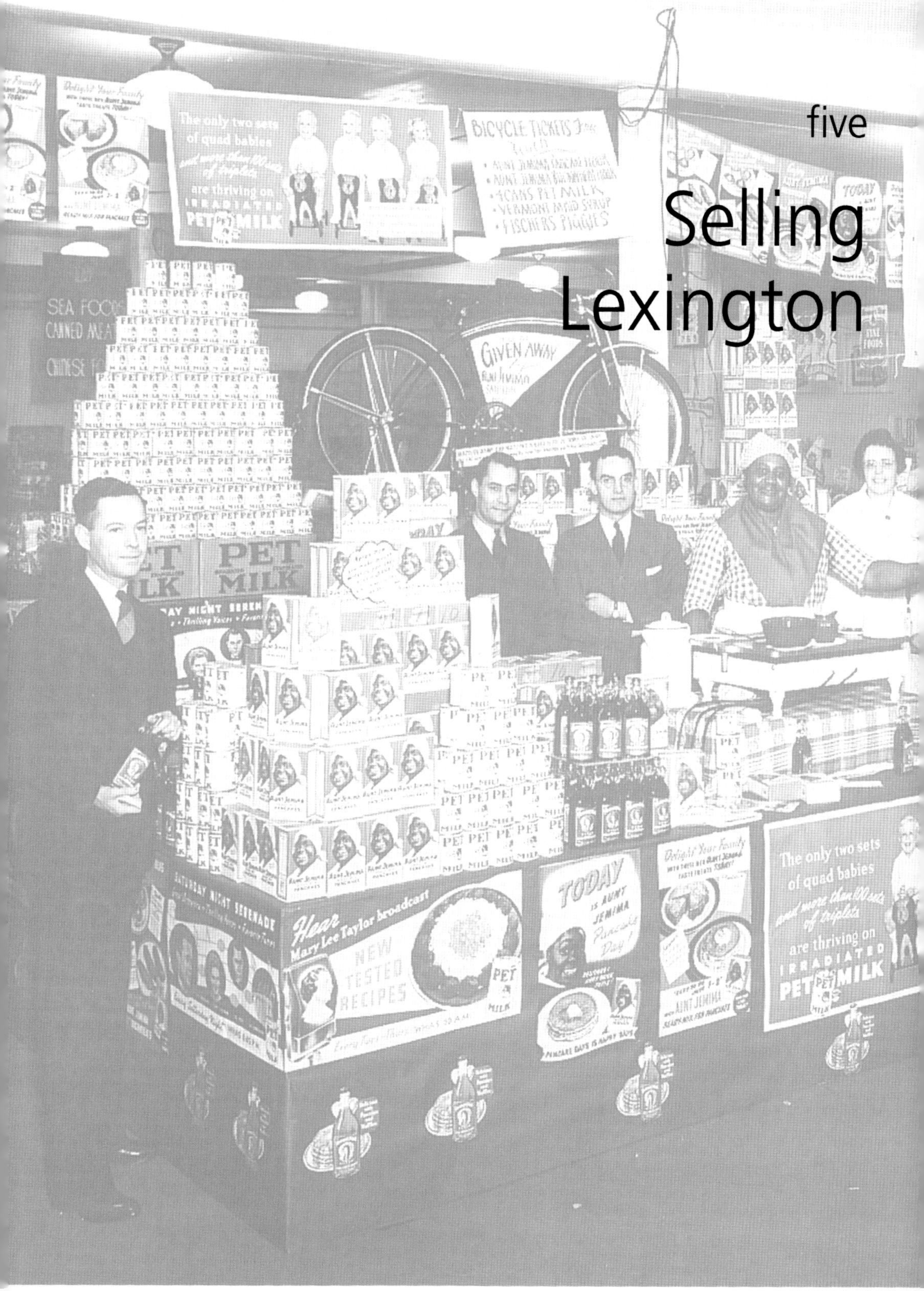

The purchase and sale of commodities in Lexington was also diverting, engaging, and prosperous. As a regional commercial center, Lexington provided a fertile environment in which local merchants could earn a livelihood. Shopkeepers and salespeople utilized creative advertising techniques and eye-catching displays to attract an ever-growing number of Lexington shoppers. Lafayette Studio prospered as it documented the activities of local businesses which commissioned photographs for various purposes.

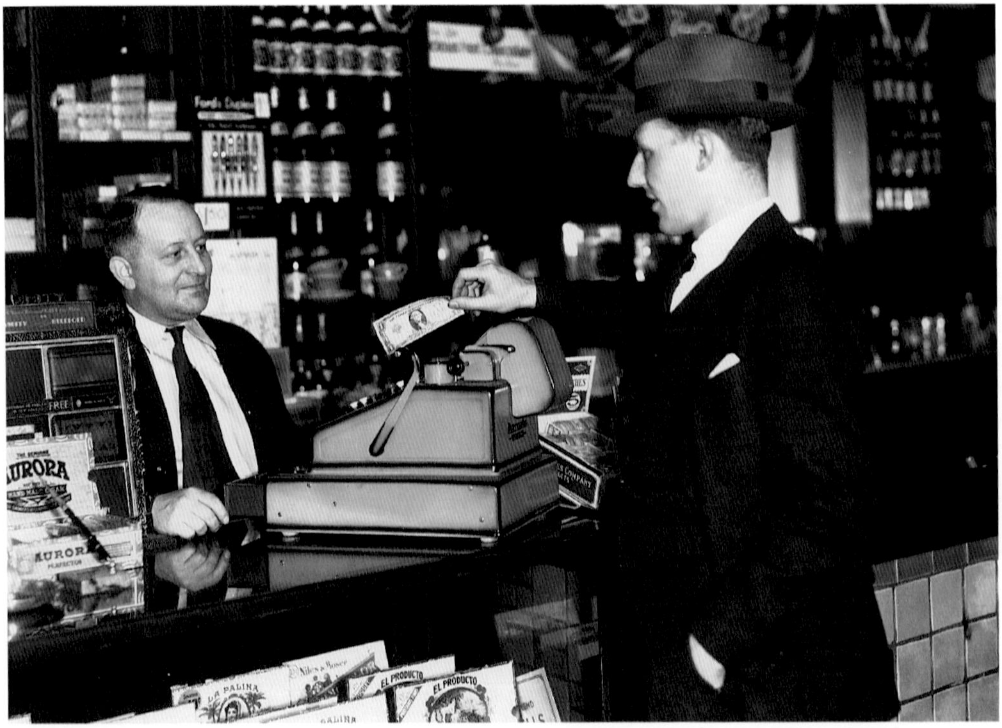

Fitzhugh's Pharmacy, February 1932. Locally owned pharmacies flourished in Lexington in the 1930s and 1940s. Clark S. Fitzhugh established Fitzhugh's Pharmacy c. 1930 at 848 East High where the business remained until it closed sometime in 1939. Fitzhugh also owned Viaduct Pharmacy and went on to open the Wigwam at 592 West Main after closing Fitzhugh's Pharmacy. (1180)

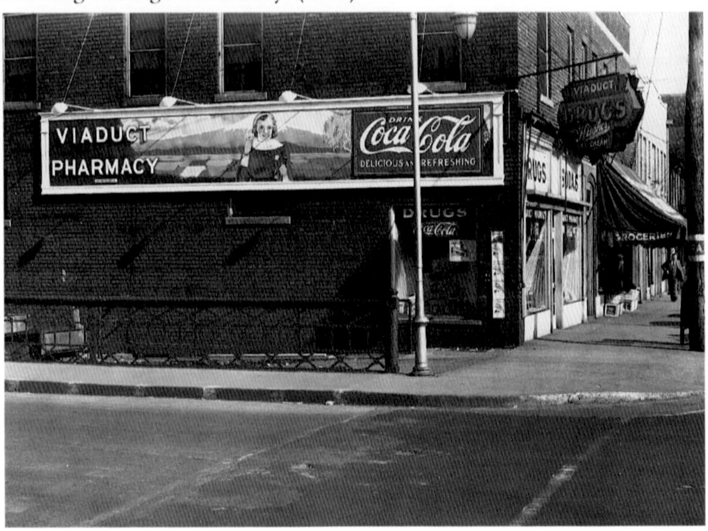

Viaduct Pharmacy, April 1934. The Viaduct Pharmacy at 169 East High Street underwent several changes in ownership over the 43 years it was in operation. In April of 1934, the store was owned by Clark S. Fitzhugh, who also owned Fitzhugh's Pharmacy farther up East High. This photograph was ordered by Coca-Cola to document this sign advertising the sale of their product at the pharmacy. (1893)

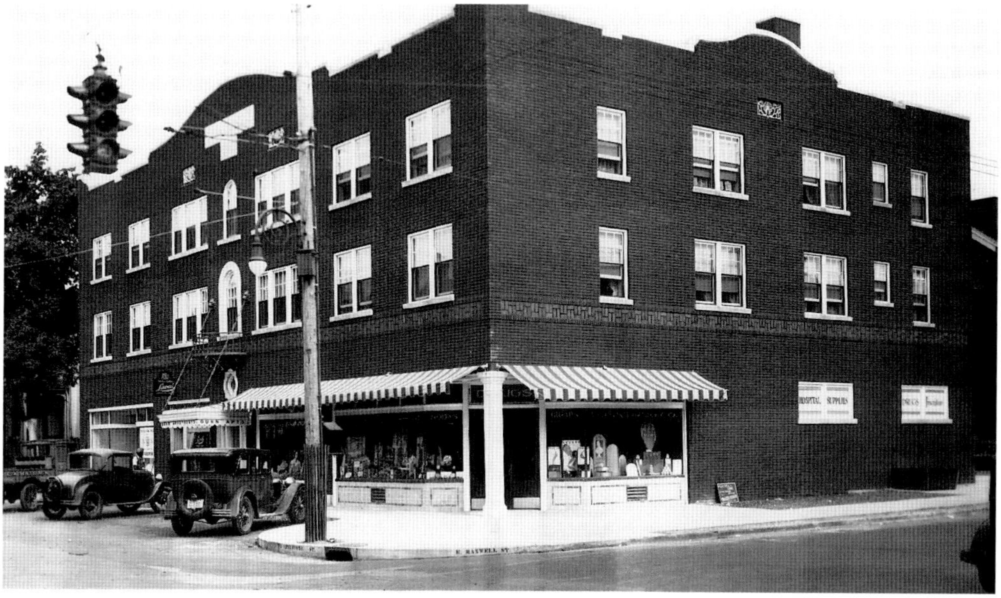

Dunn Drug's New Store, September 1930. Will Dunn became an apprentice to James E. Cooper, a Lexington druggist in 1898. In 1914, he and his brother, Peter B. 'Burt' Dunn, took over the business on 400 West Main. They opened this store at 290 South Limestone in 1930. In 1949, the West Main location closed, but the South Limestone store was maintained by the brothers and then by Will's son George until 1978, when the building housed Claywell Pharmacy. (791)

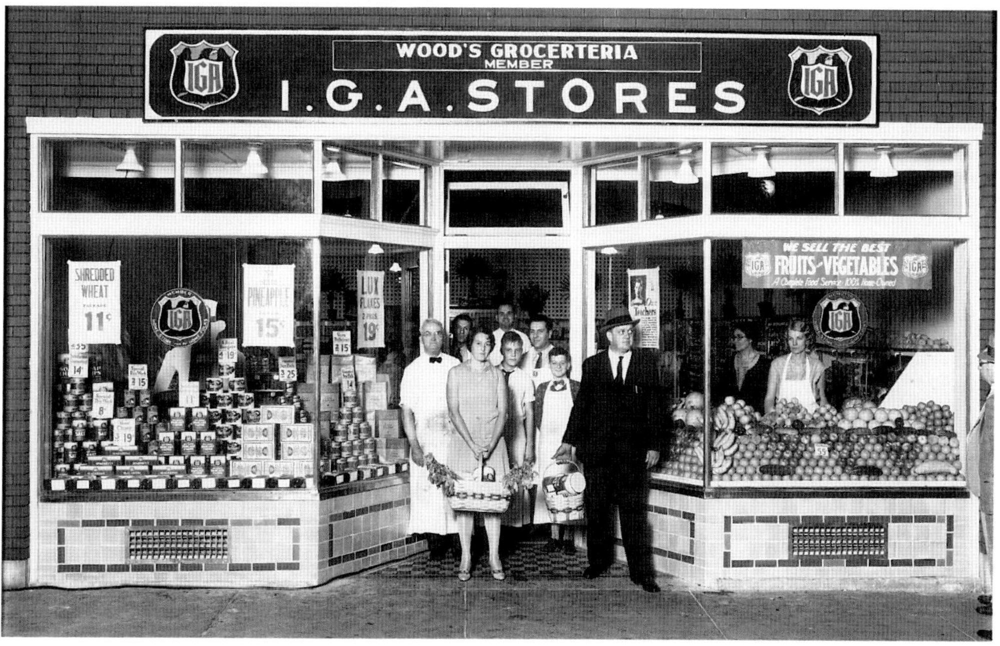

Woods Grocery, September 1930. Down the block, Louthman E. Woods established an I.G.A. grocery store at 284 South Limestone in the same year. Committed to the "home store for/by home folks" philosophy, I.G.A. (Independent Grocers Alliance) was founded in 1926 and offered Lexington entrepreneurs the support of a voluntary supermarket network, as well as the opportunity to maintain their flexibility as small business operators. (790)

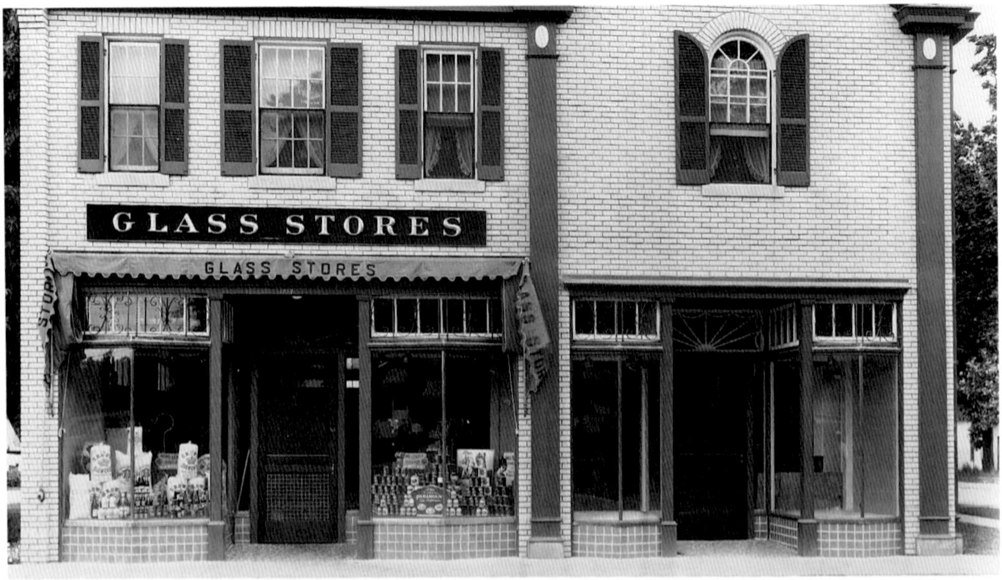

Glass Store, August 1931. The first Glass Store opened at the turn of the century at the corner of Cedar and Upper Streets. This Glass Store, located at the corner of South Limestone and Arcadia Park, was one of 30 in and around Lexington in December of 1931. In a 1938 advertisement, the stores were promoted as the "only Home Owned and Home Operated grocery chain in the Blue Grass." (1100)

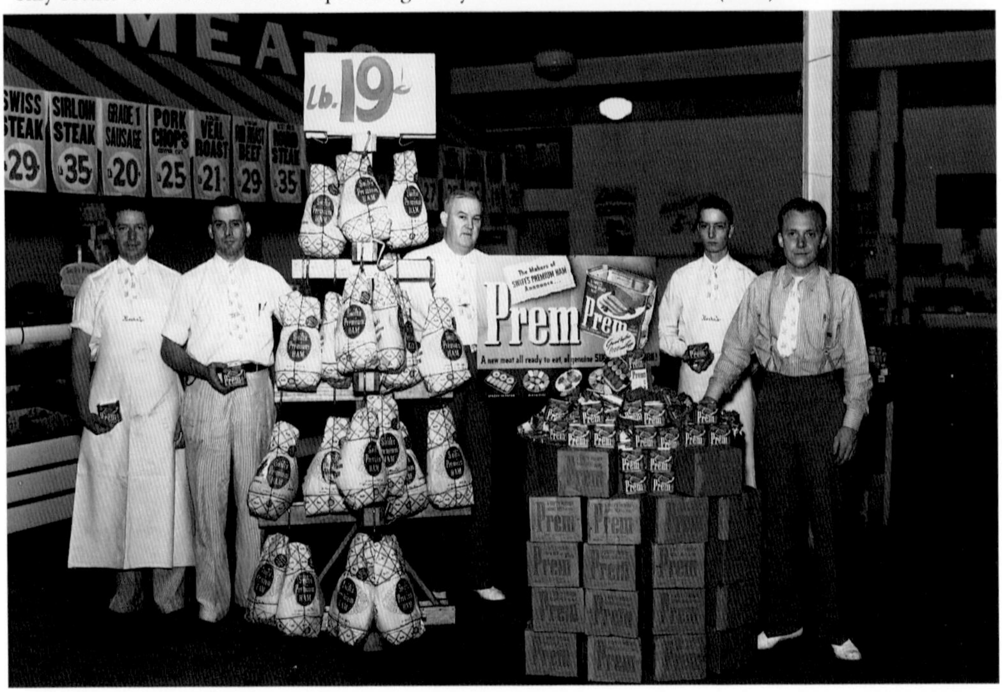

Baehr Market's Prem display, August 1940. These local businesses utilized creative marketing strategies to attract customers to new products. At the 508 West Main Baehr's Market, this in-store display advertises Prem, "a new meat all ready to eat" from the "makers of Swift's Premium Ham." Established in June of 1938 by Arthur H. Baehr, the store featured self-service aisles in the grocery and dairy departments. In 1943, Baehr opened another location at 852 East High Street. (4549)

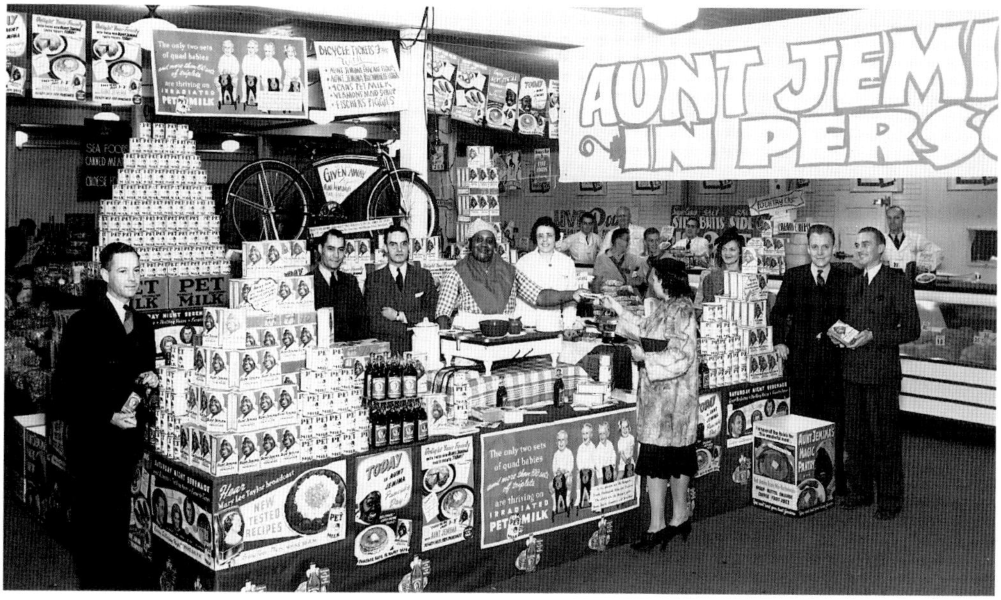

Aunt Jemima's Big Surprise Party at Baehr Market, December 1939. In another advertising campaign, Baehr's featured Aunt Jemima "in person" to promote the sale of pancake products. A bicycle was to be given away to the winner of a drawing for which tickets could be acquired by purchasing certain products from the store. By 1945, Arthur Baehr turned to selling used cars, and by 1947 both Baehr's Super Markets had closed. (4393)

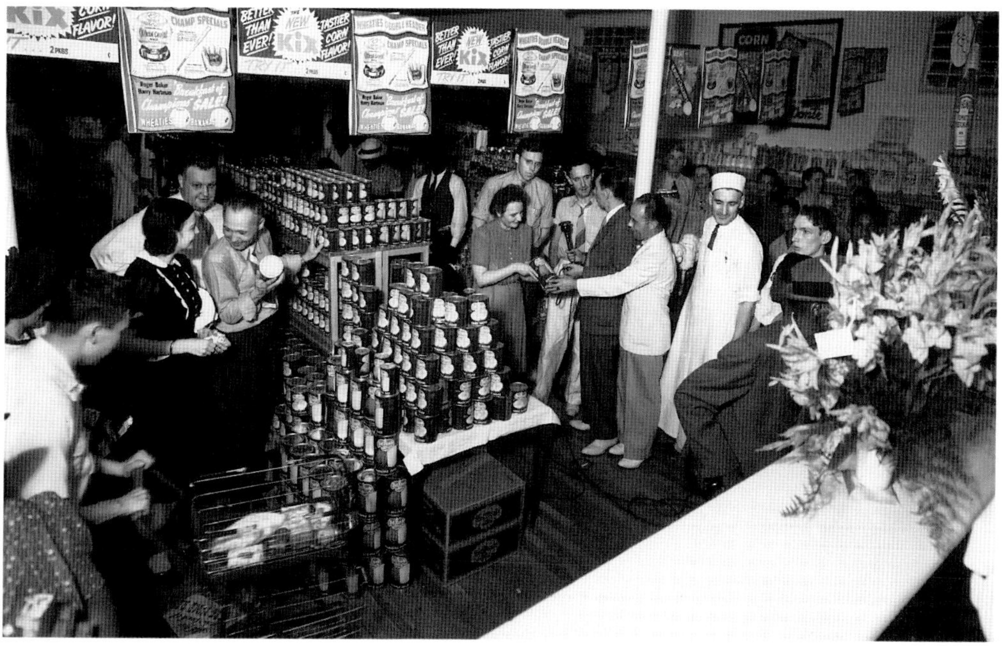

M.R.S. Super Market's Del Monte promotion, July 1941. The other supermarkets in town were also creative promoters of national brands sold in their stores. On this occasion, M.R.S. Super Market at 649 Georgetown Street held a WLAP radio broadcast to promote Del Monte products. William L. Murray, Lucian B. Reed, and Oshel C. Slone, founded M.R.S. Super Market in 1941. M.R.S. expanded to three Lexington locations, the last of which closed in the mid-1990s. (4738)

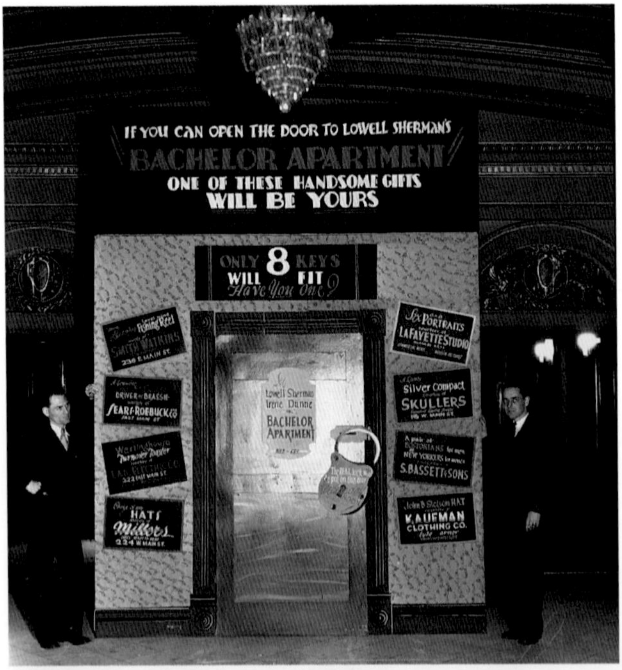

Bachelor Apartment at the Kentucky Theater. The creativity fostered by collaboration between businesses throughout the town is shown in this promotional display for the 1931 film, *Bachelor Apartment*, in the lobby of the Kentucky Theater. The promotion encourages townspeople to unlock the "apartment" to win a variety of gifts including six portraits from Lafayette Studio, a silver compact from Skullers, a pair of shoes from S. Bassett & Sons, a men's hat from Kaufman Clothing Co., a women's hat from Millers, a toaster from Lail Electric Co., a driver and brassie from Sears, and a fishing reel from Smith Watkins Hardware.

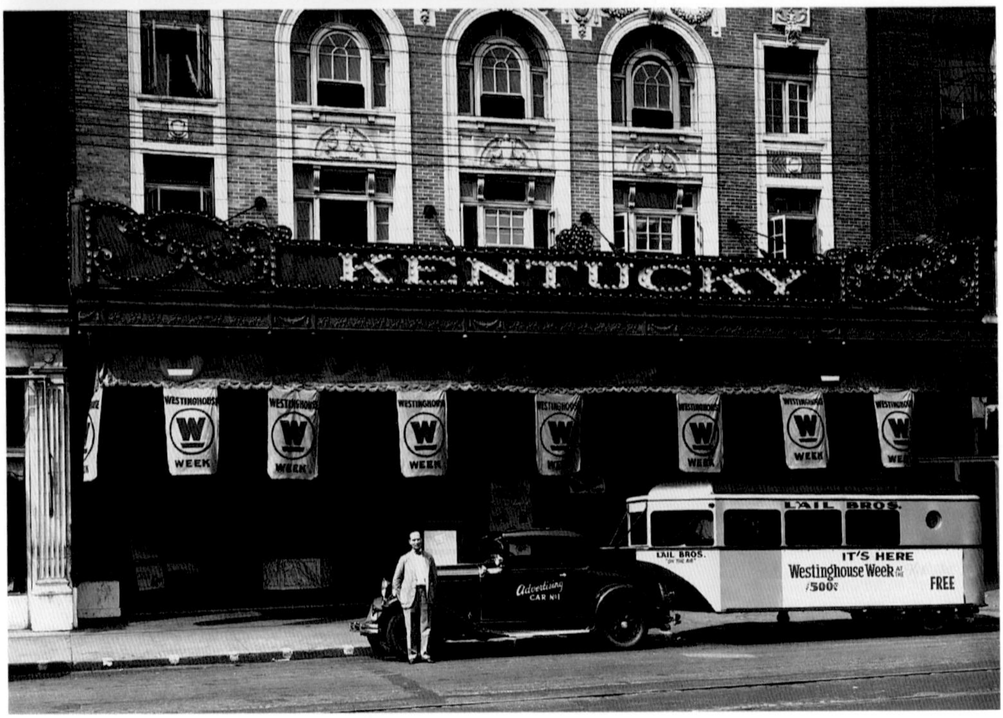

Westinghouse Week at the Kentucky Theater, August 6, 1930. The theaters often collaborated with downtown businesses to promote both movies and goods through contests. Westinghouse Week culminated in the presentation of a refrigerator to the person present in the theater on Monday night who could submit the longest list of words created from the letters in Westinghouse. Other prizes included a range, a vacuum cleaner, a percolator, a waffle iron, an oscillating fan, and an iron, all locally donated Westinghouse products. (986)

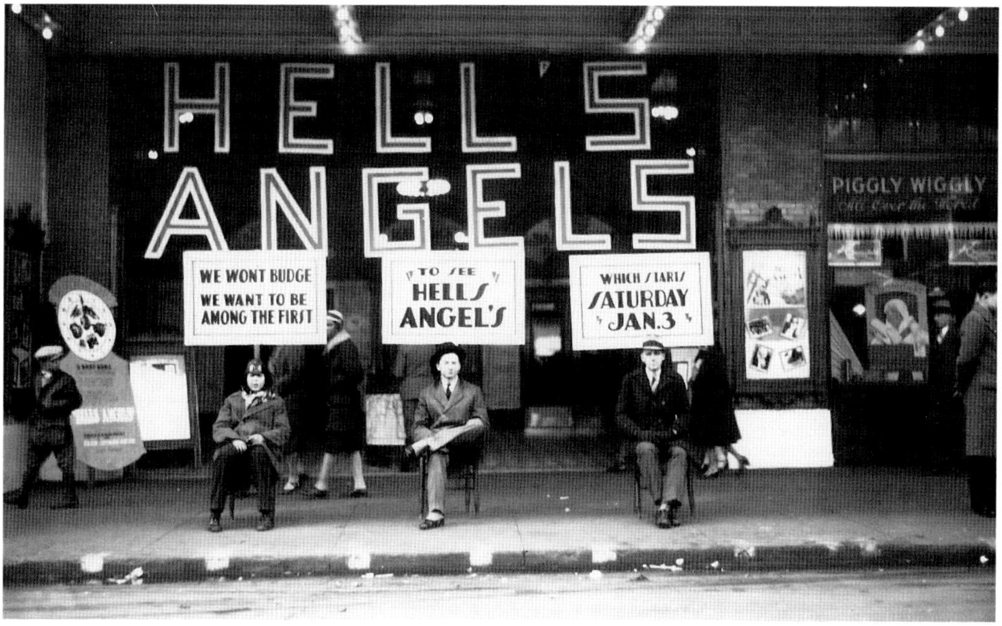

Hell's Angels Promotion at the Kentucky Theater, December 1930. In another promotion at the Kentucky, these men "refused" to leave the sidewalk in front of the theater because they wanted to be the first to see Hell's Angels, the 1930 Howard Hughes film. In addition, ads for this film featured a list of two- to four-digit numbers that were probably telephone numbers. People possessing these numbers could utilize them as passes to this movie. (827)

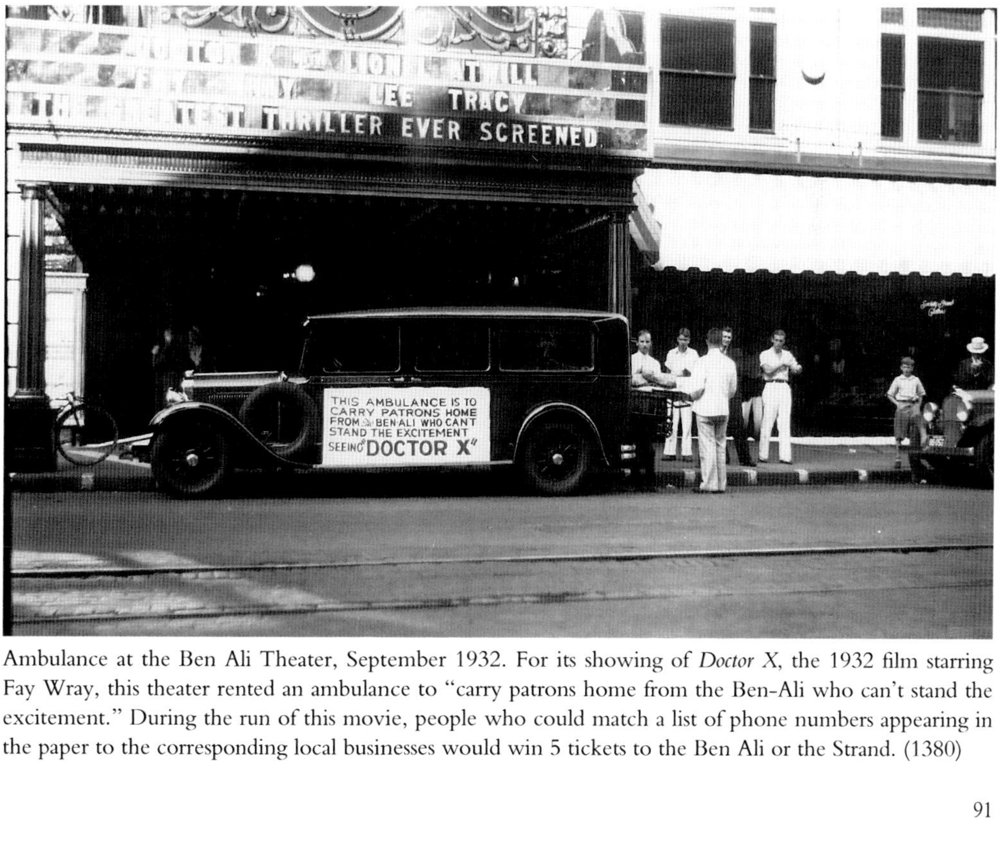

Ambulance at the Ben Ali Theater, September 1932. For its showing of *Doctor X*, the 1932 film starring Fay Wray, this theater rented an ambulance to "carry patrons home from the Ben-Ali who can't stand the excitement." During the run of this movie, people who could match a list of phone numbers appearing in the paper to the corresponding local businesses would win 5 tickets to the Ben Ali or the Strand. (1380)

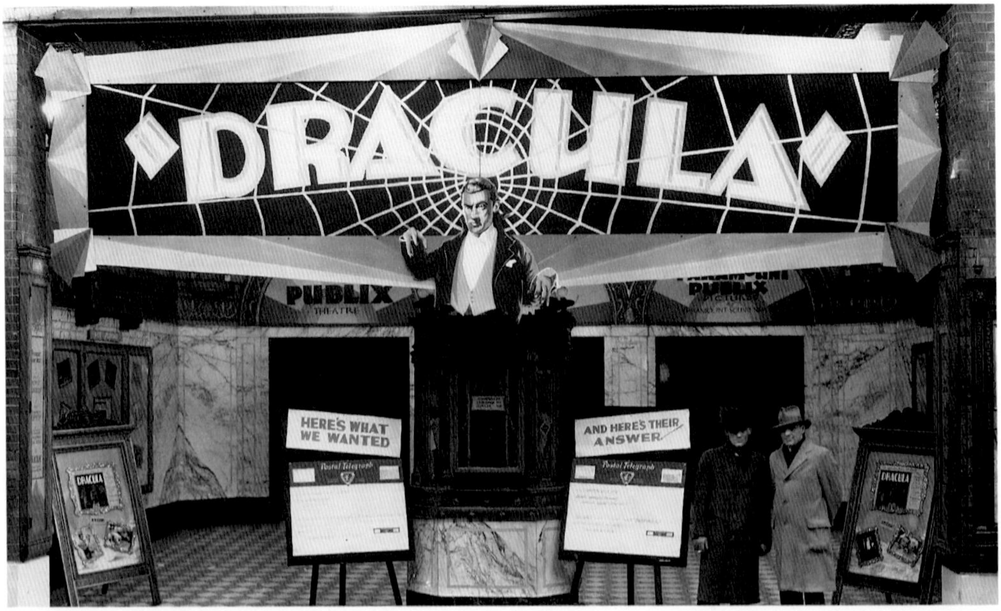

Dracula at the Kentucky Theater, March 1931. The Kentucky ran advertisements for the 1931 horror film, *Dracula*, that included the following "correspondence" with local underwriters: "WE PLAY DRACULA STARTING SATURDAY STOP CAN YOU WRITE BLANKET POLICY COVERING PATRONS FRIGHTENED TO DEATH WHILE SEEING PICTURE ADVISE IMMEDIATELY, HERMAN C. BAMBERGER, MGR. KENTUCKY THEATER." The underwriters replied, "SORRY CANNOT ACCEPT THEATER POLICY HAVE SEEN DRACULA AND RISK IS TOO GREAT, DAVIS & WILKIRSON". (1001)

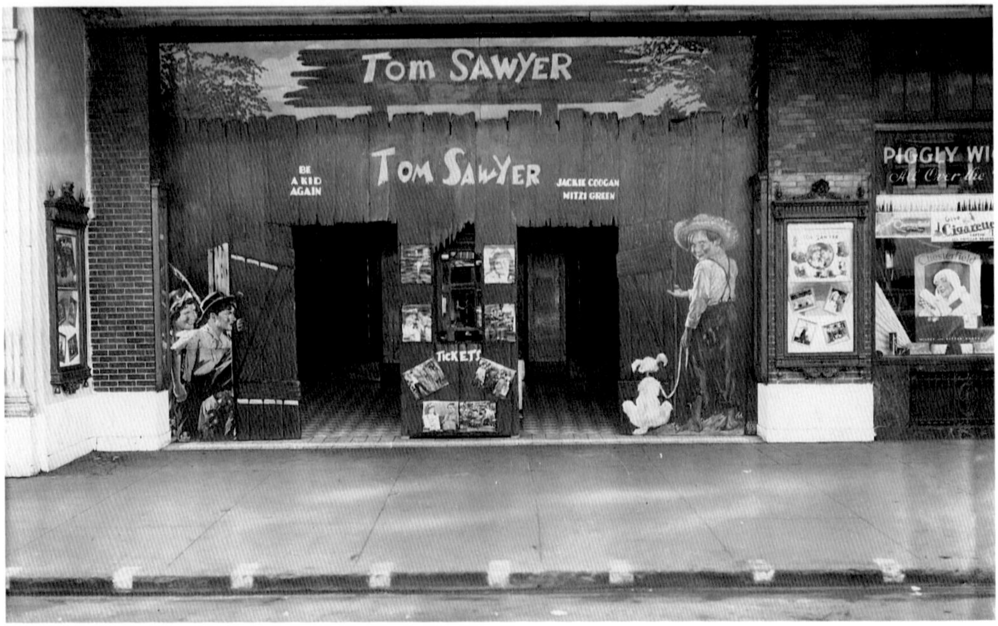

Tom Sawyer at the Kentucky Theater, December 1930. Quite often, these promotional campaigns were accompanied by extravagant signs, created by local sign companies. This display promoted the 1930 film, *Tom Sawyer*, starring Jackie Coogan. The advertisement entirely covers the front of the theater, with openings for the entrances to create the feeling that the patrons were being invited into the secret clubhouse to "be a kid again." (827)

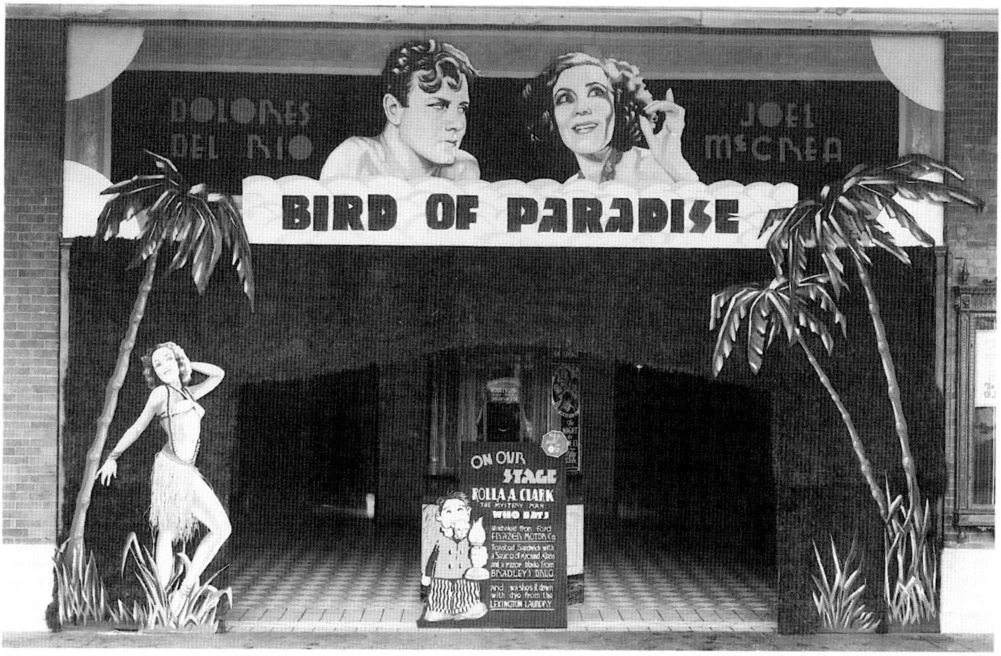

Bird of Paradise at the Kentucky Theater c. September 1932. Similarly, this display for *Bird of Paradise* encourages viewers to enter paradise with stars Joel McCrea and Dolores del Rio. A smaller sign advertises "Rolla A. Clark, the mystery man, who eats windshield from Ford Frazer Motor Company, toasted sandwich with a sauce of ground glass, and a razor blade from Bradley's Drug and washes it down with dye from the Lexington Laundry." (1383)

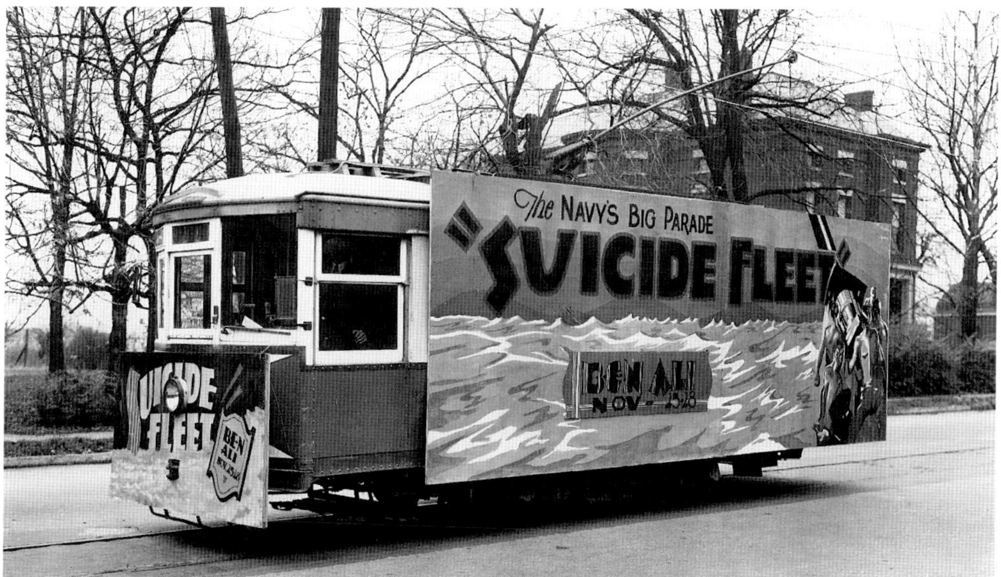

Byrd Sign Company's advertisement for *Suicide Fleet*, November 1931. The theaters even sent their advertisements on the road. With the assistance of Byrd Sign Company's distinctive style, the Ben Ali was able to turn this interurban car into a moving billboard. Byrd Sign was located at 131 Walnut Street and specialized in all kinds of outdoor advertising including neon and electric signs. (1197)

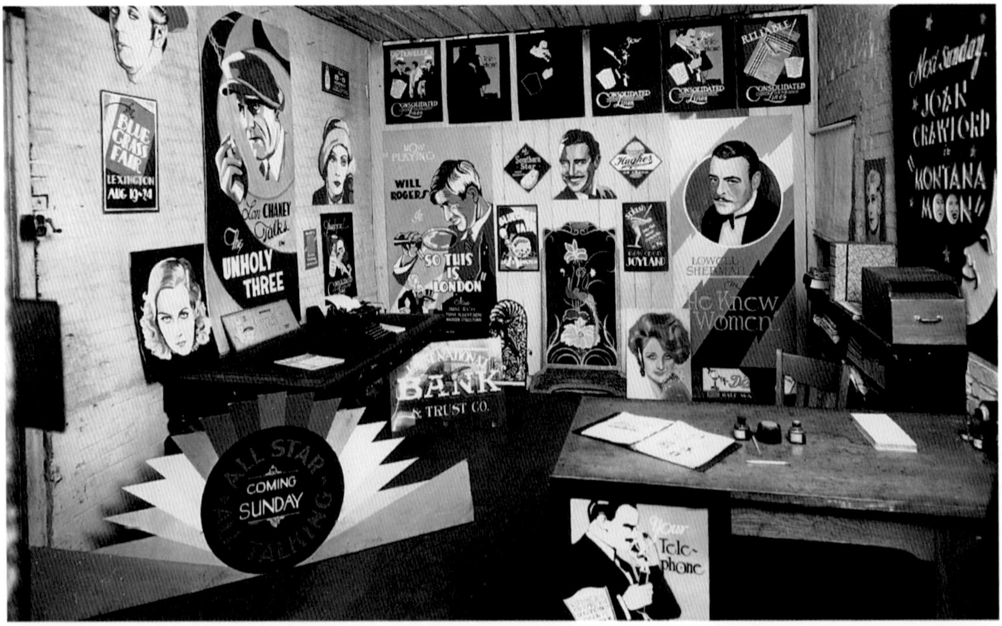

Interior of Byrd Sign Company, December 1930. Herbert Byrd started his advertising career at The Lexington Herald in 1923. He worked with Guthrie and Stiles, the outdoor advertisers, for approximately a year before starting Byrd Sign in 1928. In 1942, Byrd Sign joined with Ramsey-Witt, which provided neon commercial and highway advertising through 1947. In 1943, Herbert Byrd went to work for Lexington Signal Depot while Albert Witt managed Byrd Sign.(850)

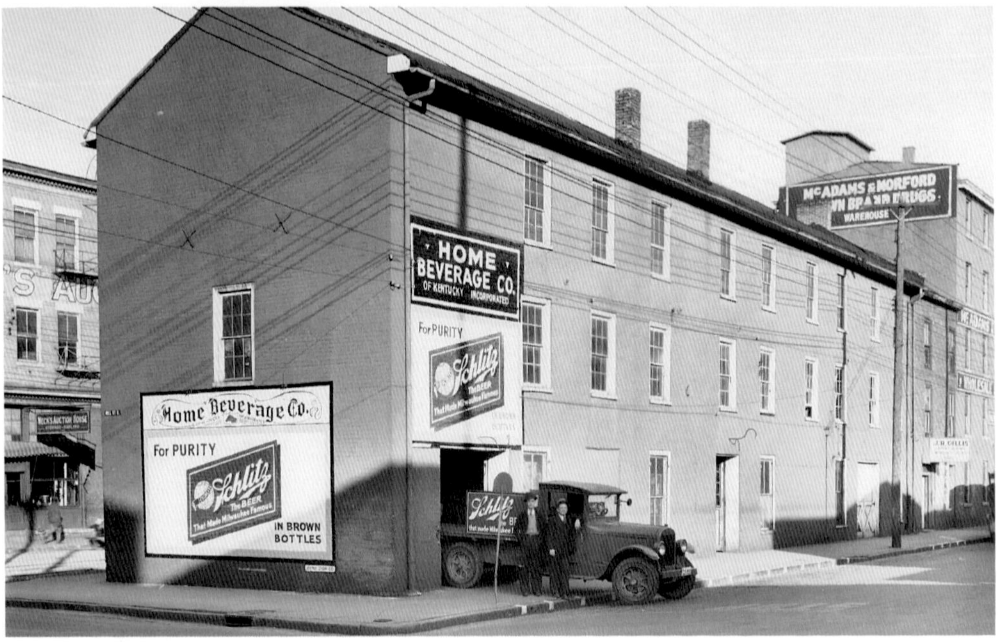

Home Beverage Company, April 1934. This wall advertisement for Home Beverage Company was also created by Byrd Sign. This photo promoted the opening of Home Beverage Company, the Schlitz beer and Drewry's ale distributors who were at 261 West Vine until 1937. The company, run by Cecil Cantrill, A.G. Owens, and Hal Hunt, delivered beer to dealers and private homes. (1906)

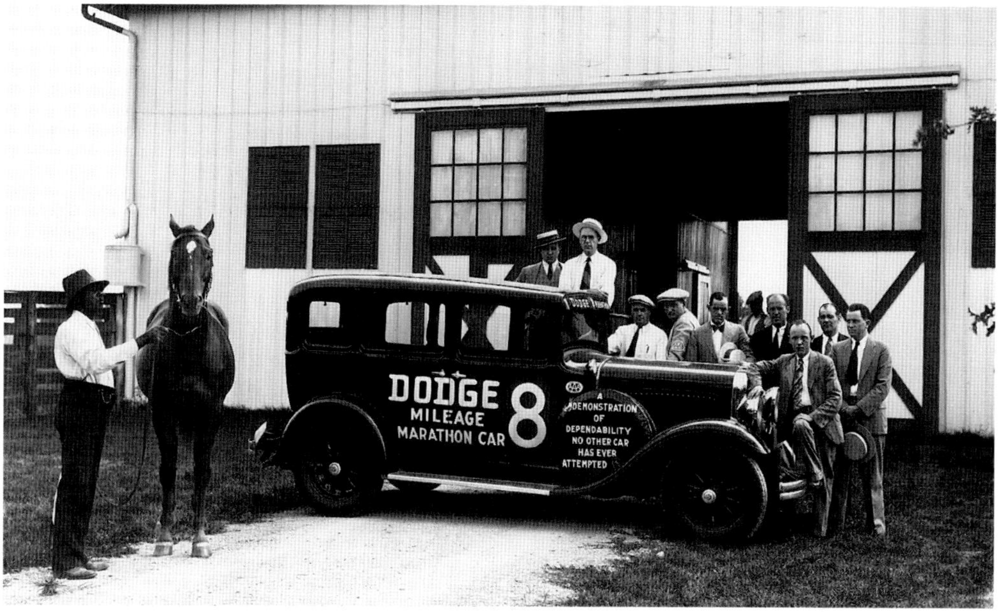

Dodge Truck and Man O' War, August 1930. Lexington's growing dependence on the automobile created a ripe environment for car companies to promote advances in automotive technology. In this photo, A.A.A. representatives pose with a Dodge mileage marathon car and Kentucky's famous thoroughbred, Man O' War, to promote the dependability of the Dodge engine in a demonstration that "no other car has ever attempted." (774)

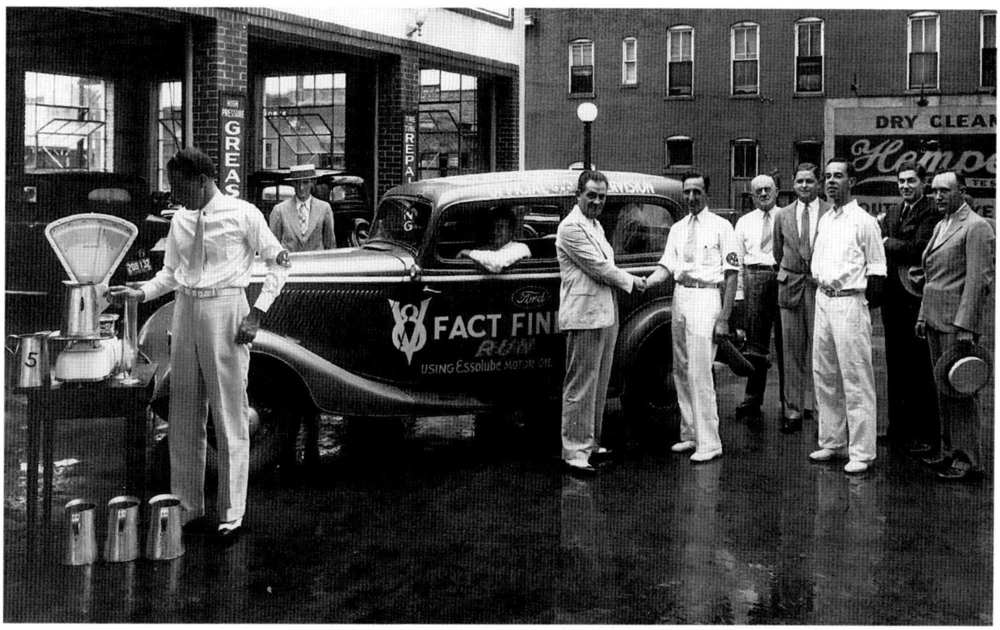

Ford Car at Standard Oil Company, September 5, 1933. In a similar promotion, A.A.A. supervised Ford's eight-day, continuous run of its new V-8 engine. The car stopped at the Standard Oil station at Main and South Eastern twice daily for control checks. Holmes Motor Company sponsored a contest in which people estimated the total mileage and miles-per-gallon of the cars and submitted slogans about Ford's V-8 economy. (1708)

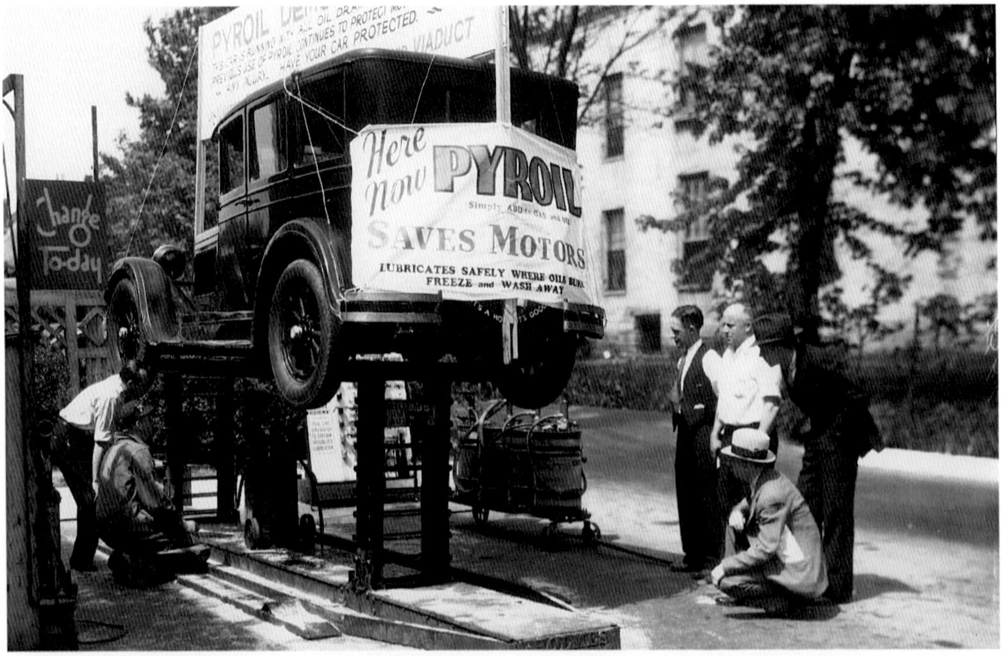

Pyroil demonstration at United Service Company, May 1932. In another demonstration of improved automobile technology, this car was left running "with all oil drained from motor." The demonstration attempted to show that "previous use of Pyroil continues to protect moving parts from any injury." The United Service Company at 176 East High, opposite the Harrison Viaduct, was established by Frank J. Rees in 1931 and advertised as "the Complete One Stop Service Station." (1799)

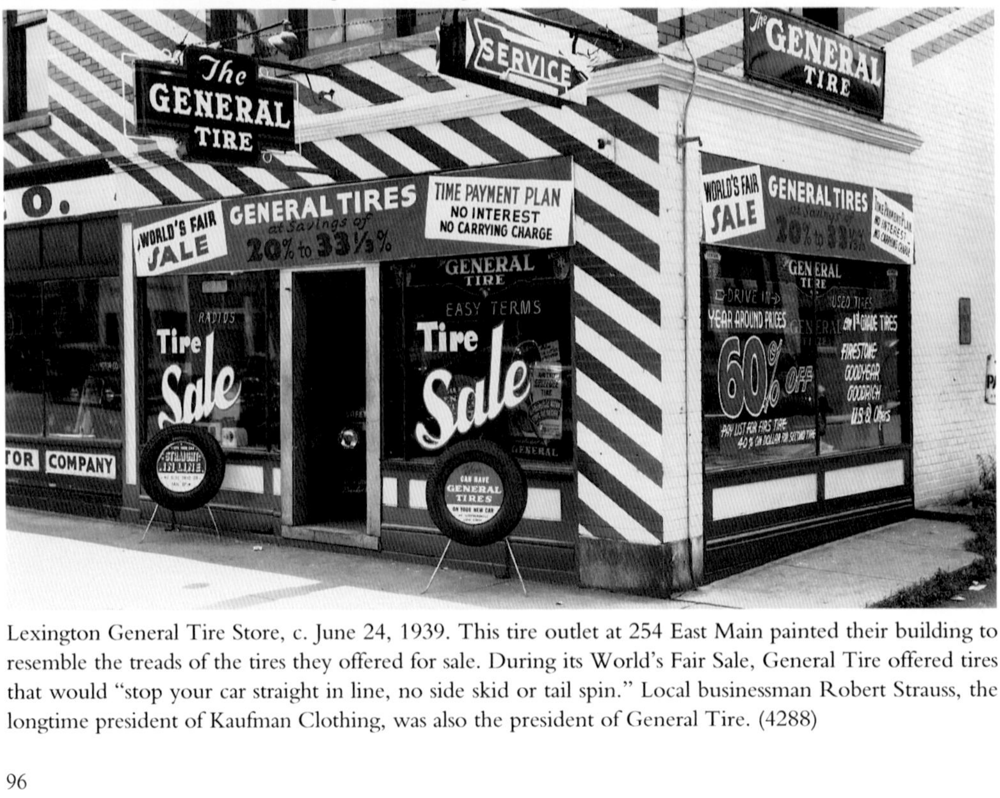

Lexington General Tire Store, c. June 24, 1939. This tire outlet at 254 East Main painted their building to resemble the treads of the tires they offered for sale. During its World's Fair Sale, General Tire offered tires that would "stop your car straight in line, no side skid or tail spin." Local businessman Robert Strauss, the longtime president of Kaufman Clothing, was also the president of General Tire. (4288)

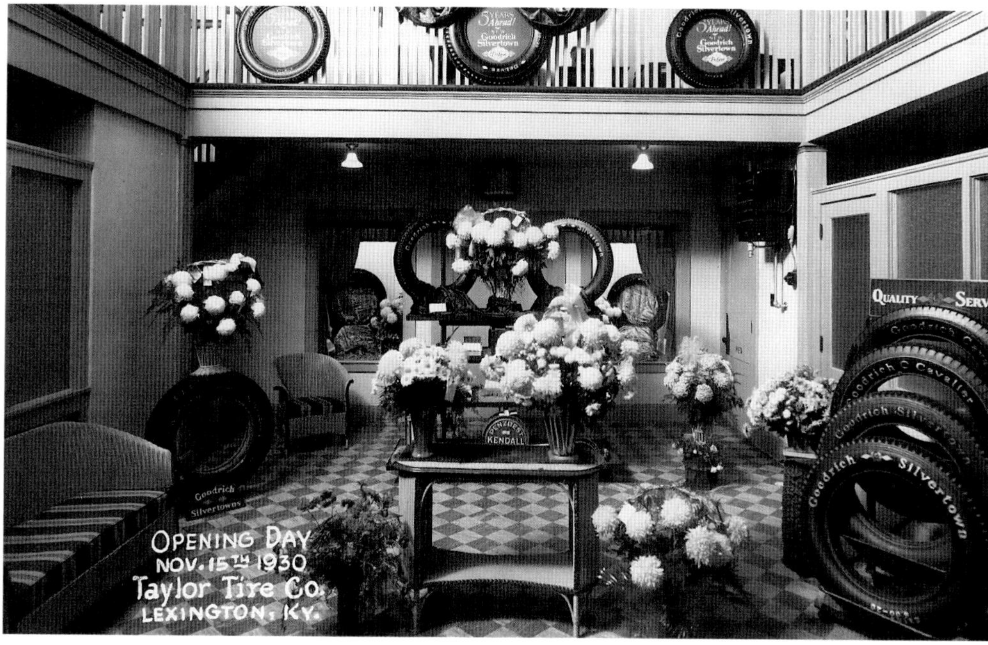

Taylor Tire Company opening, November 15, 1930. Another tire store celebrated opening day at its new location at 400 East Vine with wreaths and flowers. J.S. Taylor started his company in 1923 on East Main Street. His longtime vice president, Harry S. Tucker, took over the business in 1969 when Taylor died. Taylor's son-in-law, J.H. Banes, managed the operation after Tucker passed away until the store closed down in 1980. (966)

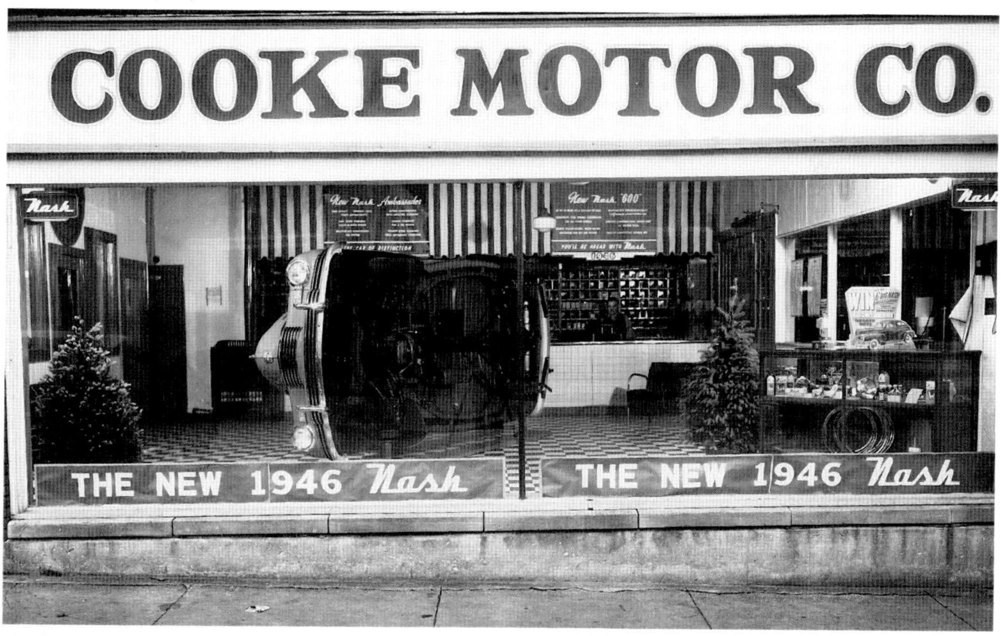

Cooke Motor Company, March 1946. Another longtime presence in Lexington's automobile market, Leamon R. Cooke, moved his Chevrolet dealership to this location on East High Street around 1945. This promotion of the new 1946 Nash creatively displays the technology beneath "the car of distinction." Customers could "Win one of 6 big Nash Ambassadors" in a contest that was co-sponsored by Quaker Oats. (5546)

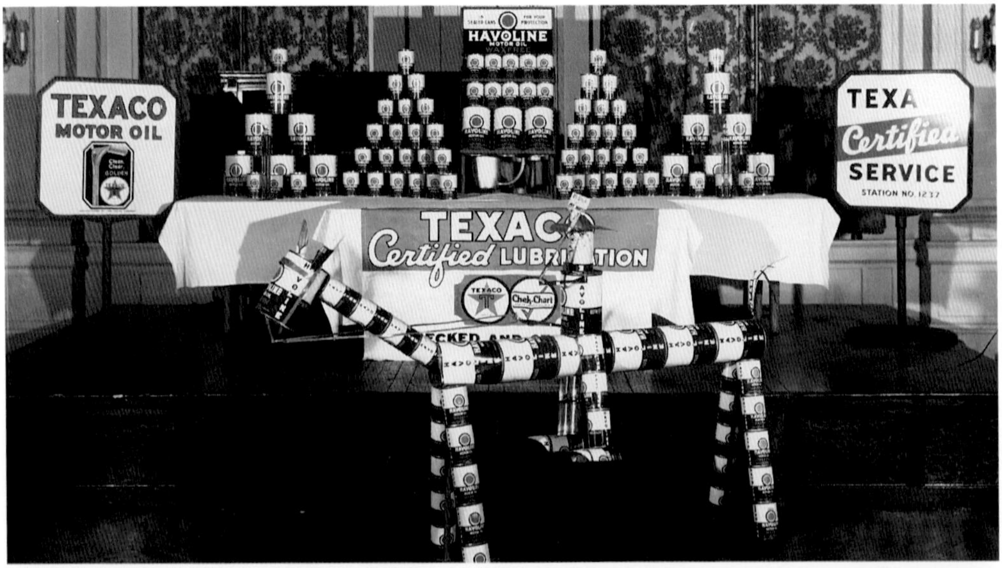

Indian Refining Company's Texaco Display, March 1934. The district manager of Indian Refining Company's Lexington office was Cecil E. Cantrill. Four years before his death in 1935, Cantrill left to preside over the Home Beverage Company and Kentucky Oil Products. His wife, Mrs. Florence Shelby Cantrill, became the second woman elected to the Kentucky Legislature and the first woman to serve on the Lexington City Council and as mayor pro-tem. (1881)

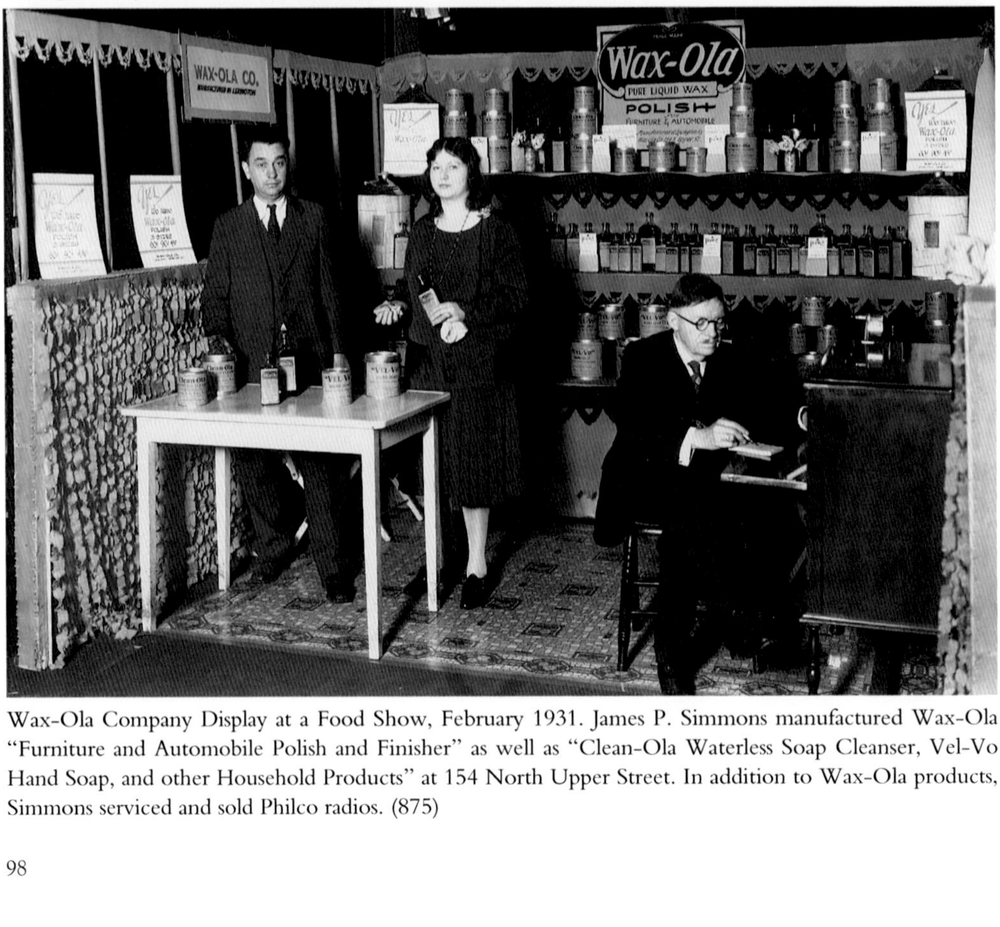

Wax-Ola Company Display at a Food Show, February 1931. James P. Simmons manufactured Wax-Ola "Furniture and Automobile Polish and Finisher" as well as "Clean-Ola Waterless Soap Cleanser, Vel-Vo Hand Soap, and other Household Products" at 154 North Upper Street. In addition to Wax-Ola products, Simmons serviced and sold Philco radios. (875)

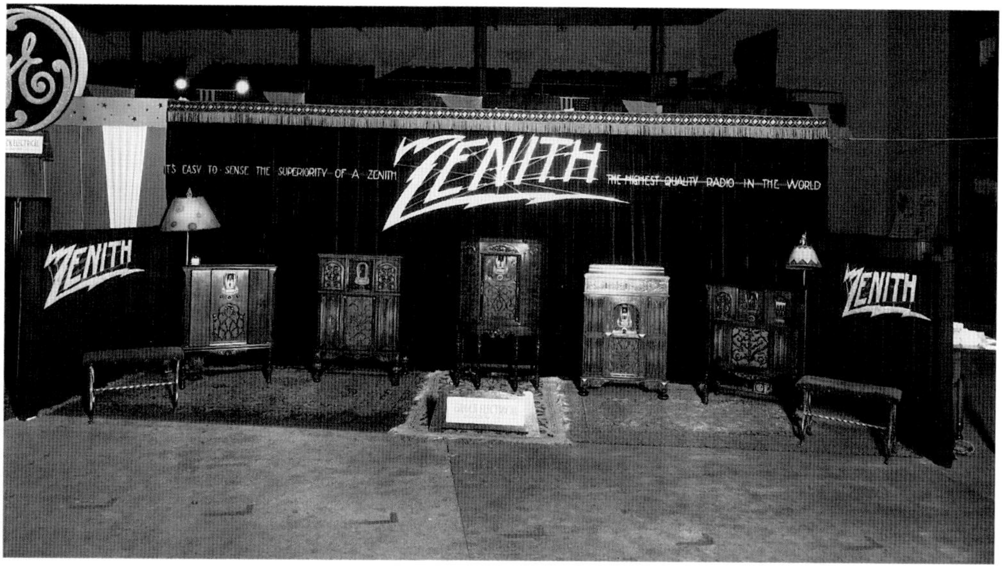

Zenith Radio Display, October 1930. As the popularity of radio grew in Lexington, a variety of businesses took up the sale of this new equipment. Brock Electrical Engineering Company at 235 East Main promoted Zenith as "the highest quality radio in the world" during this event, which was probably the third annual Lexington Radio Show. At the show, the public had the opportunity to visit booths such as this one and watch live performances by well-known radio stars and personalities. Lexingtonians would have to wait another four years before they could hear local broadcasts on Lexington's first commercial radio station, WLAP. (800)

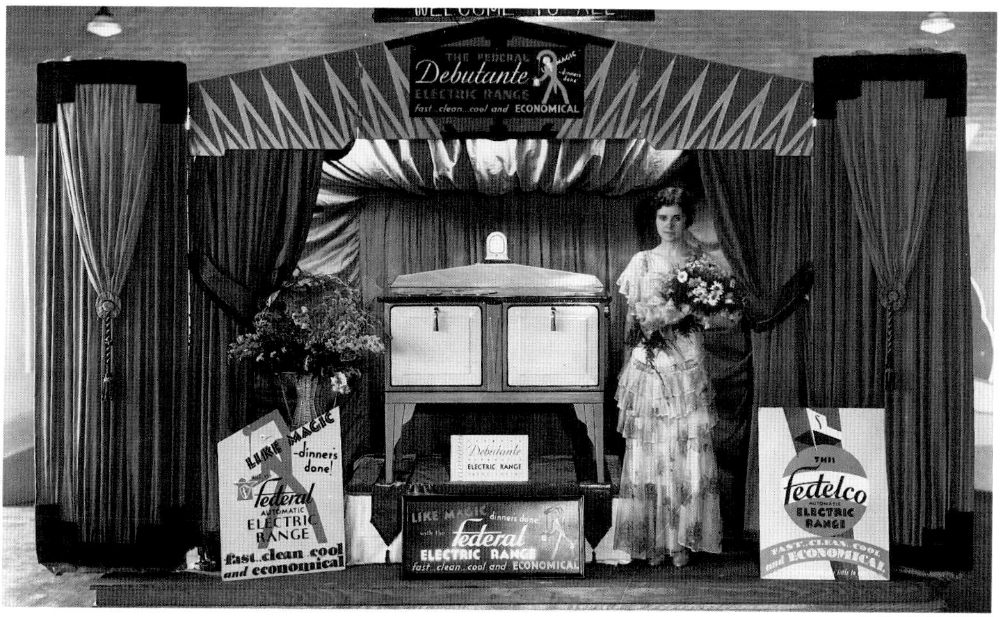

Lexington Utilities Company Electric Range Display, April 1931. Lexington Utilities Company also promoted the convenience of electrical appliances during trade shows. A human "debutante" helped to advertise Federal's Debutante Automatic Electric Range in this display promoting the stove as "fast, clean, cool, and economical." Lexington Utilities sold Federal products through its electronic shop on the northwest corner of West Main and North Broadway. (1003)

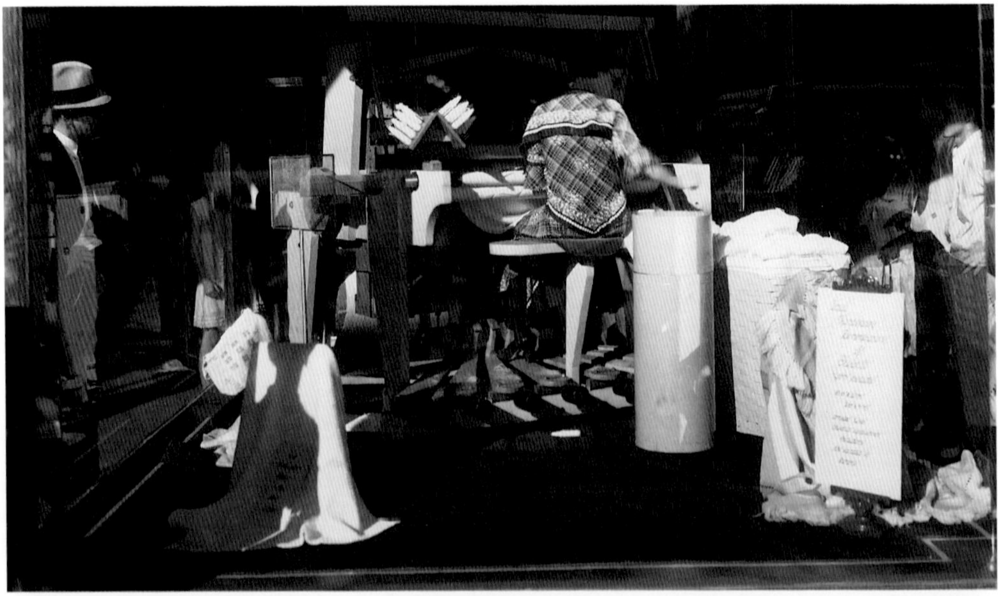

Window at Denton's featuring the Churchill Weavers, September 16, 1931. The use of human talent also attracted attention in window displays on Lexington streets. Denton's inaugurated a new department that featured the hand-woven products of Churchill Weavers by presenting an experienced weaver from the organization at work in their center window. Churchill Weavers originated on August 1, 1922 in Berea, Kentucky and has developed a national reputation for fine, hand-crafted work. (1759)

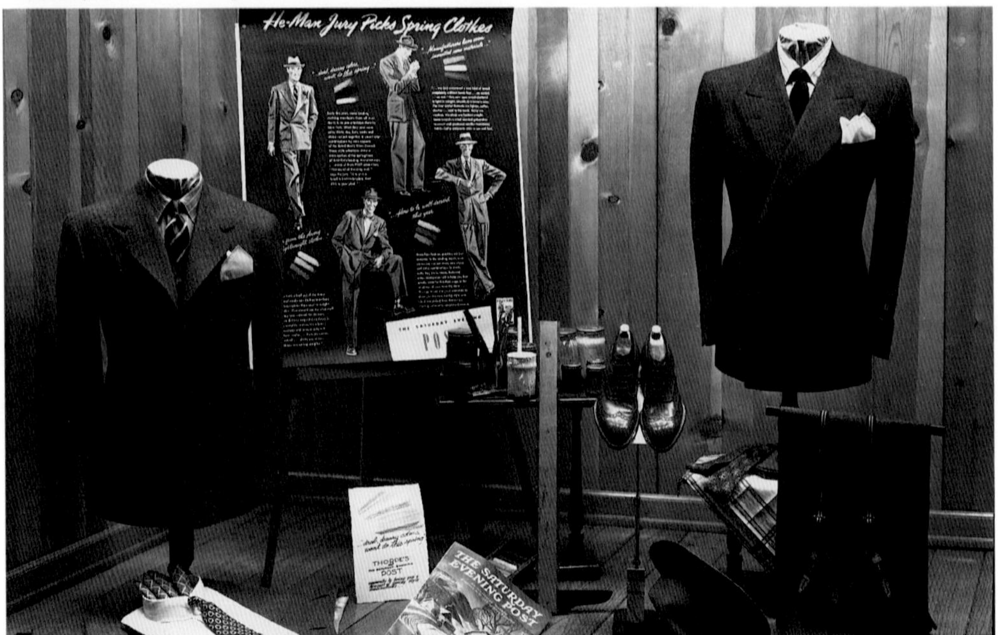

R.S. Thorpe & Sons, March 1942. In this window display, Thorpe presented its spring men's line in cooperation with the Saturday Evening Post. R.S. Thorpe established his first store in Macon, Georgia, in 1908. He often visited Lexington and opened a store on the corner of Main and Mill Streets in 1920. In 1930, the store moved to 123-27 East Main where it remained until it closed in 1954. (4865)

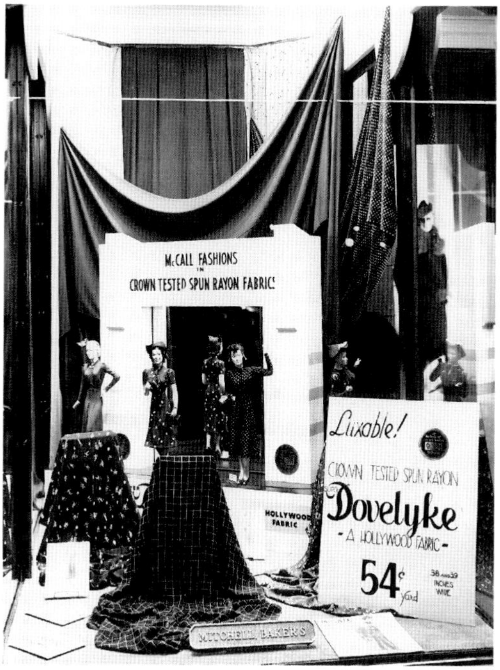

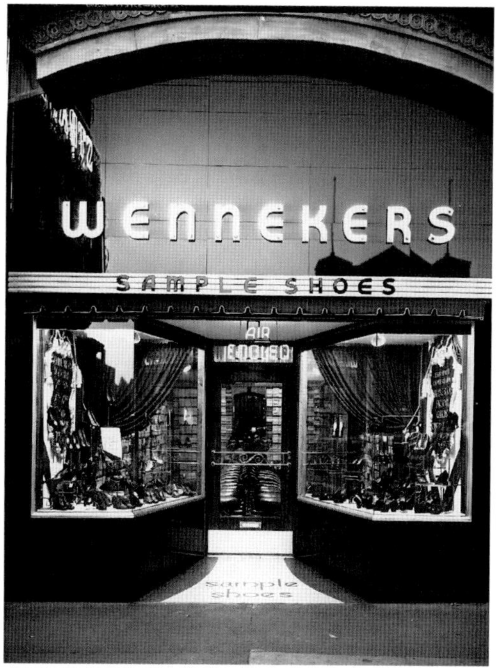

Above left: Mitchell, Baker, Smith promoted "Luxable! Crown Tested Spun Rayon Super Dovelyke, a Hollywood Fabric" for 54¢ a yard in this eye-catching display. Mitchell, Baker, Smith's long history included numerous name changes as the owners varied, starting out in the late 1860s as a dry goods store called Gibney and Cassell. It became Mitchell, Baker, Smith in 1933 when Walter G. Rehm purchased the store. (4060)

Above right: Wennekers Sample Shoe Store, September 1940. Taken at the reopening of Wennekers after a major renovation, this photograph shows the reflection of the Strand Theater next door and the roof of Union Station across the street. Al and Mary Wenneker rented the small store front in 1935, and with eight kitchen chairs and empty boxes for shelves, they built a business that thrived at 153 East Main Street until it closed on April 30, 1979, and eventually relocated in the malls. (4564)

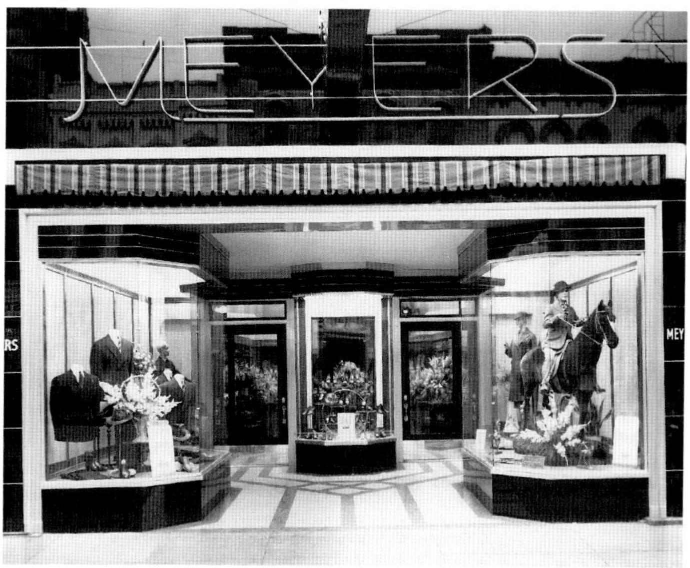

Right: Meyers Bros. Inc., August 1938. This window display celebrated Meyers Bros. Inc.'s move from Main and Mill to a larger store at 340 West Main Street. While Meyers Bros. was established in Lexington as an Army surplus store, by 1938, the firm had developed into a large department store, nationally known for its high quality riding apparel. The store continued to thrive under Marvin B. Meyers into the 1980s. (4032)

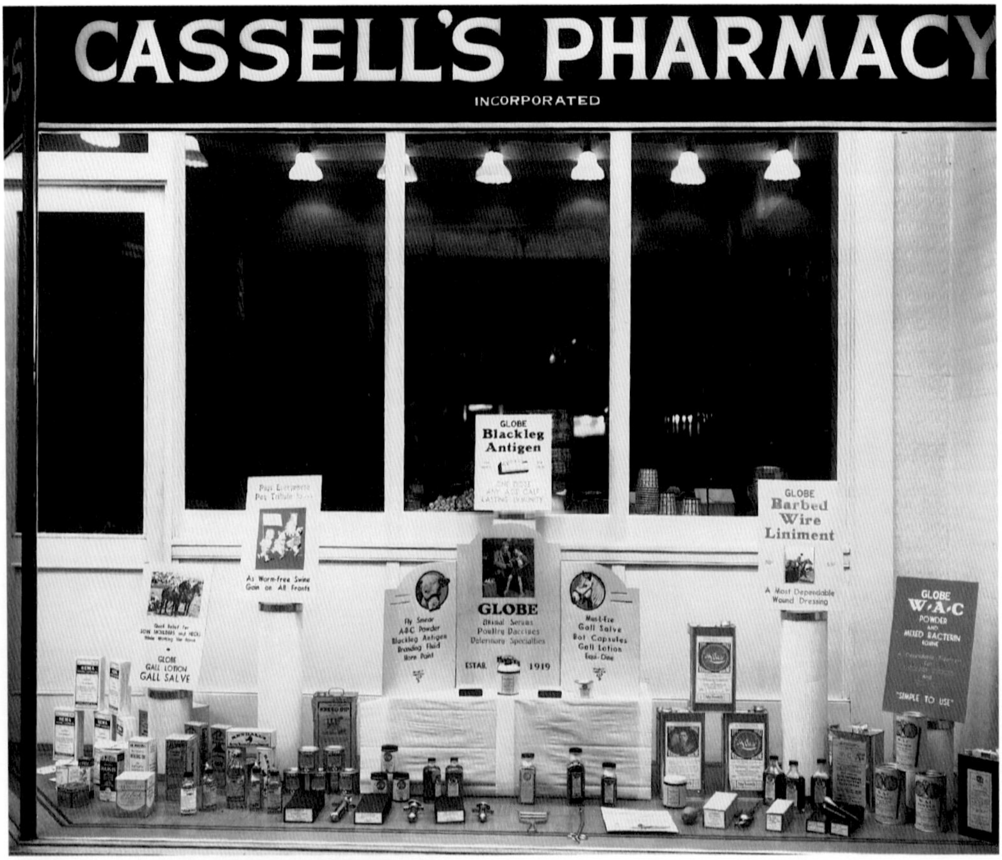

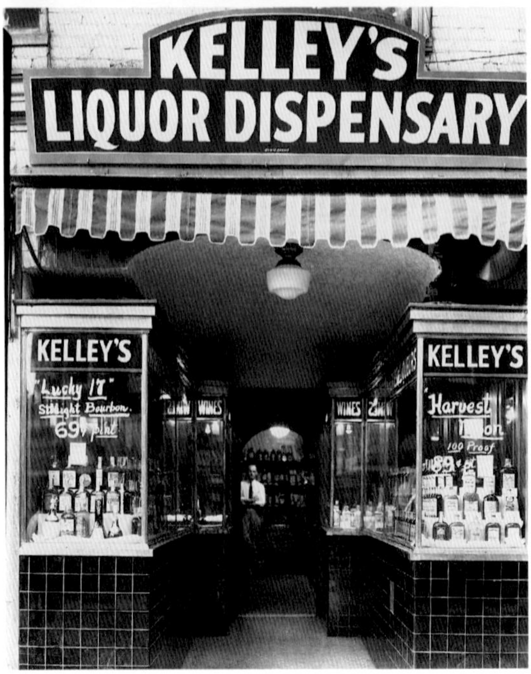

Above: Lee Cassell's Drug, September 1940. R. Lee Cassell opened a pharmacy at 167 West Short in 1904. In 1935, he moved the business to this site at 140 North Upper. By 1962, the store was relocated to 1006 North Limestone by Joe Warren Sr., who purchased the firm in 1951. While Cassell's offered pharmaceuticals for human patients, it also provided barbed wire liniment, blackleg antigen, and vaccines for animals. (4567)

Left: Kelley's Liquor Dispensary, July 1934. This photograph appeared on March 29, 1935 in The Lexington Herald to announce Kelley's first anniversary. Carl S. Kelley established this liquor store at 105 East Main after having operated a fish market at 126 North Broadway. During this celebration, Kelley's gave away a bottle of wine with each purchase. Within a few years, Kelley closed the fish market and moved the liquor store to North Broadway. (1599)

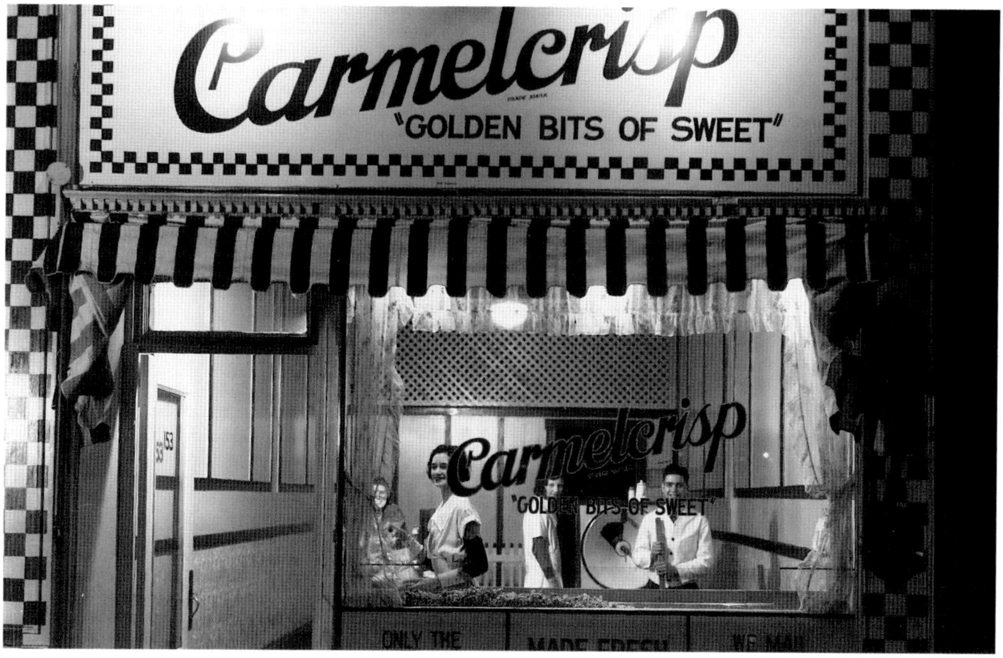

Carmelcrisp Candy Store, November 1931. The exact location of this candy store is unknown, although this photograph documents that they sold their "golden bits of sweet" from the address of 153 on some Lexington street. Like other Lexington businesses, they hoped that their inviting storefront would draw customers in from the street to purchase the merchandise they had to sell. (1196)

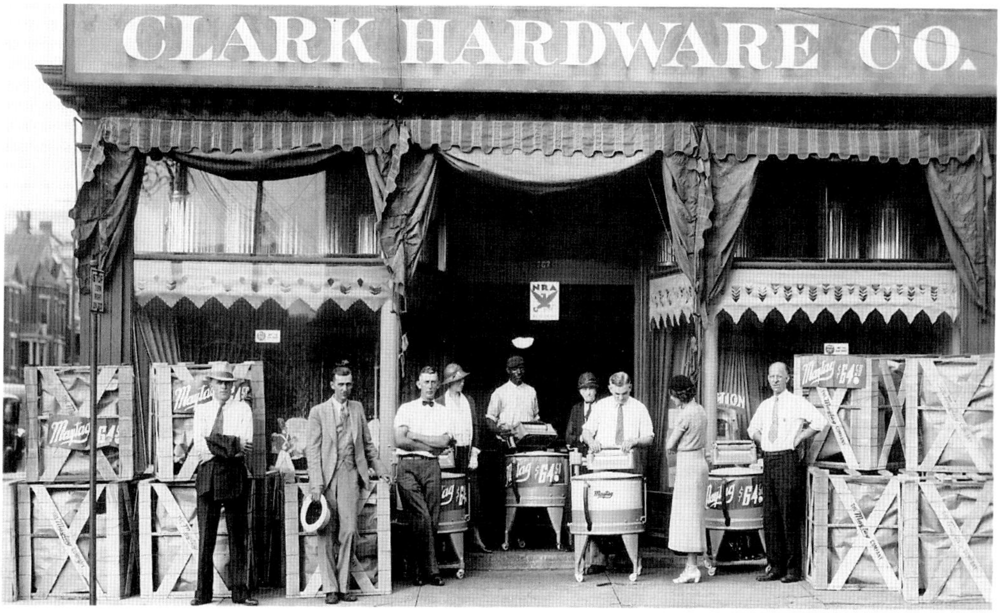

Washers at Clark Hardware Company, September 26, 1933. A new shipment of Maytag washers had just arrived at Clark Hardware on 367 West Short Street when this photograph was taken. Shown here demonstrating the $64.58 washers, R.D. Warren took over the business in 1954 when the founder, Jack W. Clark died. In 1933, Clark Hardware participated in the National Recovery Act, depicted by the blue eagle posted above the business's door. (1693)

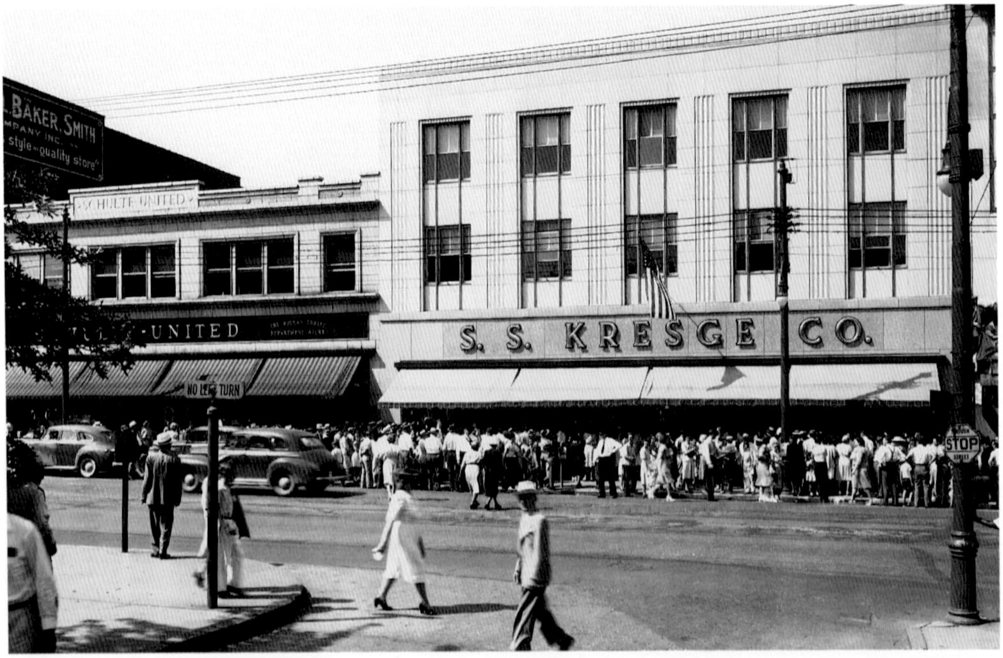

S.S. Kresge re-opening, July 25, 1947. S.S. Kresge, a Detroit, Michigan company, brought their 5 and 10¢ stores to Lexington in 1912. The popularity of their Lexington store at 250 West Main can be seen here as this crowd gathers for a re-opening sale, celebrating the building's major expansion in July of 1947. Twenty years later the store would close to make way for the Downtown Urban Renewal Project. (5850)

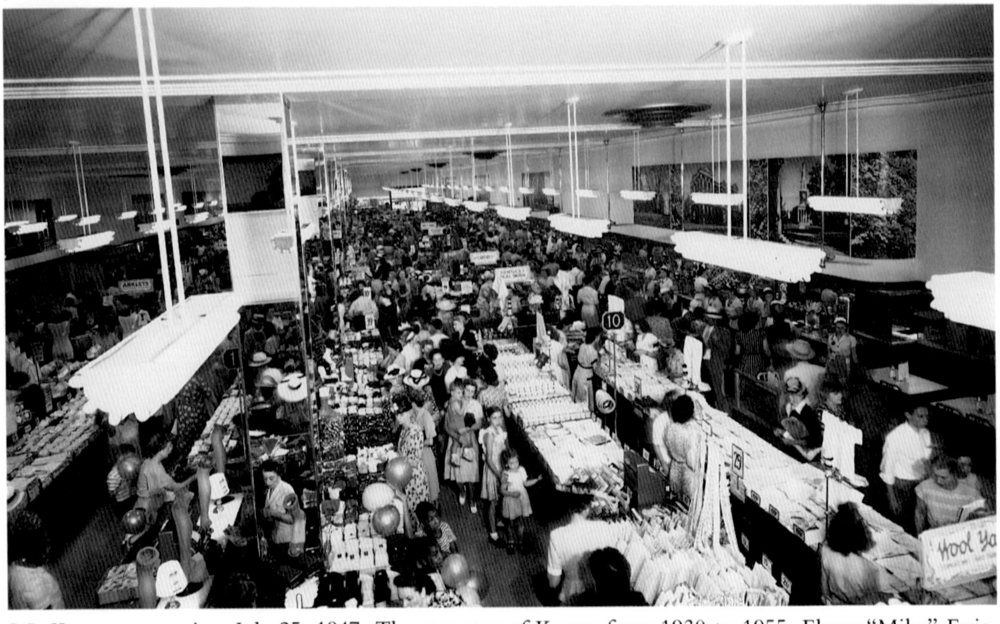

S.S. Kresge re-opening, July 25, 1947. The manager of Kresge from 1930 to 1955, Elmer "Mike" Essig, was credited by *The Lexington Leader* with developing a changed attitude among Lexingtonians toward chain stores. A well-known businessman and active civic leader, Essig cultivated a personal influence and an interest in Lexington's future, which, along with modernized facilities, low prices, and improved displays, positioned Kresge as a favorite venue for thrifty family shopping. (5850)

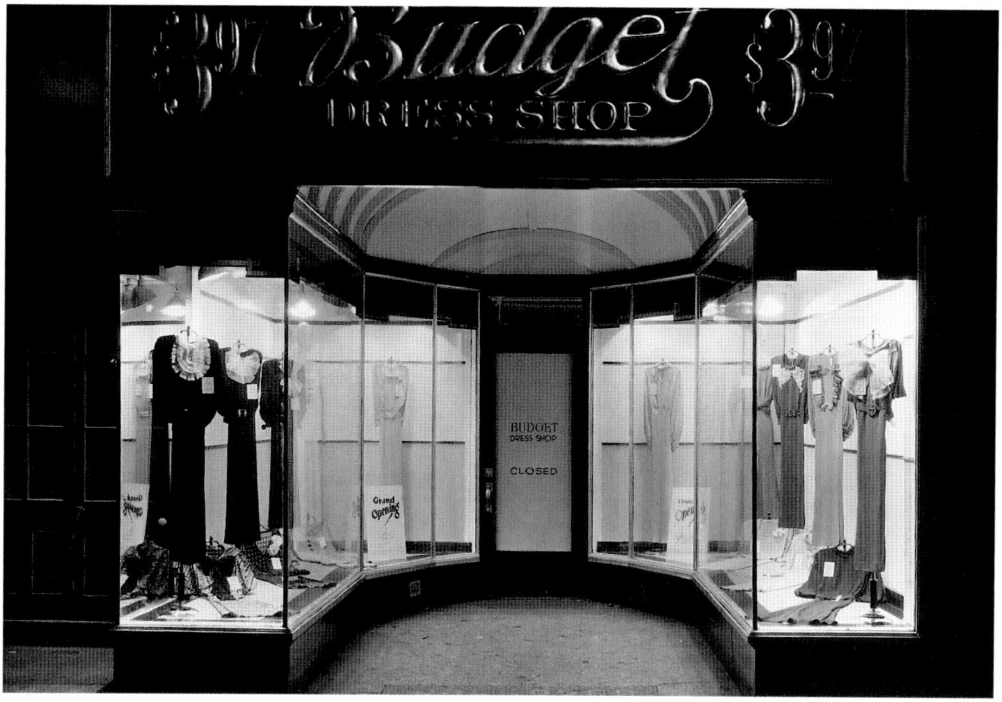

Budget Shop, March 1934. Shoppers looking for bargains on Main Street only had to walk down the block from Kresge's to 206 West Main to find additional savings at the Budget Dress Shop. The boutique opened in March of 1934 to feature "hundreds of new spring dresses featured at one price, $3.97." Frances P. Wilkerson managed the shop following its renovation in 1936 until it closed in 1960. (1875)

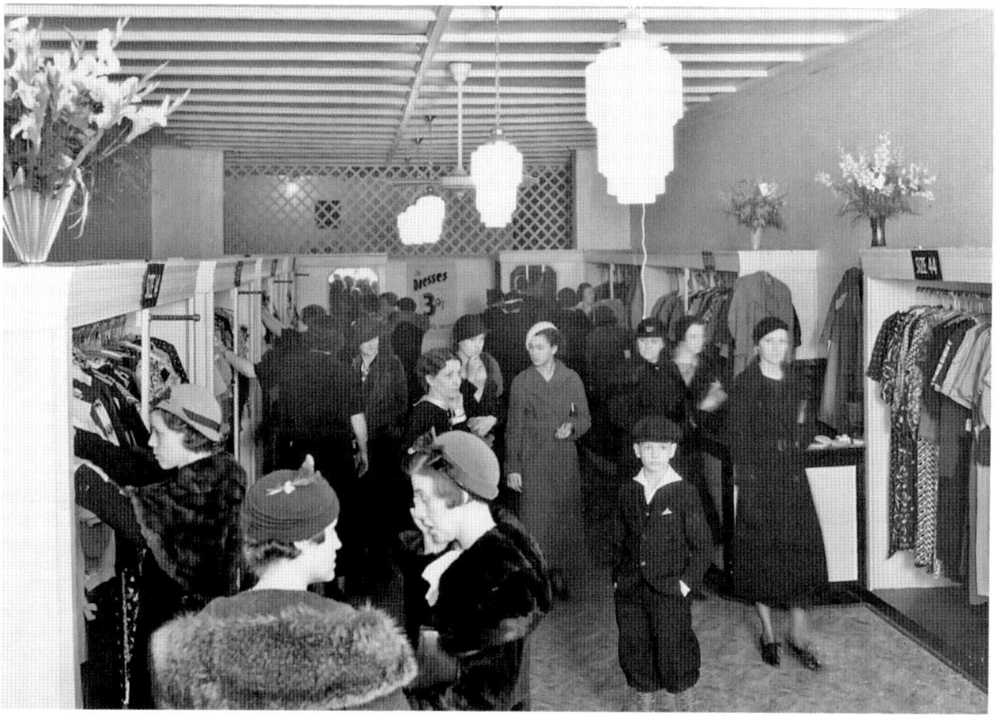

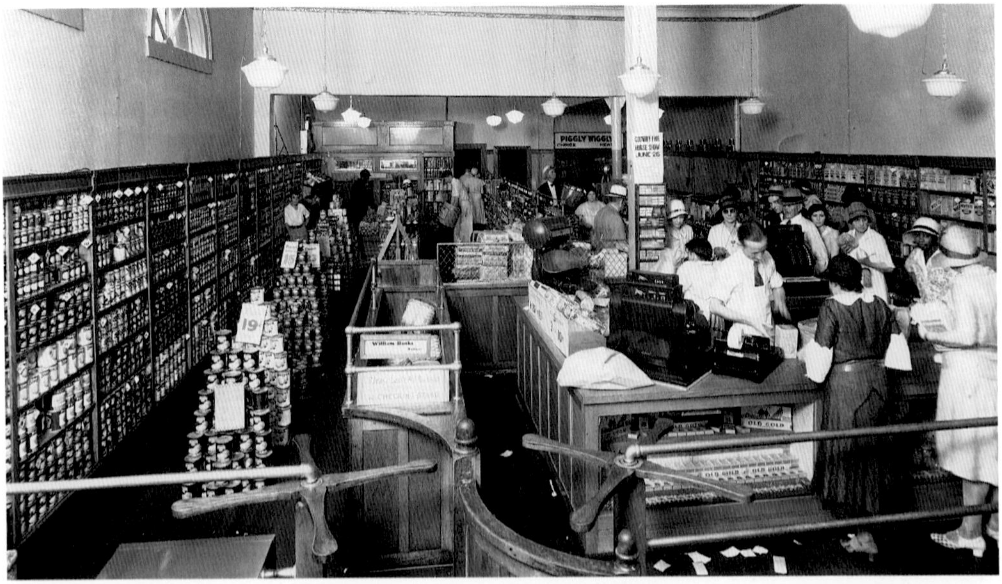

Interior of a Piggly Wiggly. Clothing stores and large department stores were not the only places to find bargains downtown. The Piggly Wiggly grocery store chain placed its first Lexington store at the corner of Broadway and Short Streets in April 1920. The stores featured the new self-service system, which displayed merchandise on open shelves, allowing the customer to choose from a variety of brands without the assistance of clerks. (U-276)

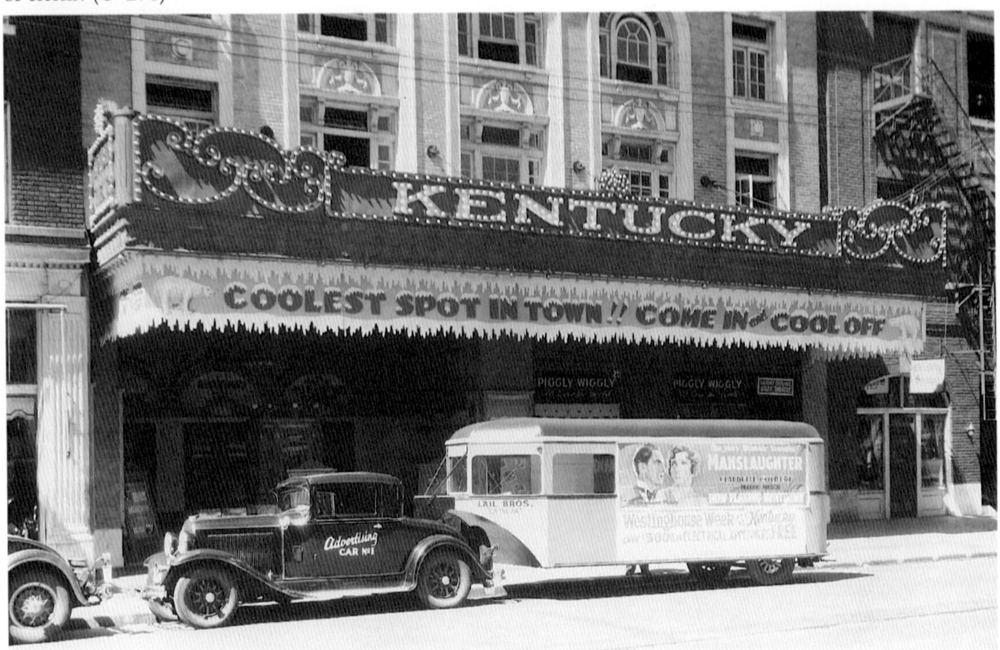

Kentucky Theater and the East Main Piggly Wiggly, August 1930. By 1922, when the Kentucky Theater was in its first year, there were Piggly Wigglys at Short and Broadway, at Woodland and Maxwell, and at 214 East Main, in the Kentucky Theater building. Like the alignment of the Piggly Wiggly and the Kentucky, the union of shopping and entertainment downtown reflected the ever-growing impact of commerce on Lexington's culture. (751)

six

Lexington at Work and on the Move

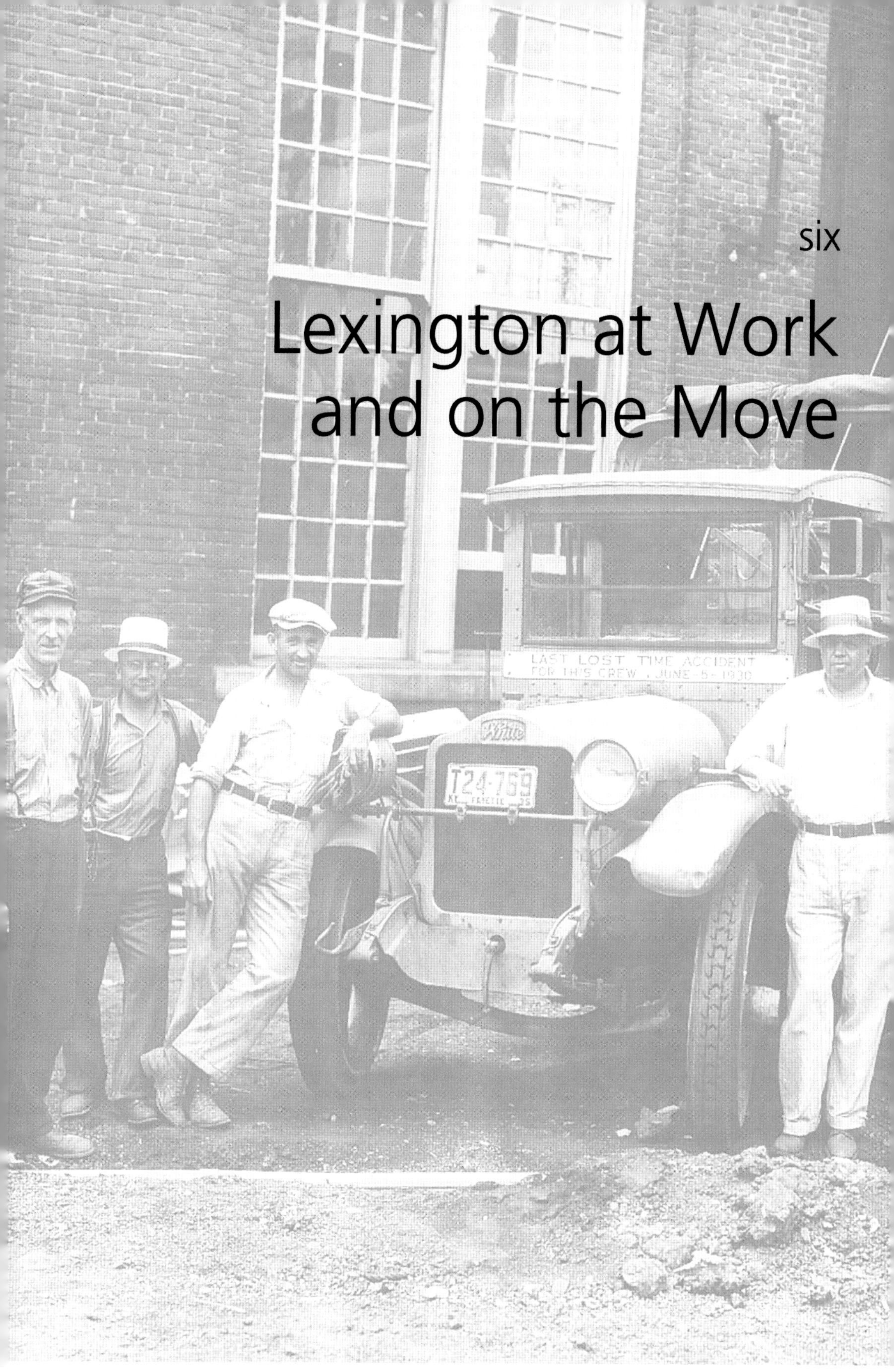

As Lexington expanded as a commercial center, its hardworking citizens kept the town moving forward through a variety of occupations. The growing diversity of services provided, the unemployment during the Depression, the expansion of traditional Kentucky industries, and the changing transportation infrastructure made the 1930s and 1940s decades of transition for Lexington. This period of growth is represented by the laborers and industries Bob Long chronicled with his cameras.

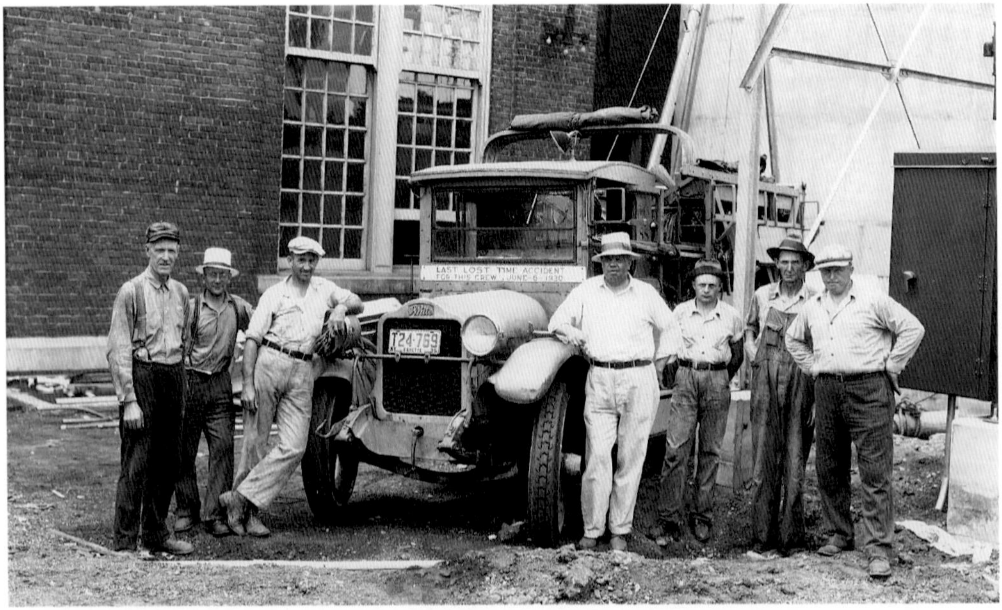

Lexington Utilities Company employees, July 1935. Lexington Utilities Company, along with its parent, Kentucky Utilities Company, was a major employer in Lexington. In 1938, the company employed 201 people. Three years earlier, these men posed for this photograph with their truck, which features the claim that the "last lost time accident for this crew" was June 6, 1930. (3268)

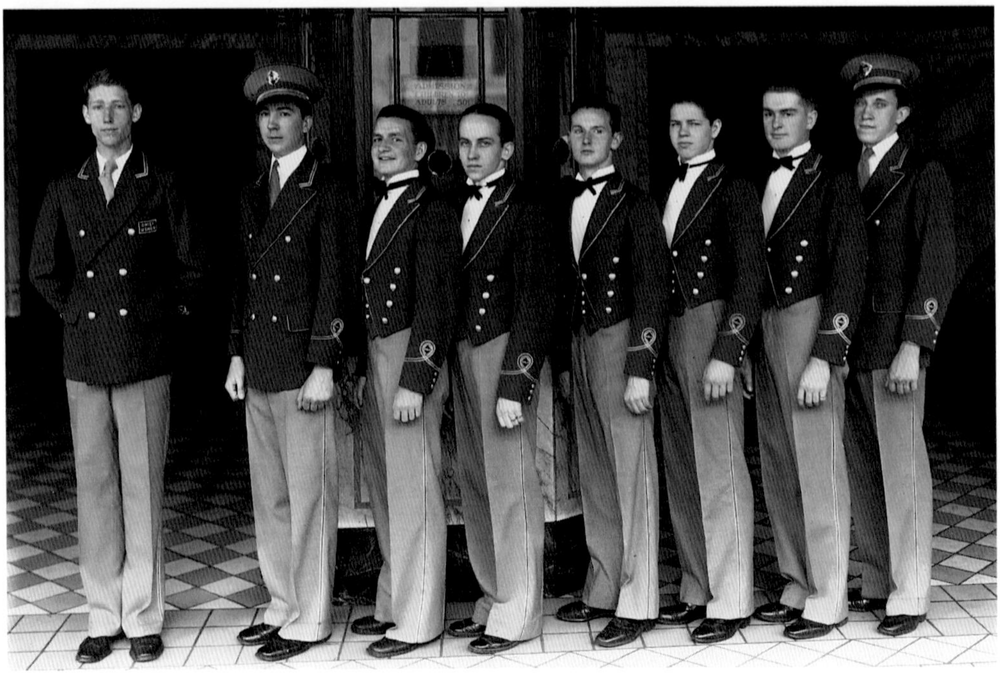

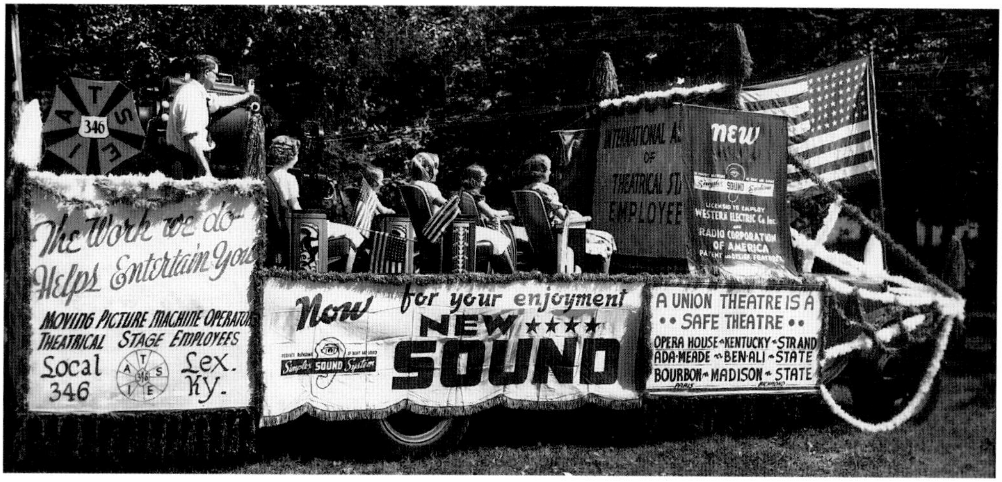

Motion Pictures Machine Operators Union. The Motion Pictures Machine Operators and Theatrical Stage Employees Union was just one union of many in Lexington during this time. As this float suggests, these unions celebrated Labor Day with the rest of the United States through parades and picnics. While unions were active in the city from the 1880s, they did not unite until the Central Labor Council was established in 1903.

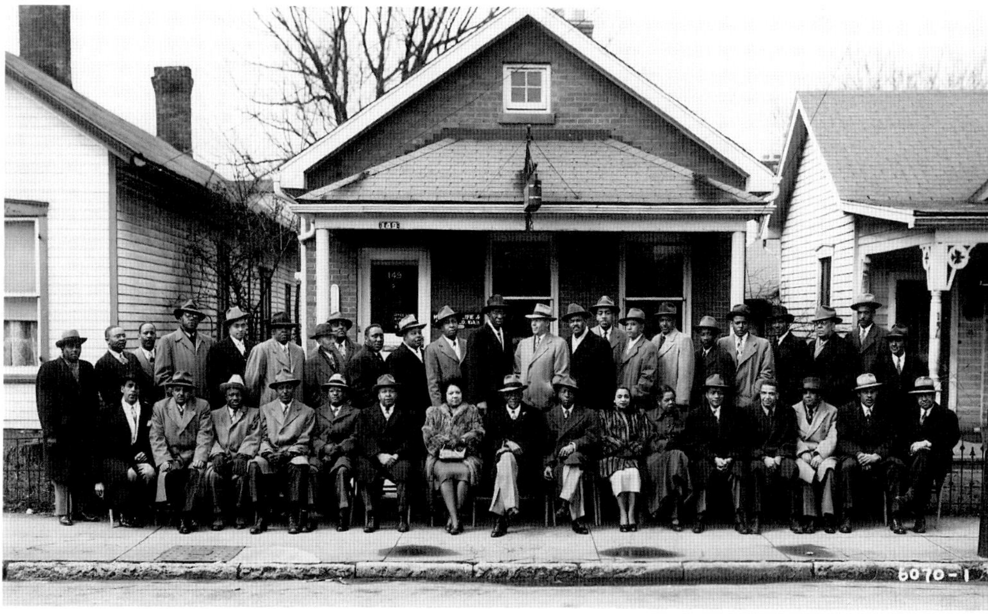

Above: Mammoth Life Insurance Company, February 1949. Kentucky's largest black-owned business was Mammoth Life and Accident Insurance Company, founded in 1915. Lexington's first district manager was Joshua P. Black, who was also the president of Mammoth Printing Company. Originally at 269 East Second Street, Mammoth Life moved to 149 Deweese around 1942. Felix F. Bowles served as district manager from approximately 1927 to 1967, after which time Walter J. Moore took over. (6070)

Opposite below: Kentucky Theater ushers, c. May 30, 1931. A sign in the ticket booth behind the ushers indicates that the admission prices were 10¢ for children and 50¢ for adults at this Paramount Publix Theater. During the weekend this photograph was taken, the Kentucky Theater hosted "Smiling" Ed McConnell, a popular radio star of the time. The manager of the theater in 1931 was Herman C. Bamberger. (1039)

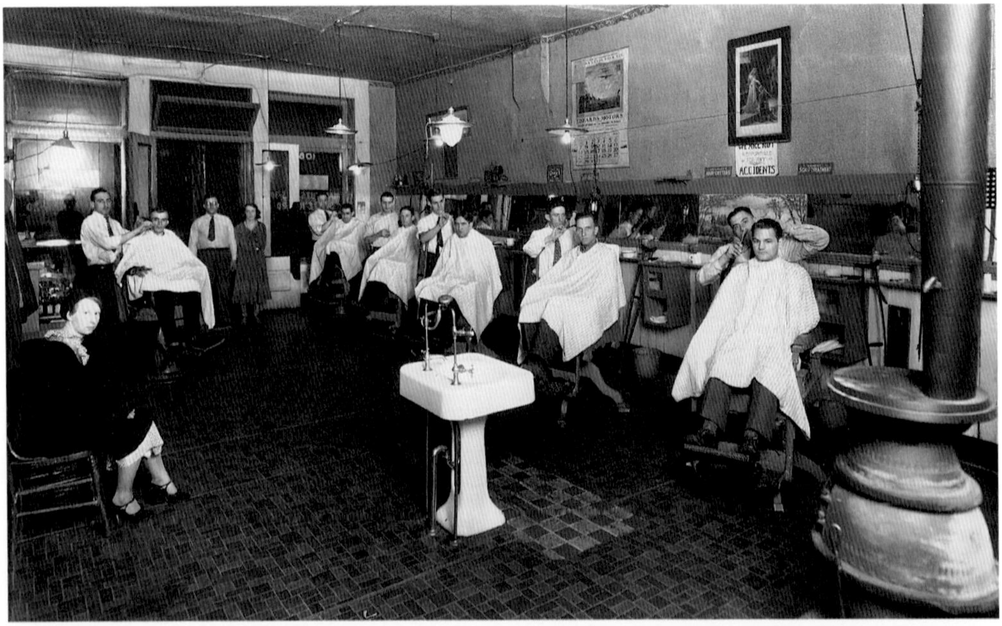

Barber shop, December 1930. This unidentified barber shop was probably Hampton's Barber College, which was located at 108 North Broadway from approximately 1930 to 1932 and was operated by Walker B. Cunningham. The previous occupant of that location was Fredrick D. Bostic who was also a barber but moved to 114 North Mill in 1930. In addition to the December 1930 calendar, signs adorn the walls including notification that the barbers "are not responsible for any 'accidents.' "

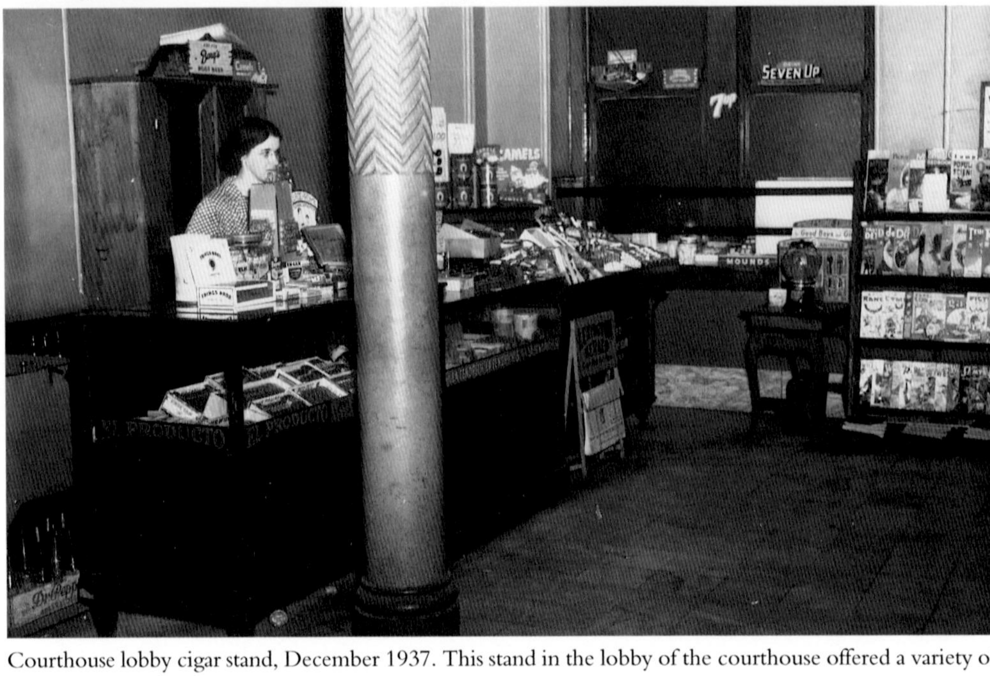

Courthouse lobby cigar stand, December 1937. This stand in the lobby of the courthouse offered a variety of confections, magazines, *The Lexington Herald*, and tobacco products. From 1937 to 1944, the City Directory lists Beatrice Bateman as selling cigars in the lobby of the courthouse. In 1945, Mrs. Beatrice B. Taylor is recorded as running the confectionery. The stand and Mrs. Taylor are not listed in 1947. (3865)

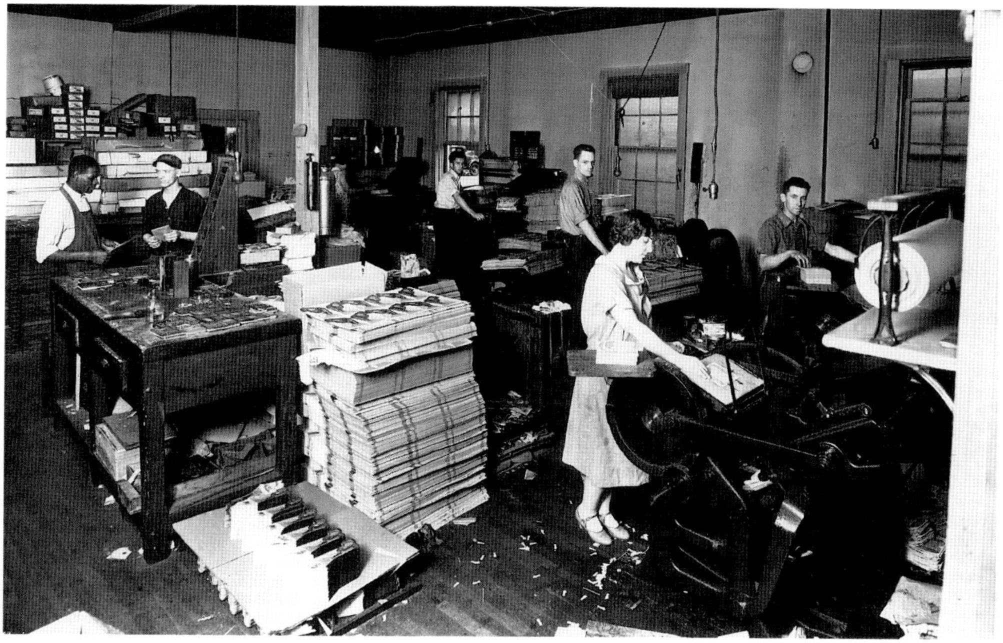

Spotswood Specialty Company's printers, May 1930. The son of a well-known Lexington lumberman, Frank D. Spotswood established Spotswood Specialty Company in the early 1900s to print advertising novelties. Spotswood managed the print shop until his death in 1927 when J. Howard King began his longtime association with the firm. Hugh G. King III became president around 1984, and Tyler King took over the shop at 218 Jefferson c. 1995. (680)

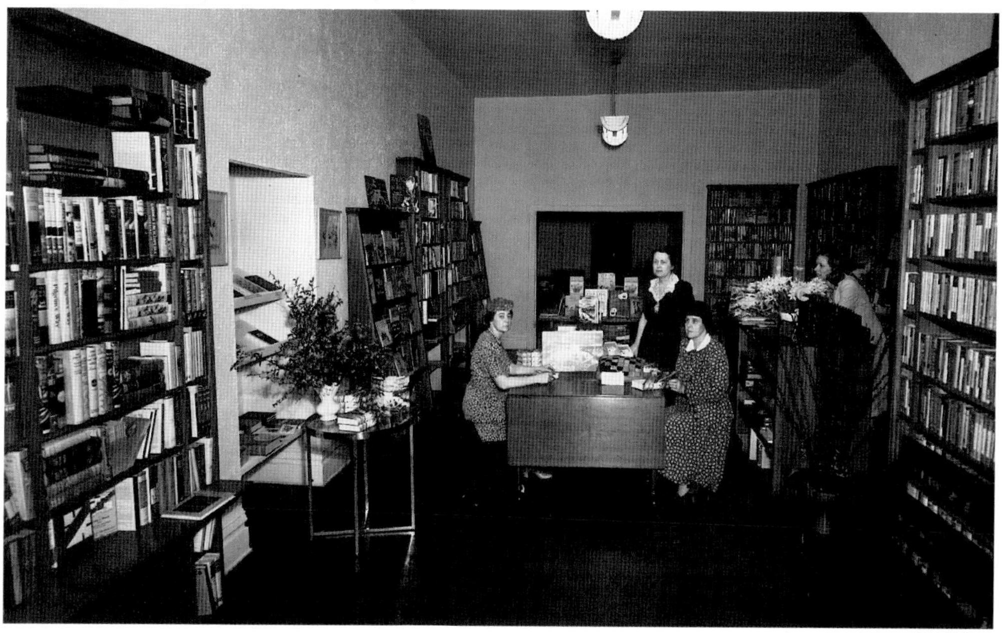

Morris book shop, April 1941. Ethel R. LeBus assumed proprietorship of the Morris Book Shop and moved it to 110 Walnut Street shortly before this photograph was taken. The shop had been established five years earlier by James E. Morris, the book store manager at the University of Kentucky. LeBus turned the business over to H. Joseph Houlihan in 1946, who moved the store to 228 East Main around 1970. (4695)

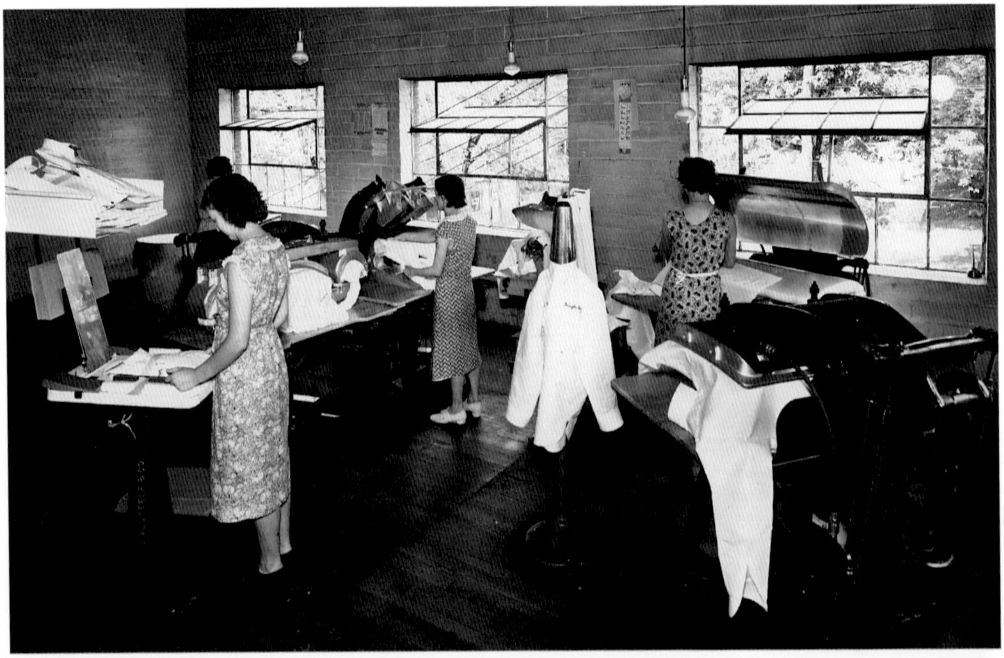

Ideal Laundry's employees and new equipment, July 1938. J.W. Kelley Jr. and H. de Waegenaere, partners in laundry, rug cleaning, and dry cleaning ventures, always promoted their businesses as having the latest in technology to assist their workers in providing excellent service. This photograph was used to advertise the new Prosperity Dowed Unit, demonstrated here by four women who were specially trained to handle the latest equipment in shirt finishing. (4017)

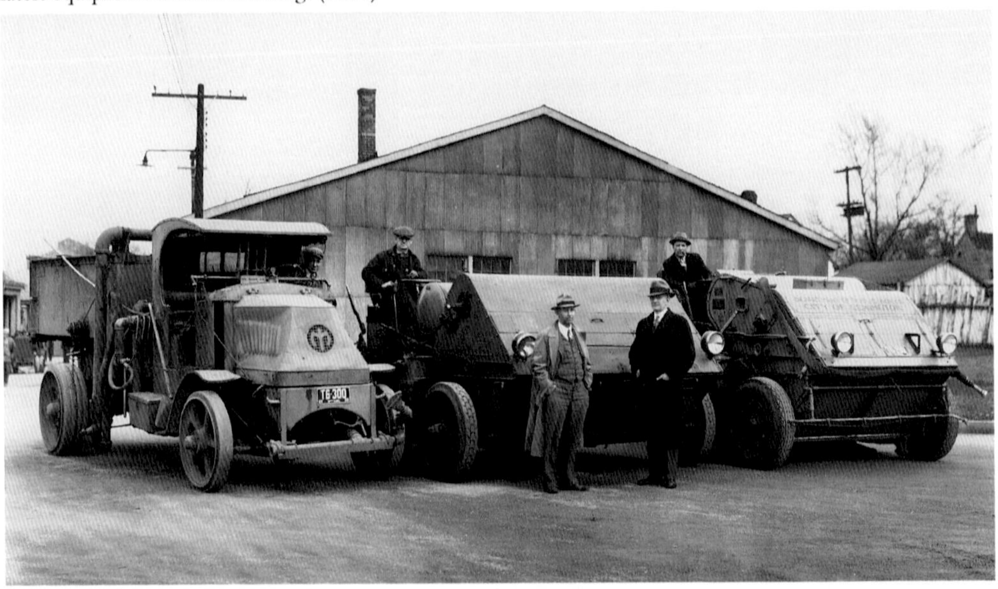

City of Lexington Street Sweepers, January 1933. Street maintenance has been a long-standing challenge for city workers. In the photograph above, city employees pose with a truck and two Elgin Corporation power brooms that enabled the sweeping of approximately two tons of trash from the city streets each night. In addition, snow removal, sewer drainage, and flooding problems continuously hindered Lexington's efforts to keep its busy streets clear. (1474)

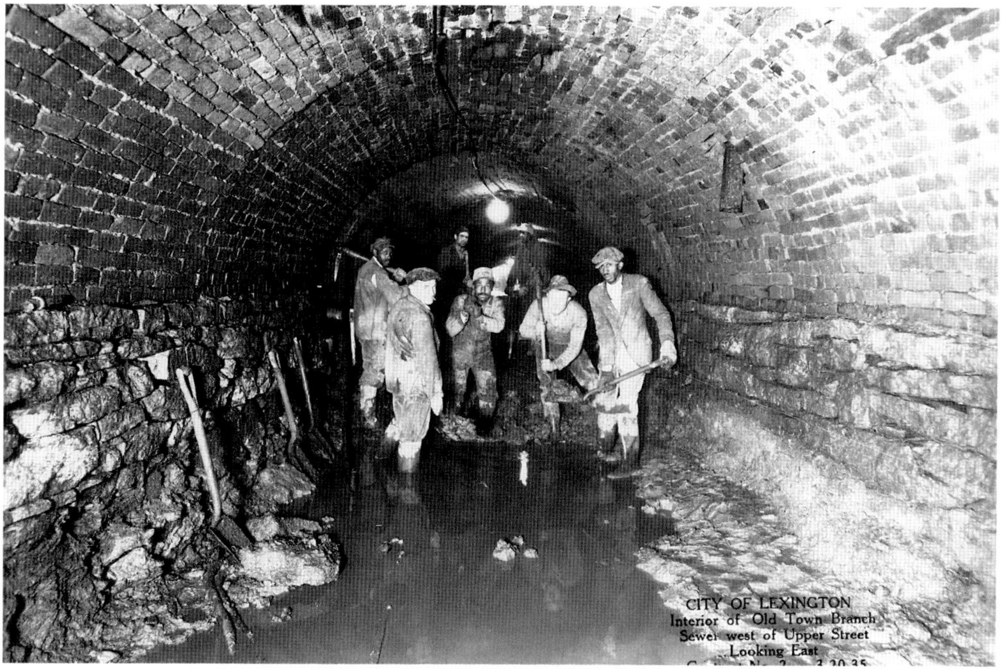

Sewer construction, March 20, 1935. The laying of the central district sewer in 1934 and 1935 alleviated the flooding problems on Vine, Water, and Main which had plagued the city since its origins in 1779. These floods were caused by the Town Branch, which originated from near the present intersection of Seventh Street and Winchester Road and followed a route roughly parallel to Midland and Vine Streets, between Old Frankfort Pike and Leestown Pike to join South Elkhorn near the Fayette and Scott County lines. (3401)

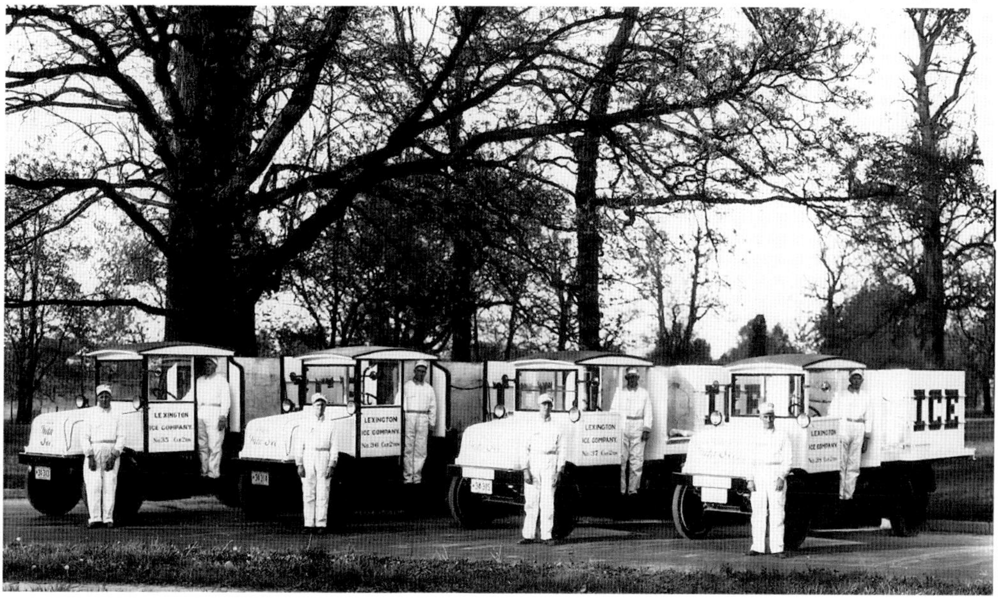

Lexington Ice Company's Delivery Service. From the 1890s to around 1940, the employees of City Ice Company, which later became Lexington Ice Company, transported ice to the residents of the city. These drivers delivered the ice from the company plants on Maxwell Street and Loudon Avenue at Limestone to their customers, who were encouraged by the motto painted on the hood of these trucks to "Chill with Ice."

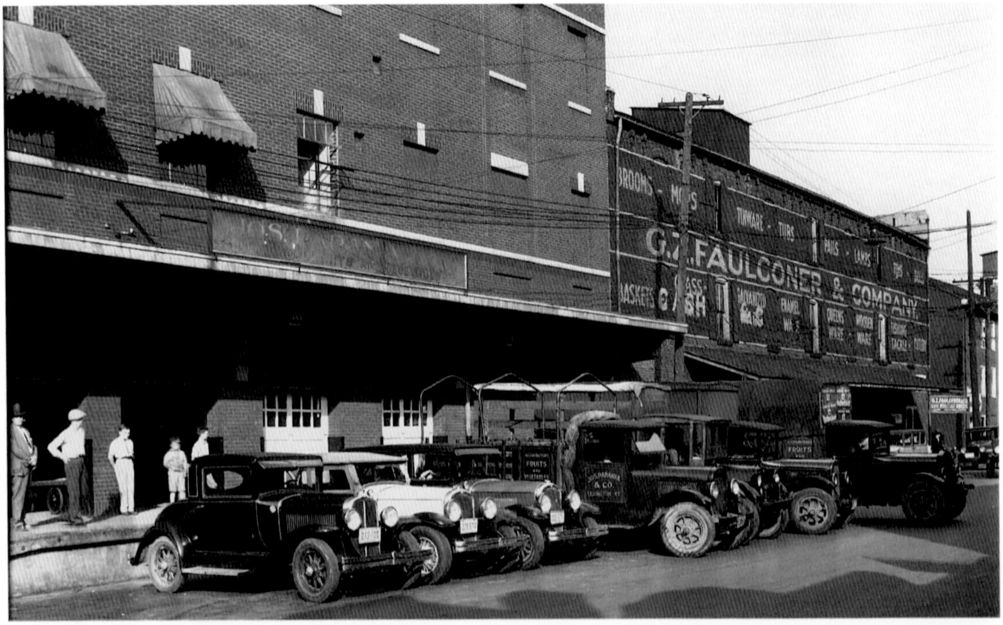

Jos. Papania & Company's delivery service, June 1930. Also making deliveries, Jos. Papania & Company provided fresh fruits and vegetables to businesses throughout Central Kentucky. Joseph V. Papania established this family-run business at the turn of the century on South Broadway. Around 1917, the produce wholesalers moved to this three-story warehouse at 242 West Vine. The fourth generation of Papanias continue to provide personal, Lexington-based service from 115 Zesta Place. (706)

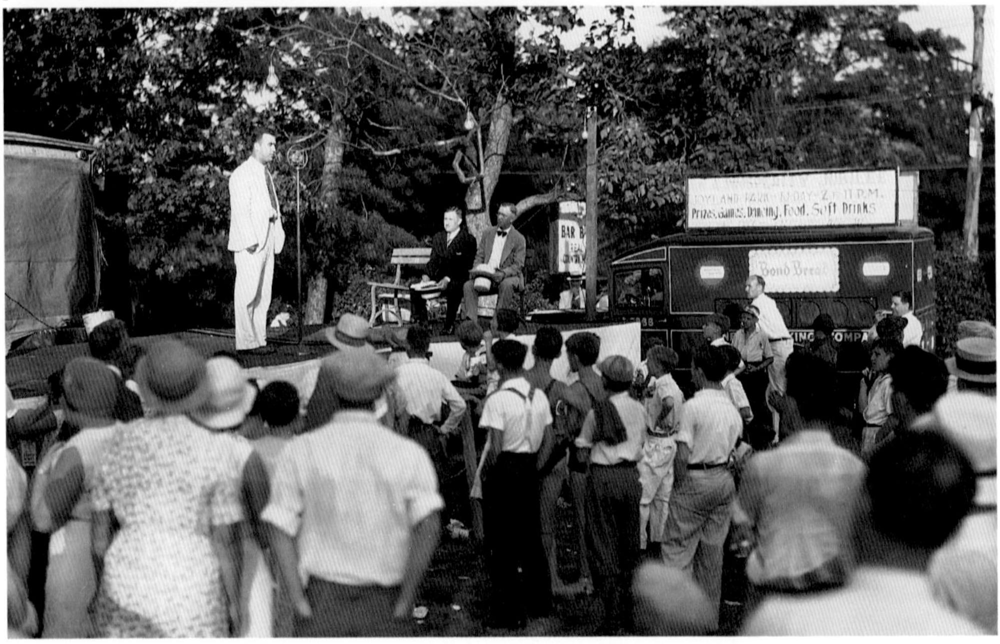

I.G.A. Prosperity Jubilee, June 29, 1932. Lieutenant Governor A.B. Chandler spoke to the attendees of this Independent Grocers Alliance picnic. J. Frank Grimes, president and founder of I.G.A., was also slated to speak at the event. C.T. Crowe, president and general manager of W.T. Sistrunk and Company, a supplier for local I.G.A. stores, sponsored the jubilee, where a free lunch and soft drinks were offered to the public. (1347)

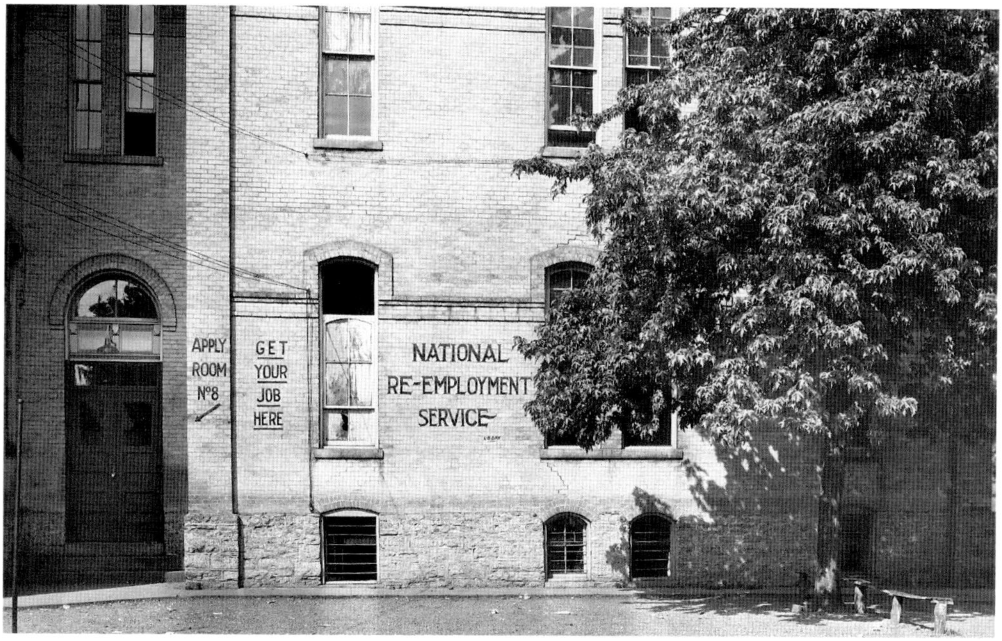

National Re-employment Bureau, May 1934. The Great Depression and the unemployment of the early 1930s concerned Lexington as it did the rest of the country. Several support systems developed in Lexington throughout the decade. The National Re-Employment Service provided an organized means by which Lexingtonians could learn about and apply for jobs. Shown in the photograph below are stations for people seeking construction positions as well as commercial and professional positions. (3340)

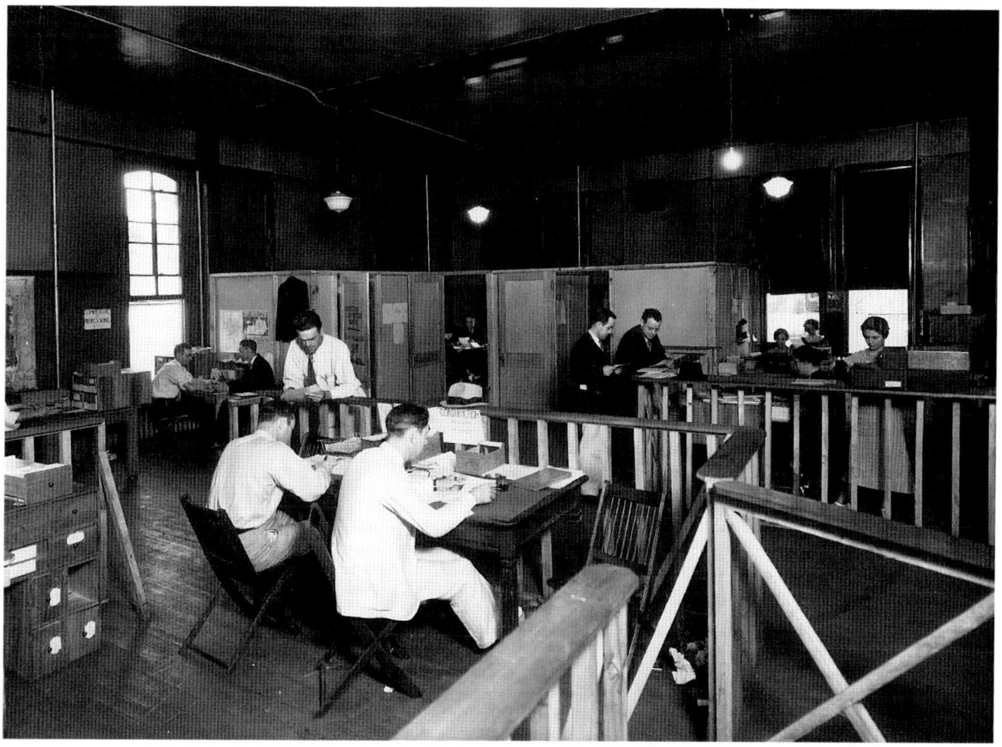

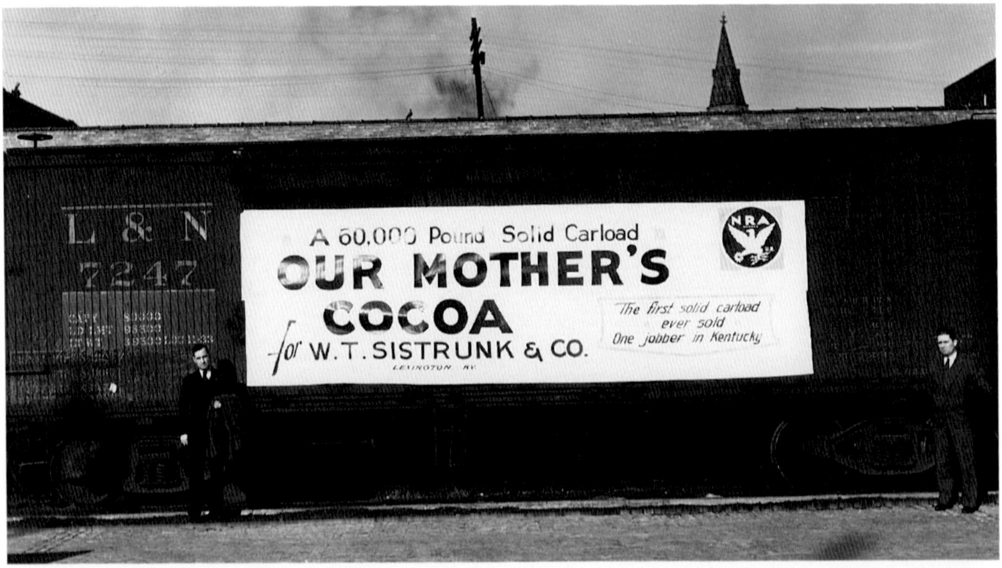

W.T. Sistrunk Boxcar, March 1934. W.T. Sistrunk Company was just one of many Lexington employers to sport the blue eagle symbol of the National Recovery Act and apply its formula in an effort to revitalize the city's economy. Sistrunk furnished groceries and produce to local hotels and restaurants. The company, established in 1891 by W.T. Sistrunk, employed over a hundred people in 1934, when it was managed by C.T. Crowe. (1869)

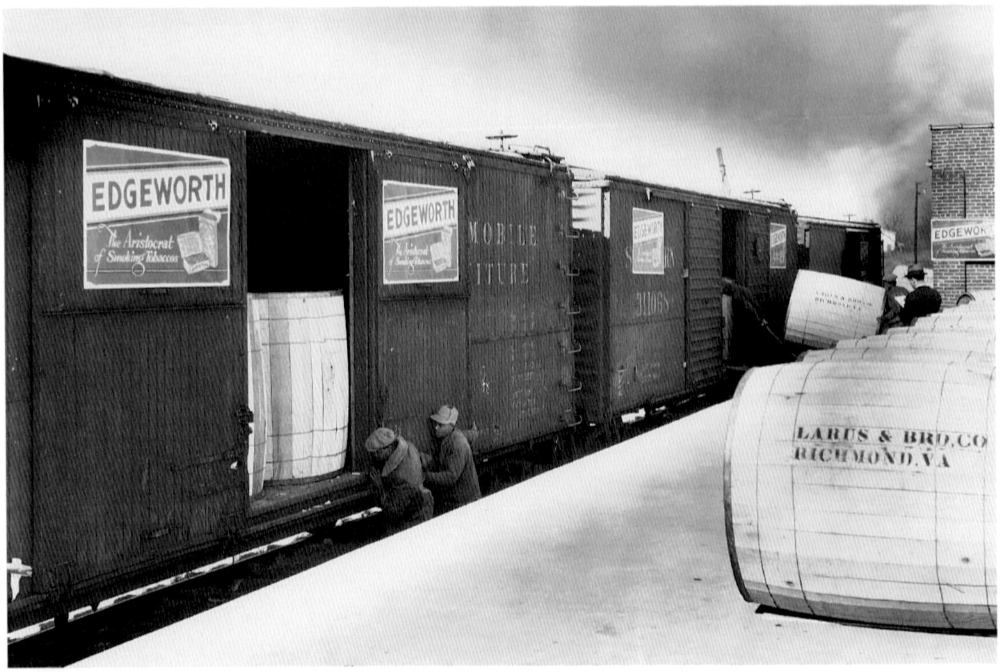

Loading Tobacco for Edgeworth Tobacco Company, February 1934. The tobacco industry has been an historically important source of work in Kentucky. More efficient handling, cooperative acreage controls, and price support systems benefited the entire industry. Whether a person was a farmer, buyer, warehouseman, or boxcar loader, tobacco meant jobs, profits, and continued growth throughout the 1930s and 1940s. Here, men load railroad cars with tobacco for shipment by Edgeworth Tobacco. (1855)

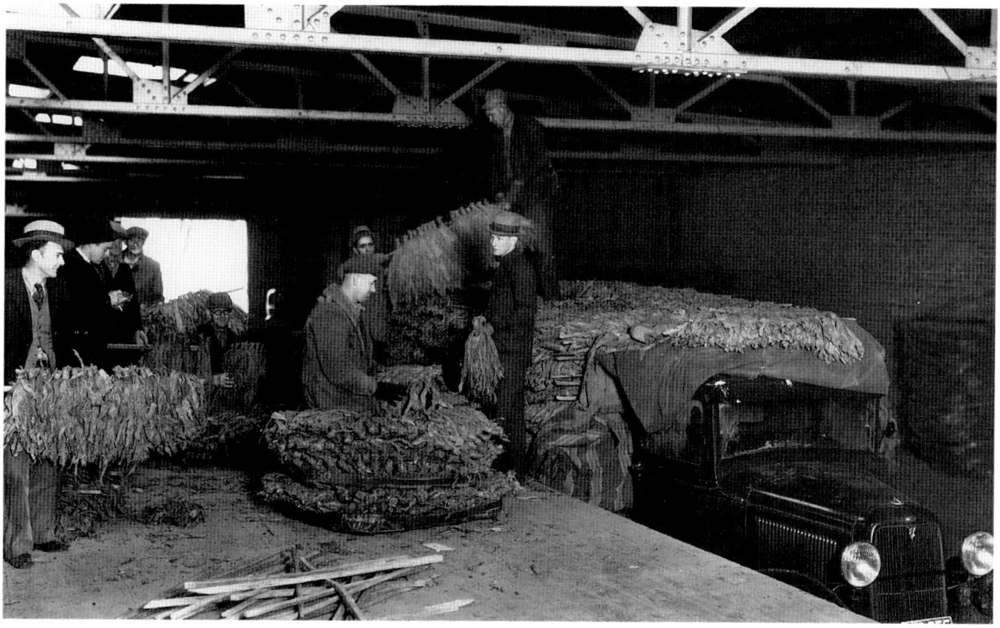

Loading Tobacco for Shipment, February 1934. As these men unloaded tobacco from trucks in February of 1934, they were looking forward to higher prices as a result of lower production under the first acreage control plan of the Agricultural Adjustment Act of 1933. Lexington, considered a major center of tobacco commerce during this time, was proud of its prosperous tobacco district. (1855)

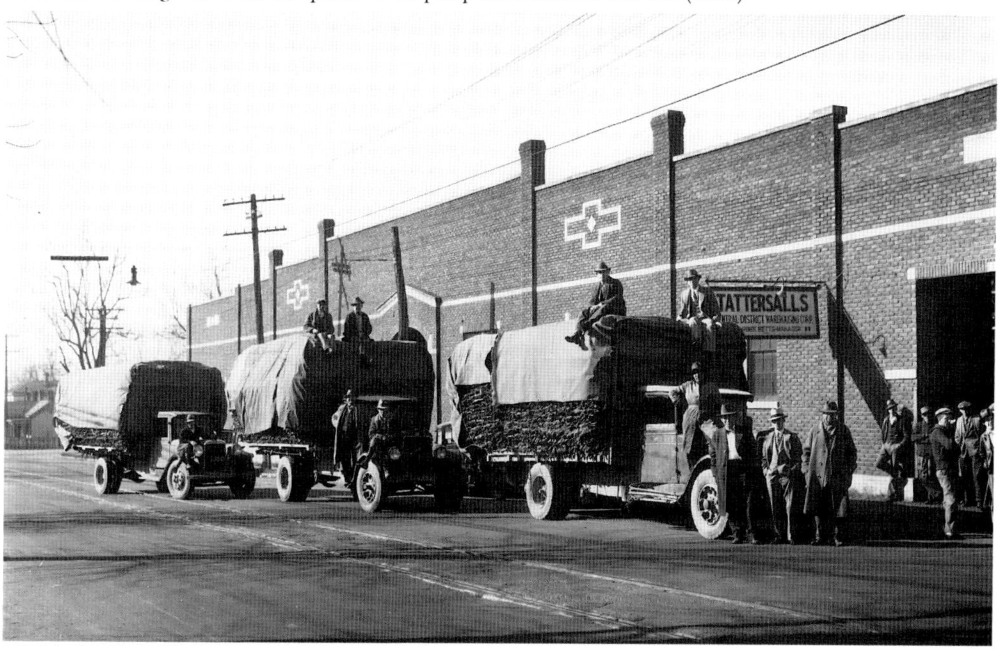

Looking North on South Broadway in the Tobacco Warehouse District, December 1931. The South Broadway area, including Angliana Avenue and Bolivar and South Upper Streets was a major hub of activity for buying and selling tobacco in Lexington. These views, looking north and south on South Broadway, reflect the bustling traffic of trucks, cars, and horse-drawn wagons transporting tobacco to and from Lexington's warehouse district. Tattersall's, pictured here at 845 South Broadway, also dealt in livestock. (1124)

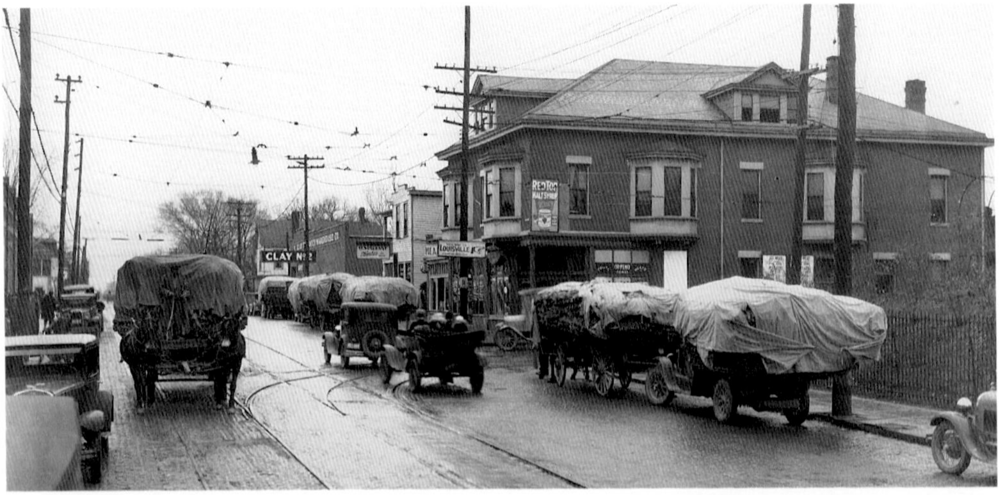

Looking south on South Broadway in the tobacco warehouse district, December 1931. The company that ordered these photographs, American Tobacco at 574-92 South Upper at Bolivar, was surrounded by over two dozen tobacco warehouses and the vigorous activity of the Burley market. Because of the efficient services provided by these warehouses, many tobacco dealers found it worthwhile to travel long distances to sell in Lexington. (1124)

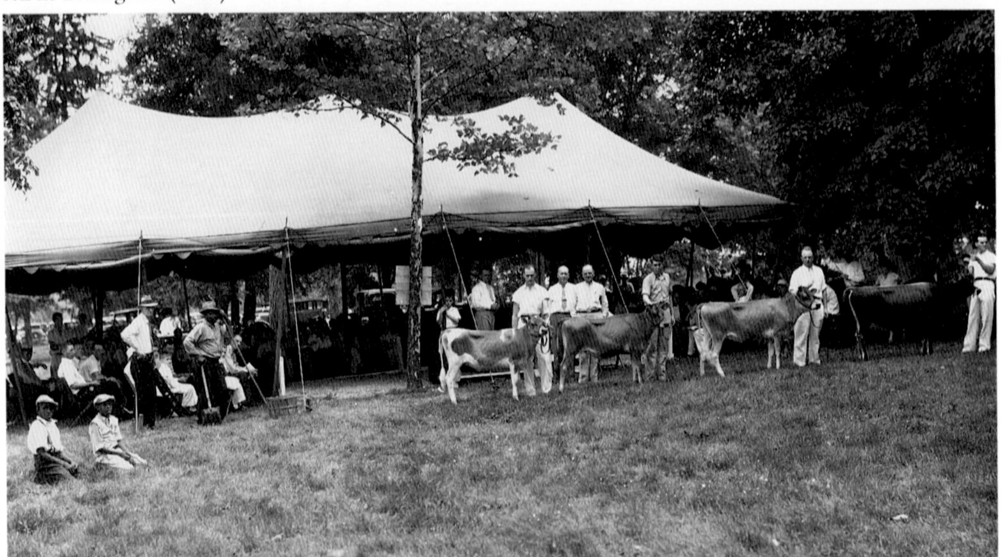

Above: Forward farm auction, August 1934. Like many other Central Kentucky farmers, J.D. McKibben and J.R. Hill at Forward Farm on Georgetown Pike took pride in their Jersey herds. In Lexington, cattle farming provided a lucrative alternative to horses and tobacco in the 1930s and it experienced noticeable growth in the late 1940s. While agriculture would continue as Kentucky's top industry, much of Lexington's farmland would be lost to urban growth. (1579)

Opposite below: Turkey farming, November 1939. In addition to tobacco and horse farming, Lexington's agricultural tradition included a variety of crops and livestock. Poultry farming was a growing industry in Lexington around the turn of the century, but it had fallen behind other agricultural pursuits by 1939, when this photograph was taken for Ubiko, a poultry feed developer, whose products were sold locally through Blue Grass Elmendorf Grain Corporation. (4377)

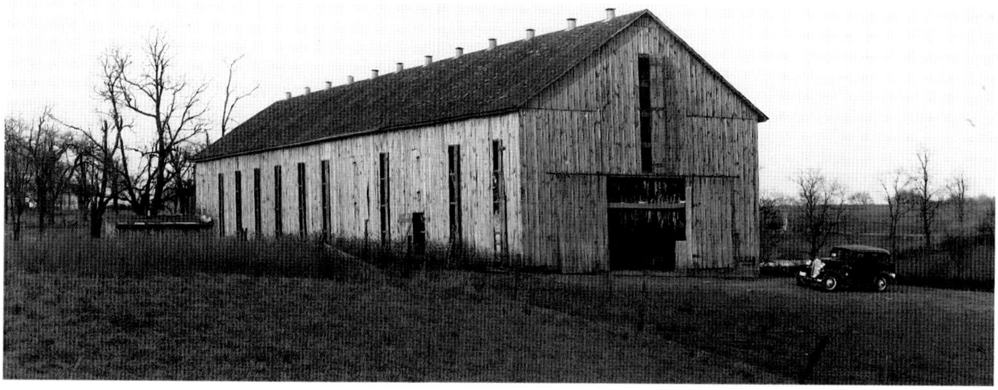

Tobacco hanging in barn, February 1934. According to studio records, Bob Long made a 13-mile round trip to photograph this barn located on Lawrence Britton's farm in Versailles. Tobacco barns like this one still stand on farms throughout the Blue Grass and remain a symbol of the significant role this crop has had in the region's agricultural economy. (1853)

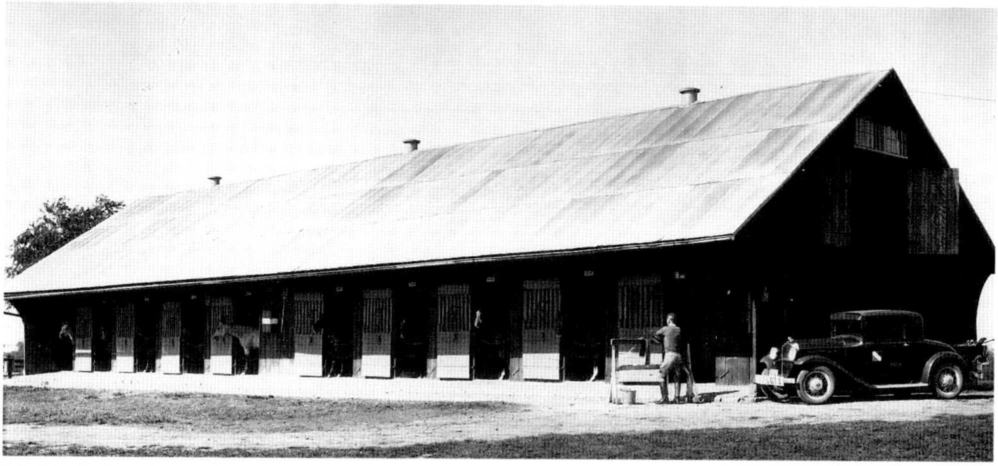

Madden's Hamburg Place, October 1932. Horse farms such as Calumet, Elmendorf, Gainesway, and Hamburg Place have played a significant role in Lexington's cultural and economic life. John E. Madden established Hamburg Place in 1898 with the $40,001 he received from the sale of the champion colt, Hamburg. In recent years, a considerable portion of the farm has been developed into a commercial shopping center. (1401)

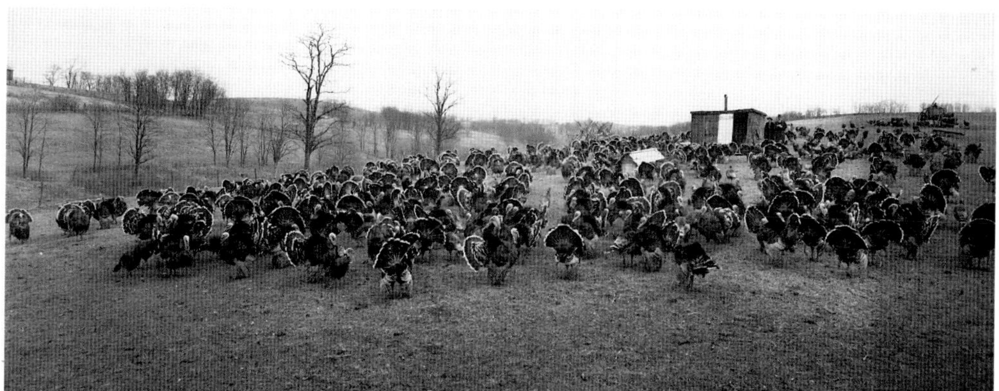

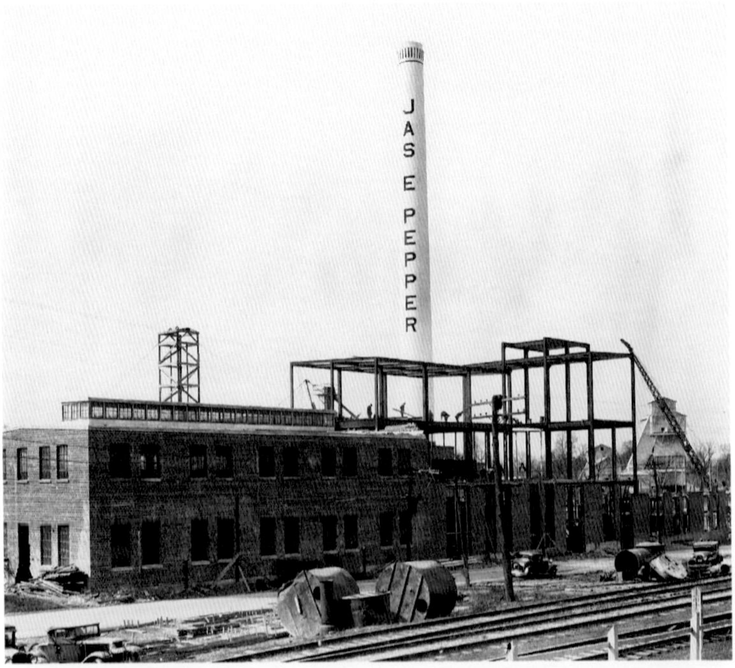

Old Pepper Distillery construction, February 1934. Distilling, a significant Lexington industry in the 19th century, continued to impact Lexington culture into the 20th century. James E. Pepper established his Old Pepper Distillery on Old Frankfort Pike in Lexington in 1880. After a period of inactivity, during which whiskey produced before prohibition was stored in the plant, the Schenley Products Company of New York began these renovations in February 1934. (1856)

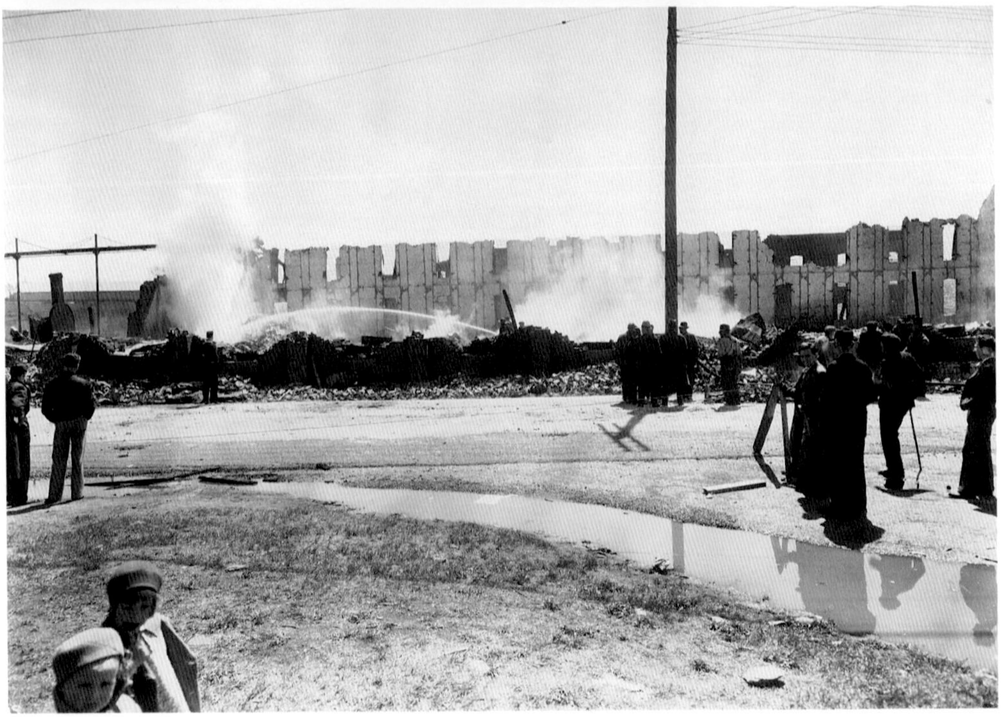

Fire Scenes at the Pepper Distillery, April 28, 1934. Two months after renovations began, a night watchman mistook gasoline for kerosene and started a fire. The badly burned man was overcome before he could sound the alarm. Seven buildings and 15,500 barrels of whiskey were destroyed before firemen contained the blaze. Schenley immediately began to rebuild and by August 1936, the new plant had been operating for 23 months, producing 97,000 barrels of whiskey and employing 100 men. (1914)

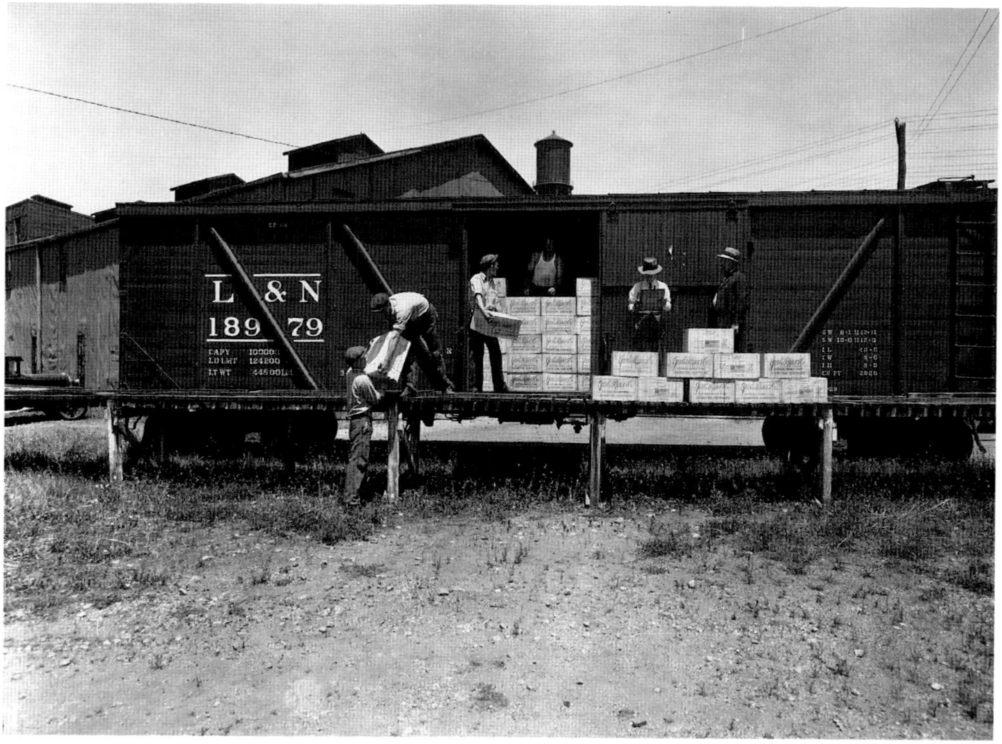

Above: Loading Jas. E. Pepper whiskey into an L & N boxcar, June 1932. Like other Lexington industries, distilleries transported local goods to national markets by railroad. These men are loading Jas. E. Pepper Whiskey into an L & N car. The first railroad tracks west of the Alleghenies were laid at Mill and Water Streets, on October 21, 1831, by the Lexington and Ohio Railroad, which was purchased by Louisville & Nashville Railroad in 1881. (1334)

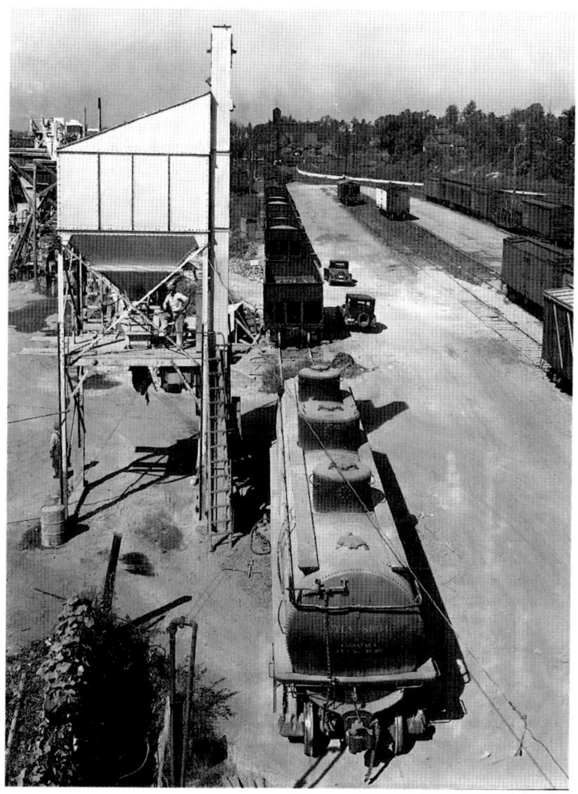

Right: Freight car on railroad tracks near Vine Street, October 1934. For 135 years, Lexington profited from the railroad that ran through the heart of its commercial area, two blocks from Main Street. Passenger service to Union Station brought businessmen, tourists and shoppers to town. More significantly, Lexington commodities were transported primarily by rail until the advanced highway development of the late 1940s. While the idea of removing the railroad tracks from the downtown area originated in 1947, the tracks were not relocated until 1968. (1944)

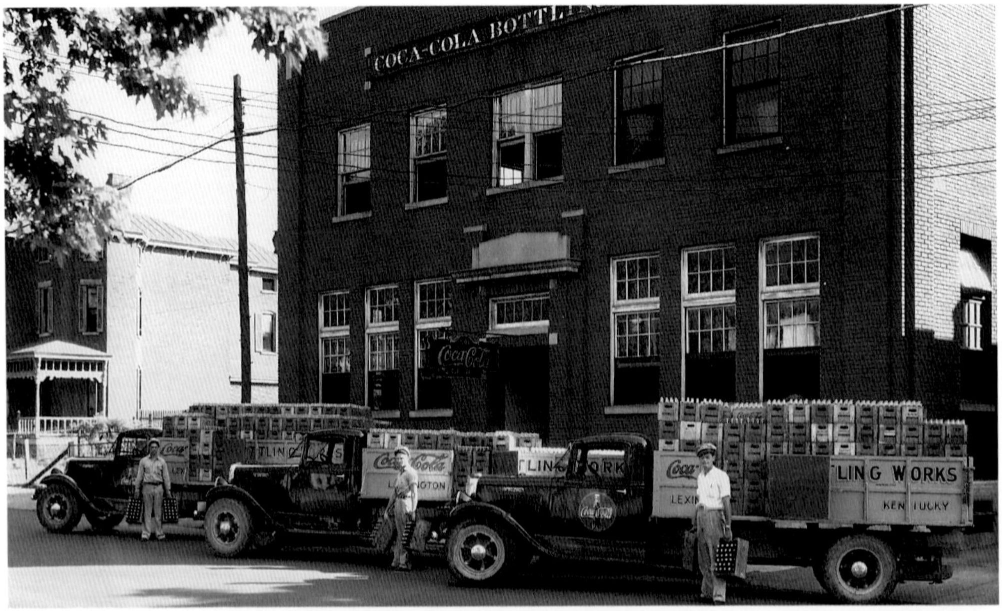

Coca-Cola Bottling Company Trucks, July 1935. While the 1930s and 1940s became the twilight of the railroad's importance in downtown Lexington, they also saw the dawn of highway transportation's impact on the city's growth. Through the use of these trucks, Coca-Cola was able to bottle their product in Lexington and transport it throughout Central Kentucky. This photograph advertised the purchase of these trucks from the International Harvester Company. (3259)

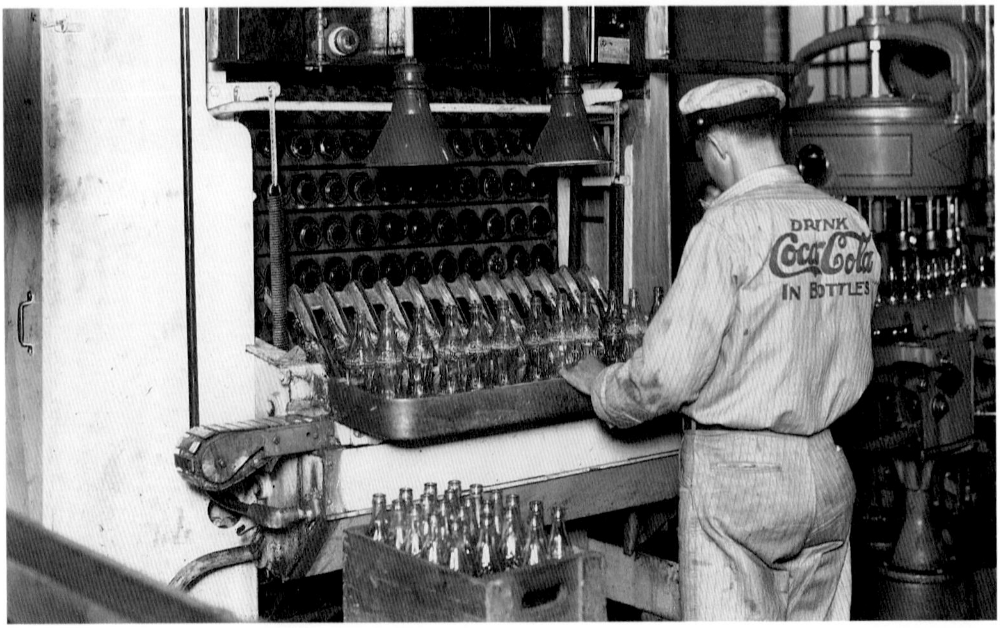

Coca-Cola bottling machine and operator, June 1938. Coca-Cola's bottling plant in Lexington was managed by Charles Mitchell until his death in 1927, when his wife, Myrtle Mae Mitchell, took over. She was manager in June of 1938, when this photograph appeared in a full page Lexington Leader advertisement celebrating the longtime presence of Coca-Cola in Lexington. The Meyer-Dunmore Machine and operator pictured here could sterilize 120 bottles a minute. (3985)

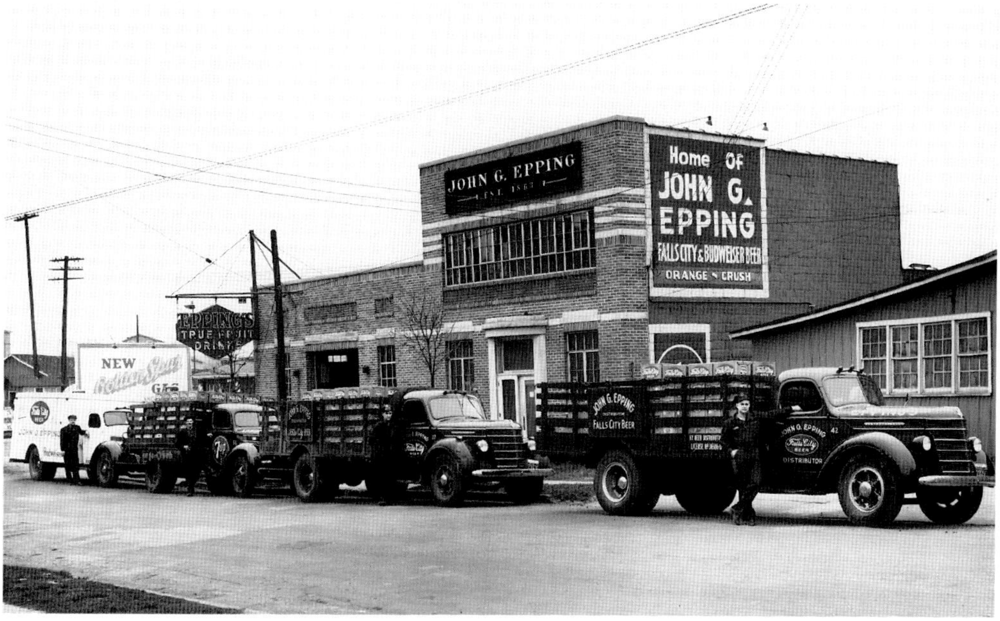

John G. Epping bottling works, March 1942. Another bottler with a long-standing presence in Lexington, Louisville-based Epping opened a plant on East Third Street in the mid-1920s. The factory moved to 264 Walton around 1932 where it produced Orange Crush and 7-Up until it closed in 1966. In 1942, when this photograph was taken, the Epping plant employed 20 people who distributed soda and Falls City Beer to a 50-mile area around Lexington. (4873)

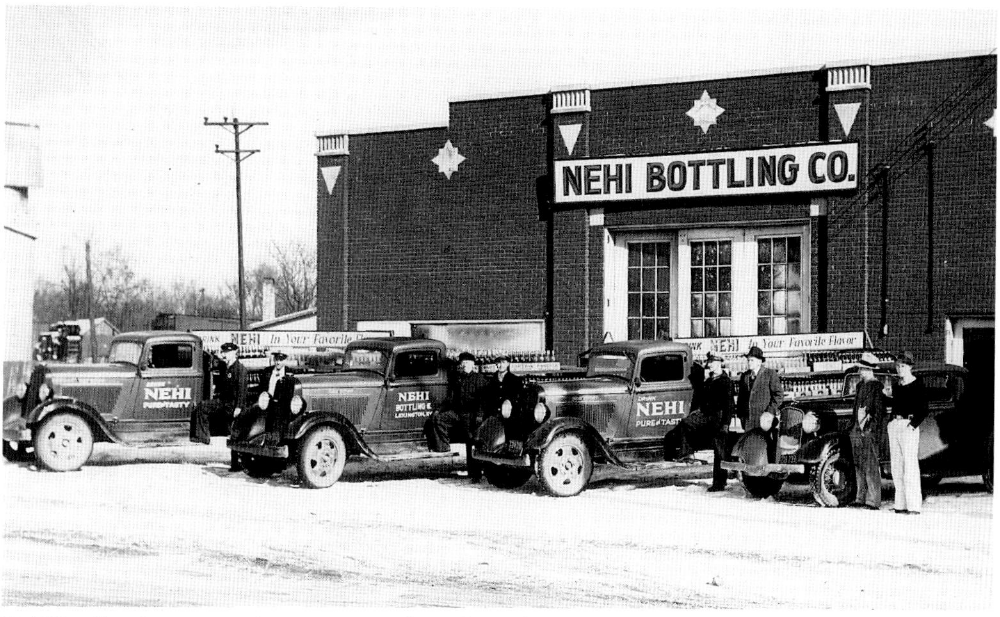

Nehi Bottling Company, February 1936. Nehi, makers of Nehi, Royal Crown, and Par-T-Pak beverages, was established in 1934 by Robert D. and Robert F. Head at 326 Georgetown Street. Later located at 628-640 East Third, the firm employed 25 Lexingtonians. In a 1941 advertisement, Mr. Head emphasized that "there are no outside interests whatever" involved in the firm, possibly alluding to his competitors, including Epping and Coca-Cola, which were regionally headquartered in Louisville. (3101)

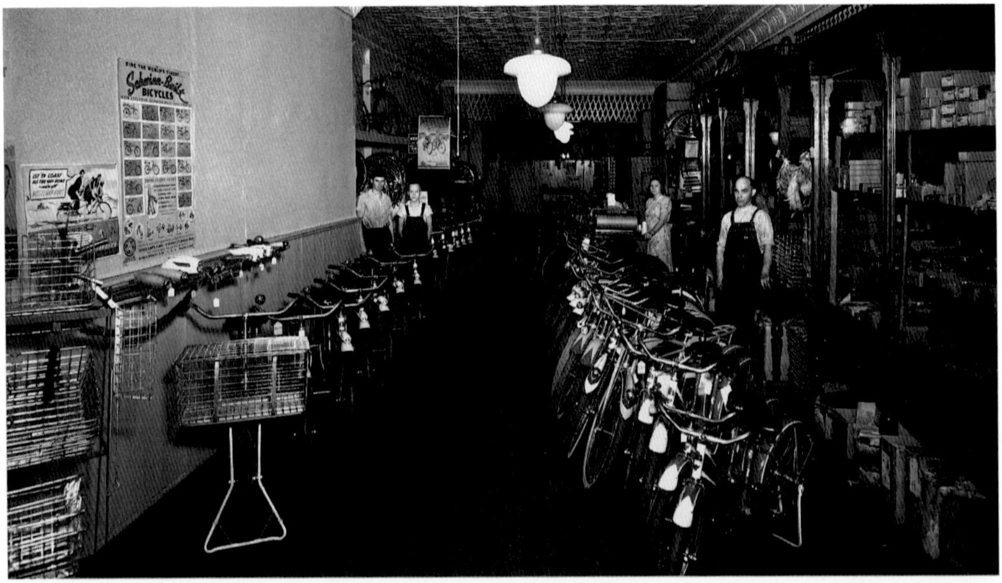

Joyner's bicycle shop, August 1940. John B. Joyner managed a bicycle shop at 115 South Mill until around 1936 when he opened this store at 109 North Mill. "The largest sales and service store for bicycles in Lexington," Joyner's maintained a large stock of Schwinn's popular American Flyers, as well as used bicycles. After 1945, the shop moved to 221 North Limestone where William B. LeMay assumed proprietorship in the 1960s. (4546)

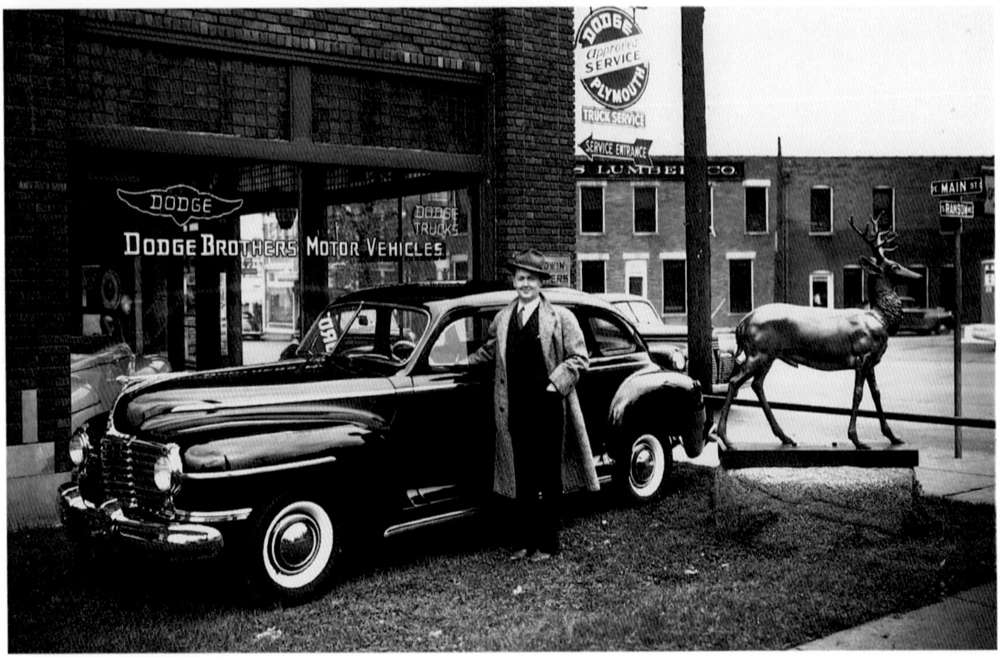

Goodwin Brothers, November 1941. Across town at 444 East Main, the Goodwin Brothers were developing a successful business selling cars. Having started their business in 1916, George E. and Joseph A. Goodwin helped to pioneer the automobile business in Lexington. Many of their family members were also involved in running the business, including their mother and father. Their nephews, William I. Goodwin and Dwight Goodwin Tenny, took over after Joseph's death in 1953. (4788)

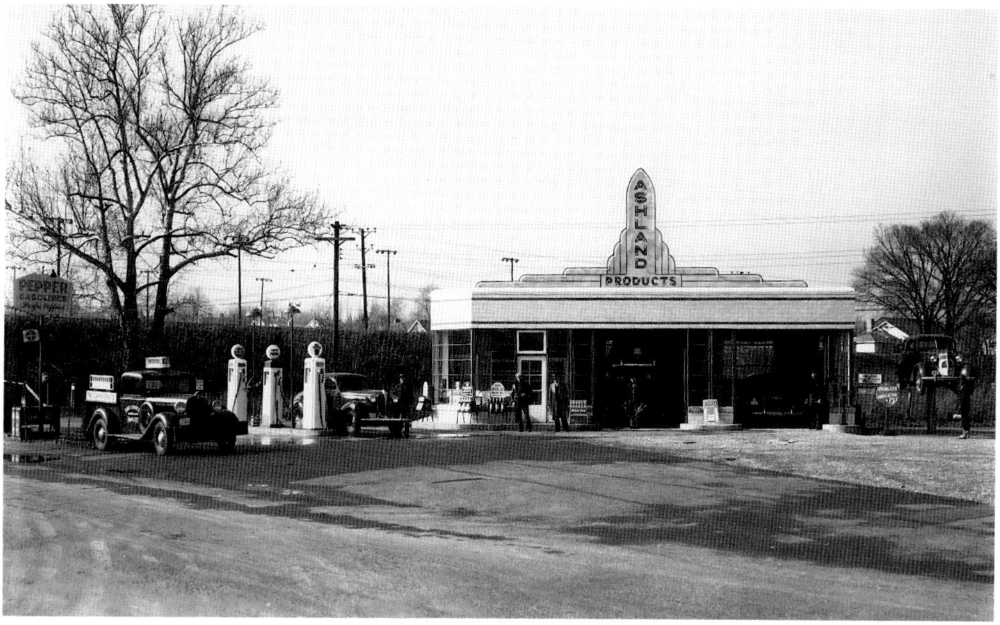

Two Carrs gas station, December 1940. Earl M. Carr invited Lexington's motoring public to stop at the Two Carrs Gas Station on the corner of North Broadway and Russell Cave Road, where he offered a complete service, a variety of automobile products, and clean restrooms. Carr operated the station until c. 1944 when he became a maintenance superintendent with Lexington Railway System Inc. (4608)

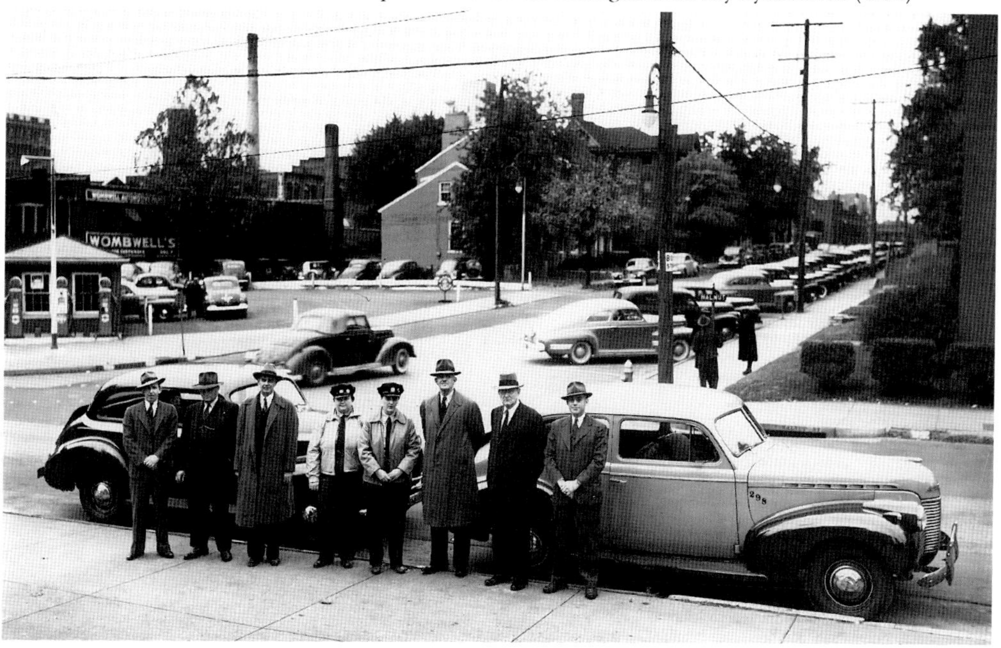

Lexington Yellow Cab, October 13, 1942. When 28 of its male employees entered the armed services, Lexington Yellow Cab hired its first women drivers, Marie Plowman and Mable B. Grimes. The first passengers were Mayor T. Ward Havely, County Judge W.E. Nichols, and City Manager Will White. Yellow Cab's president, Leroy M. Smith, assured customers that women would be employed only when men were unobtainable and only during daylight hours. (4951)

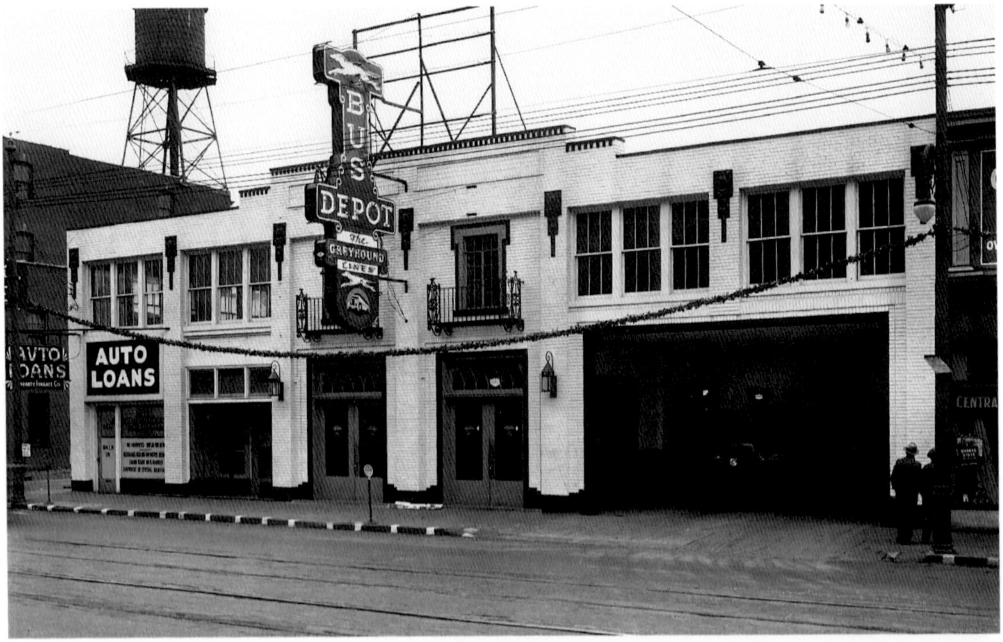

New Greyhound Station, December 1934. For transportation to and from Lexington, people increasingly chose to travel by bus. On August 14, 1934, The Lexington Herald reported that "Lexington, per capita, has more regular daily schedule buses and handles more bus passengers than any other city in the United States, 108 buses entering and leaving the Lexington terminal [at Walnut Street] daily." (1300)

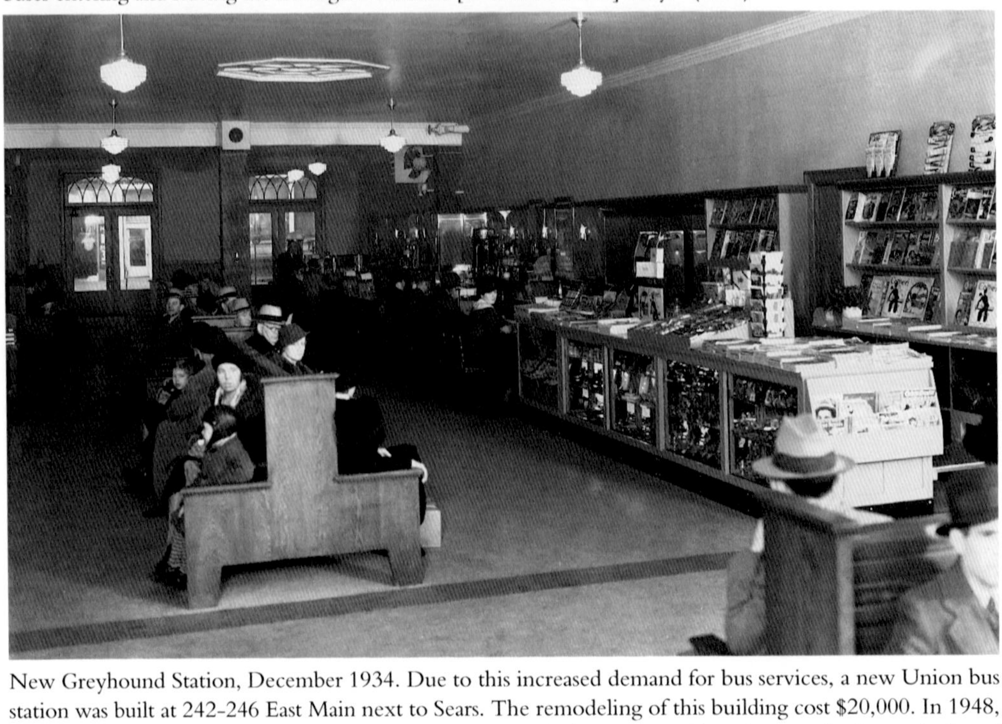

New Greyhound Station, December 1934. Due to this increased demand for bus services, a new Union bus station was built at 242-246 East Main next to Sears. The remodeling of this building cost $20,000. In 1948, the bus station was moved again to a new million-dollar facility on East Short Street, after bus arrivals and departures had increased to 270 with 300,000 passengers daily. (1300)

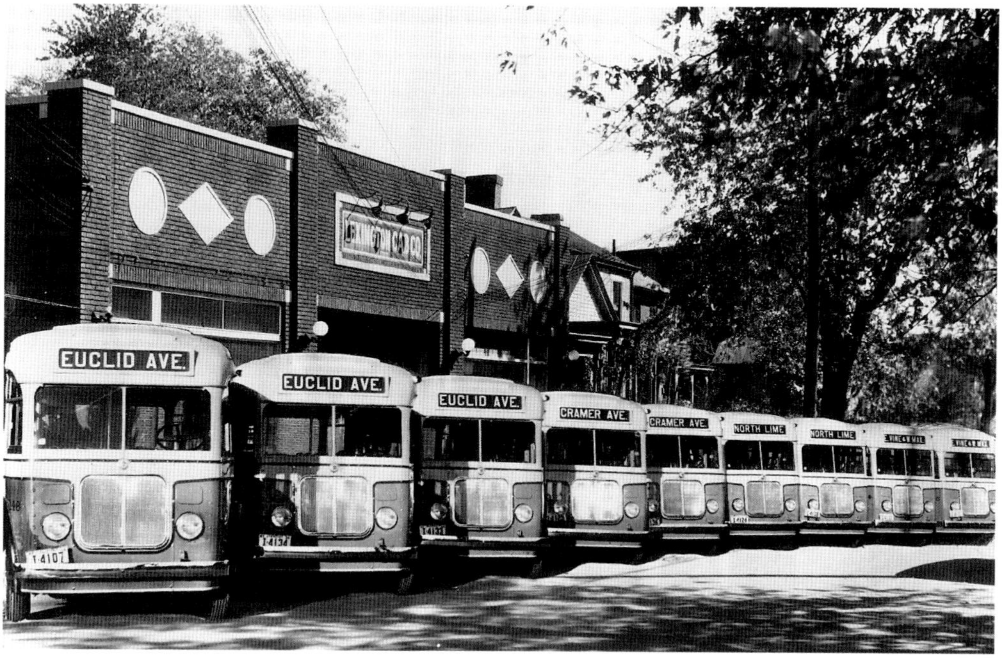

Lexington Cab Company, October 1934. Bus travel within the city was provided by the Lexington Cab Company, which, in October of 1934, gained an exclusive franchise purchased from the city for $2,750. The fare was 5¢ for travel anywhere in the city with free transfers available to the streetcar lines. Thirteen new buses were placed in operation on six different routes around the city. (1945)

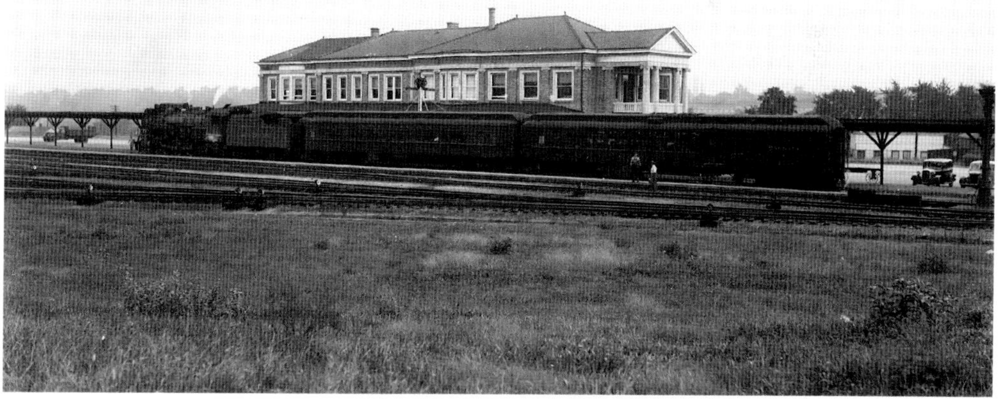

Kentucky Railway System and the Q & C Train, September 1947. An advertisement for the Lexington Cab Company's city bus service in the June 6, 1938 edition of *The Lexington Leader* advertised that the city "known the world over for its culture and progressiveness, is in every respect 'the biggest little city on earth.' Its industries, the envy of every city of equal size . . . its wealth surpassing that of many larger cities." As Lexington turned its attention to the later half of the century, it would grow in ways that were unimagined. And yet, it would remain a city at work and on the move. Lexington is greatly indebted to Bob and Ida Long for capturing such a remarkable visual history of a significant period in its development. (5881)

ADDITIONAL READINGS AND SOURCES

Birdwhistell, Terry L. "WHAS Radio and the Development of Broadcasting in Kentucky, 1922-1942." The Register of the Kentucky Historical Society 79 (Autumn 1981): 333-353.

Coleman, J. Winston, Jr. The Squire's Sketches of Lexington. Lexington, KY: Henry Clay Press, 1972.

Kerr, Bettie L. and John D. Wright Jr. Lexington: A Century in Photographs. Lexington, KY: Lexington-Fayette County Historic Commission, 1984.

Kleber, John E., ed. The Kentucky Encyclopedia. Lexington, KY.: The University Press of Kentucky, 1992.

Lancaster, Clay. Vestiges of the Venerable City: A Chronicle of Lexington, Kentucky, Its Architectural Development, and Survey of Its Early Streets and Antiquities. Lexington, KY: Lexington-Fayette County Historic Commission, 1978.

Milward, Burton. A History of the Lexington Cemetery. Lexington, KY: Lexington Cemetery Company, 1989.

Sutton, Barbara, ed. Lexington As It Was. Lexington, KY: Paddock Publishing, Inc., 1981.

Waller, Gregory A. Main Street Amusements: Movies and Commercial Entertainment in a Southern City, 1896–1930. Washington, D.C.: Smithsonian Institution Press, 1995.

White, Tom. A Century of Speed: The Red Mile, 1875–1975. Lexington, KY: Thoroughbred Press, Inc., 1975.

Wright, George C. A History of Blacks in Kentucky: In Pursuit of Equality, 1890–1980. Frankfort, KY: Kentucky Historical Society, 1992.

Wright, John D. Jr. Lexington: Heart of the Bluegrass. Lexington, KY: Lexington-Fayette County Historic Commission, 1982.